ate Due

META-ANALYSIS IN SOCIAL RESEARCH

META-ANALYSIS IN SOCIAL RESEARCH

Gene V Glass, Barry McGaw and Mary Lee Smith

SAGE PUBLICATIONS   Beverly Hills   London

For information address:

SAGE Publications, Inc.
275 South Beverly Drive
Beverly Hills, California 90212

SAGE Publications Ltd
28 Banner Street
London EC1Y 8QE, England

Printed in the United States of America

Library of Congress Cataloging in Publication Data

Glass, Gene V, 1940
  Meta-analysis in social research.

  Bibliography: p.
  Includes index.
  1. Social sciences--Research. I. McGaw,
Barry. II. Smith, Mary Lee. III. Title.
H62.G517   300'.72   81-5673
ISBN 0-8039-1633-7   AACR2

SECOND PRINTING, 1982

CONTENTS

Ben-Adhem picked up a stone from beside the road. "It had written on it, 'Turn me over and read.' So he picked it up and looked at the other side. And there was written, 'Why do you seek more knowledge when you pay no heed to what you know already?' "

Shah (1968, p. 110)

PREFACE

This may be precisely the right time to write this book or precisely the wrong time. Readers ought not to assume that since this book lies before them that we came eventually to believe that the former was true. For we may have persevered in the face of ambivalence and written in spite of our doubts. Propitious or not, this book will be written in this moment and not some later one. The reader who has ever struggled with writing a book will understand when we say that we now have *that* feeling that if we do not write it now, it will never get written.

Our subject is the methods of integrating empirical research. The problems we address lie at the center of a tiny revolution in the way social scientists and researchers attempt to extract knowledge from empirical inquiry and communicate it. The revolution was spawned by necessity. The findings of empirical research grew exponentially in the middle 50 years of the 20th century. Evidence—even the organized, analyzed, and codified evidence of the archival journals—has multiplied beyond the ability of the unaided human mind to comprehend it. In the last 10 years, scientists and methodologists have worried about how the findings of research can be synthesized and organized into coherent patterns. We worried along with them, and we hope that our efforts helped clarify the problem if not solve small bits of it.

Because of our efforts and our colleagues' efforts and the efforts of a few dozen scholars around the world who have addressed the same problems, persons who start out to review and integrate a body of research literature today have at their disposal some guidelines, examples, and tricks that stand a good chance of enriching their understanding of that literature. The methods to which we refer have now been applied a few dozen times, perhaps, and the experiences have been reported as being moderately satisfactory. (They have hardly escaped all criticism, but then what does?) In our minds, this counts as a hopeful beginning. But it is only a beginning—and hereby lie our doubts about timing. A new field in its early stages should not have to contend with the conservative drag of a textbook, the existence of which too often cuts off inquiry instead of stimulating it ("Well, if it's not in Grinch's *Atlas of Organizational Dynamics,* it must not be a problem"; or "Grinch says that's not so."). But, then, how does one weigh the disadvantages of a premature textbook against the disadvantages of no textbook at all? That question was ours, and we decided, "Better early than never."

We are indebted to several institutions and individuals who have aided us in our work. Foremost among them are our universities: the University of Colorado and Murdoch University. Time that the first and last authors spent at the University of California, Los Angeles, contributed to this work. Some financial support was contributed by the Australian Education Research and Development Committee, the Spencer Foundation of Chicago, the Far West Laboratory for Educational Research and Development of San Francisco, the National Institute of Education, and the National Institute of Mental Health through grants (NIMH # 278-77-0049MH and # 278-78-0037MH) to Drs. Herbert Schlesinger and Emily Mumford of the University of Colorado Health Sciences Center. Several persons contributed more directly to our thinking: Gavin Andrews of Sydney, Australia; Mark A. Barton, Princeton, New Jersey; Gregory A. Camilli, Boulder, Colorado; Larry V. Hedges, University of Chicago; Ingram Olkin, Stanford University; Robert Rosenthal, Harvard University; Karl R. White, Utah State University; John Willett, Stanford University; and Leonard S. Cahen, Arizona State University. We are indebted to each.

GVG
BMcG
MLS

CHAPTER ONE

THE PROBLEMS OF RESEARCH REVIEW AND INTEGRATION

The mathematician David Hilbert once said that the importance of a scientific work can be measured by the number of previous publications it makes superfluous to read. There is a hint in Hilbert's complaint of the despair that scholars in all fields increasingly feel. What is one to make of the cornucopia of research literature? Can one make anything of it, or does one inevitably founder in the riches of empirical inquiry and sink to confusion? The house of social science research is sadly dilapidated. It is strewn among the scree of a hundred journals and lies about in the unsightly rubble of a million dissertations. Even if it cannot be built into a science, the rubble ought to be sifted and culled for whatever consistency there is in it.

Maccoby and Jacklin's (1974) review of research on the psychology of sex differences encompassed 1,600 works published before 1973. If one considers the literature on that topic since 1973 and realizes that many studies not focused specifically on sex differences (or not mentioning them in their title) may contain data on the question, then a population of over 5,000 studies can be imagined. Dozens of educational problems could be named on which the available research literature numbers several hundred articles: ability grouping, reading instruction, programmed learning, instructional television, integration, and others. When Miller (see Smith et al., 1980) set out to determine the effects of drug therapy on psychological disorders, he found published reports of clinical experiments in such abundance (numbering literally thousands of studies) that he was forced to impose a sampling frame on the immense body of literature and take a survey sample of studies. Social and behavioral research is a large and widely scattered enterprise. On problems of importance, it produces literally hundreds of studies in only a few years. The research technique used, the measurement taken, the type of person studied—each may vary in bewildering irregularity from one study to the next even though the topic is the same. The research enterprise in education and the social sciences is a rough-hewn, variegated undertaking of huge proportions. Determining what knowledge this enterprise has produced on some question is, itself, a genuinely important scholarly endeavor.

Styles of research integration have been shaped by the size of the research literature. In the 1940s and 1950s, a contributor to the *Review of Educational Research* or *Psychological Bulletin* might have found one or two dozen studies on a topic. A narrative integration of so few studies was probably satisfactory. By the late 1960s, the research literature had swollen to gigantic proportions. Although scholars continued to integrate studies narratively, it was becoming clear that chronologically arranged verbal descriptions of research failed to portray the accumulated knowledge. Reviewers began to make crude classifications and measurements of the conditions and results of studies. Typically, studies were classified in contingency tables by type and by whether outcomes reached statistical significance. Integrating the research literature of the 1980s demands more sophisticated techniques of measurement and statistical analysis. The findings of multiple studies should be regarded as a complex data set, no more comprehensible without statistical analysis than would be hundreds of data points in one study. Contemporary research reviewing should be more technical and statistical than it is narrative. Toward this end, we suggest a name for the needed approach. The desired approach was earlier referred to as the *meta-analysis* of research (Glass, 1976), the analysis of analyses (i.e., the statistical analysis of the findings of many individual analyses). The term *integrative analysis* might serve as well, but meta-analysis has entered common parlance among some researchers fairly quickly and may become conventional. *Secondary analysis* is imprecise to the point of being misleading and should not be used interchangeably with these terms; it connotes an altogether different activity (Cook, 1974), as does *meta-evaluation.* Where a modification is needed to distinguish the meta-analysis of a body of studies from the studies individually, *primary research* could be used to denote the latter.

Jackson (1978) conducted what is perhaps the finest study yet of the practices and methods of research reviewers and synthesizers in the social sciences. He sampled at random 36 integrative reviews from the leading journals in education, psychology, and sociology. The various features of method of each review were coded according to the categories of an extensive ciding form that Jackson created. His conclusions follow:

a) Reviewers frequently fail to examine critically the evidence, methods and conclusions of previous *reviews* on the same or similar topics. [Although 75 percent of the reviewers cited previous reviews, only 6 percent examined them critically]

b) Reviewers, often focus their discussion and analysis on only a part of the full set of studies they find, and the subset examined is seldom a representative sample and it is seldom clear how it (the subset) was chosen. [Only 3 percent of the reviewers appeared to have used existing indexes—e.g., ERIC—in their search; only 22 percent selected a fair sample of studies, in the judgment of Jackson's coders; and only 3 percent analyzed the full set of studies found.]

c) Reviewers frequently use crude and misleading representations of the findings of the studies. [About 15 percent of the reviewers classified studies according to whether their findings were "statistically significant," a practice which will be criticized in Chapter 5; frequently, reviewers report test statistics (t, F, etc.) for one or more studies.]

d) Reviewers sometimes fail to recognize that random sampling error can play a part in creating variable findings among studies.

e) Reviewers frequently fail systematically to assess possible relationships between the characteristics of the studies and the study findings. [Fewer than 10 percent of the reviewers studied whether the findings of the research were mediated by characteristics of the persons studied, the study context, the nature of the experimental intervention or the characteristics of the research design.] The lack of systematic examination of these relationships is important because reviewers frequently eliminate studies from consideration because of *a priori* judgments that their findings are flawed by one or another study characteristics.

f) Reviewers usually report so little about their methods of reviewing that the reader cannot judge the validity of the conclusions.

Jackson also surveyed a small group of fewer than a dozen editors of review journals and executives of social science organizations. He attempted to determine which practices and standards prevail in their reviewing and integrating activities. He concluded that this survey was unproductive, but it was only unproductive of an articulated set of procedures and methods of study review and integration for the simple reason that such apparently does not exist. Jackson's small survey revealed clearly that the conception of research review and integration that prevails in the social and behavioral sciences is one in which the activity is viewed as a matter of largely private judgment, individual creativity, and personal style. Indeed, it is and ought to be all of these to some degree; but if it is nothing but these, it is curiously inconsistent with the activity (viz., scientific research) it purports to illuminate.

Jackson (1978) went on in Chapter Six of his report to give valuable guidelines for integrative reviewing that encompass such aspects of the process as selecting the topic, sampling studies, coding the characteristics of studies, analyzing the data, and interpreting the results. (Note coincidentally, guidelines for performing a primary research study could well be classified under the same headings.) Jackson devoted Chapter Four, "A New Alternative: Meta-Analysis," of his report to a description and critique of the approach that is the subject of this book.

Under the pressure of burgeoning research literatures, old and informal narrative techniques of research review and integration are breaking down. The fundamental problem is one of the mind's limitations and the magnitude of the task to which it is applied. The reviewer is even less able to absorb the sense of a hundred research studies than is an observer able to scan a hundred test scores and, without reliance on statistical methods, absorb the sense of their size and spread and and correlations.

Light and Smith (1971) were among the first to give serious attention to methodological and technical problems of research integration. Their article is a careful treatment of the inadequacies of simple methods of research integration. Their proposed solution—the cluster approach—is in the spirit of the solution recommended here, but it is more conservative: "Little headway can be made by pooling the *words in the conclusions* of a set of studies. Rather, progress will only come when we are able to pool, in a systematic manner, the original data from the studies" (Light and Smith, 1971: 443). This restriction to the integration of original data and the methods based on it probably discards too many informative studies for which the data are no longer available, though the summary findings remain.

Cooper and Rosenthal (1980) recently conducted an experiment in integrating research findings that illustrated the inadequacies of narrative integration even with a small body of literature. About 40 persons (graduate students or more experienced) were randomly split into two groups. Subjects in both groups were given seven empirical studies on "sex differences in persistence" to review. Subjects in Group A were told:

> Before drawing any final conclusions about the overall results of persistence studies, please take a moment to review each individual study. In generating a single conclusion from the independent studies, employ whatever criteria you would use if this exercise were being undertaken for a class term paper or a manuscript for publication.

Thus, Group A employed traditional, narrative techniques of integrating the findings of the seven studies. By contrast, Group B was instructed as follows:

> Before drawing any final conclusions about the overall results of persistence studies, you are asked to perform a simple statistical procedure. The procedure is a way of combining the probabilities of independent studies. The purpose of the procedure is to generate a single probability level which relates to the likelihood of obtaining a set of studies displaying the observed results. This probability is interpreted just like that associated with a t- or F-statistic. For example, assume the procedure produces a probability of .04. This would mean there are 4 chances in 100 that a set of studies showing these results were produced by chance. The procedure is called The Unweighted Stouffer method, and requires that you do the following:

> 1) Transfer the probabilities recorded earlier from each study to Column 1 of the Summary Sheet. [A summary sheet was provided each subject. The sheet contained the titles of the seven articles and columns for performing each step in the procedure.]
> 2) Since we are testing the hypothesis that females are more persistent than males, divide each probability in half (a probability of 1 becomes .5). If a study found *men* more persistent, attach a minus sign to it's probability. Place these numbers in Column 2. [It had been determined before hand that only two-tailed probabilities were reported.]
> 3) Use the Normal Deviations Table provided below and transform each probability in Column 2 into its associated Z-score. Place

these values (with sign) in Column 3. If the probability is .5, the associated Z-score is zero (0).
4) Add the Z-scores in Column 3, keeping track of algebraic sign. Place this value at the bottom of Column 3.
5) Divide this number by the square root of the number of studies involved. In this case, because N = 7, this number is 2.65. Thus, divide the sum of the Z-scores by 2.65. Place this number in the space below.

Z-SCORE FOR REVIEW _____

6) Return to the Normal Deviations Table and identify the probability value associated with the Z-score for review. Place this number in the space below.

P-VALUE FOR REVIEW _____

This probability tells how likely it is that a set of studies with these results could have been produced if there really were no relation between gender and persistence. The *smaller* the probability, the *more* likely it is that females and males differ in persistence, based on these studies [1980: 445].

Subjects in both Groups A and B rated their opinion of the strength of support for a conclusion of a relationship between sex and persistence in the seven studies. In fact, the combined results from the seven studies supported rejection of the null hypothesis of no difference at beyond the .02 level. The following frequencies were obtained:

Opinion (Is there a relationship?)	Group A Traditional Methods of Review		Group B Statistical Method of Review	
	No.	%	No.	%
Definitely No	3	14	1	5
Probably No	13	59	5	26
Impossible to Say	5	23	8	42
Probably Yes	1	4	5	26
Definitely Yes	0	0	0	0
		100%		100%

Numbers may not add due to rounding.

The results are remarkable. Nearly 75% of the reviewers who relied on traditional narrative methods concluded that sex and persistence were not related. The comparable figure among the group using the prescribed statistical method of review was 31%—rather strikingly different conclusions for equivalent groups trying to integrate only seven studies.

An issue of nearly equal importance concerns the magnitude of the relationship that the seven studies revealed. Again the reviewers in both groups were asked to rate their perception of the strength of the relationship.

	Group A Traditional Methods of Review		Group B Statistical Methods of Review	
Opinion (How large is the sex difference in persistence?)	No.	%	No.	%
None at all	4	18	2	10
Very Small	12	55	6	32
Small	4	18	6	32
Moderate	2	9	4	21
Large	0	0	1	5
		100%		100%

The above data repeat the general findings apparent in the previous table: Persons using the two different methods of research integration formed quite different impressions about what the studies indicated. Cooper and Rosenthal examined these processes on a small collection of studies; the entire set of seven studies occupied a total of fewer than 50 journal pages. One can imagine how much more pronounced would be the difference between these two approaches with bodies of literature typical of the size that are increasingly being addressed with meta-analytic techniques. The problems of applying informal methods of review will become more apparent to the reader who wends his way through the complex examples of research integration in the remainder of this book.

Consider another example of the contrasting conclusions arrived at through contrasting methods of review and integration. In a narrative review of experiments on the effects of teachers' use of higher cognitive questions on students' achievement, Winne (1979) concluded that the former had no beneficial impact on the latter. A meta-analysis of virtually the same studies by Rousseau and Redfield (1980) revealed that, on the average, students given higher cognitive level questions scored one-half standard deviation higher on achievement tests. Thus, informal and narrative techniques of review discredited a finding that quantitative methods of integration showed to be consistent and large.

Narrative research reviews often make no attempt at rigorous definition and standardization of techniques. Hence, conclusions are influenced by prejudice and stereotyping to a degree that would be unforgivable in primary research itself. Consider an instance encountered by Miller (1977) in his meta-analysis of experiments on the psychological benefits of drug therapy. At one point, attention focused on the question of whether the combination of verbal psychotherapy and drug therapy were superior to drug therapy alone. Three different traditional reviews completed within about five years of each other and based on largely the same literature arrived at the following conclusions:

> The advantage for combined treatment is striking . . . a combination of treatments may represent more than an additive effect of two treatments—a "getting more for one's money"—there may also be some mutually facilitative interaction benefits for the combined treatments [Luborsky et al., 1975: 1004].

> There is little difference between psychotherapy plus drug and drug therapy alone for hospitalized psychotic patients (but not for neurotic out-patients). The combination is, however, quite clearly superior to psychotherapy alone [May, 1971: 513].

> When all is said and done, the existing studies by no means permit firm conclusions as to the nature of the interaction between combined psychotherapy and medication [Unlenhuth et al., 1969: 611].

The disparity among these reviewers is not limited to their conclusions but extends even to their classification of individual experiments. Miller (1977) found five reviews (the three quoted above and two others) addressed specifically to the "psychotherapy-plus-drug" versus "drug

TABLE 1.1   Summary of Findings of Five Reviews Comparing Drug
             Plus Psychotherapy with Drug Therapy
             (After Miller, 1977)

Reviewer	Drug-plus-psychotherapy Superior to Drug Therapy	Drug Therapy Equal to or Superior to Drug-plus-psychotherapy
Group for the Advancement of Psychiatry (1975)	King (1958) Evangelikas (1961) Klerman (1974) Honigfeld (1964)	May (1964) Cowden (1955, 1956)
Gillian (1965)	Evangelikas (1961)	Cowden (1956)
Uhlcnhuth (1969)	King (1958) Evangelikas (1961)	Cowden (1956) King (1963) Honigfeld (1964) Gorham (1964) May (1964)
Luborsky (1975)	Gorham (1964) Hogarty (1974) Cowden (1956) King (1963) Luborsky (1954) Klerman (1974)	King (1960) May (1965)

Evangelikas (1961) |
| May (1971) | Gorham (1964) | King (1963, 1958) Gorham (1964) Cowden (1956) May (1964) Evangelikas (1961) Lorr (1961) |

therapy" issue. In Table 1.1, the manner in which these reviewers interpreted various studies is shown. Notice, for example, that Luborsky et al.
(1975) classified the Gorham study, the Cowden study, and the King
study as finding that "drug-plus-psychotherapy" was superior to "drug
therapy" alone, whereas both Unlenhuth (1969) and May (1971) classified
the same studies as showing either no difference or a difference in the
reverse order.

Obviously, different reviewers sometimes see things differently. The
only way to force all reviewers to see the same thing would be to demand

a standardization of definitions and techniques of research integration. We do not suggest such; indeed, it would be ill-advised, since the little "reliability" that would be gained would probably be more than off-set by the creativity that would be staunched by uniformity. It is not uniformity in research reviewing and integrating that is desirable, rather it is clarity, explicitness, and openness—those properties that are characteristic of the scientific method more generally and which impart to inquiry its "objectivity" and trustworthiness.

It is often said of experimental research that it must be *replicable* to be scientific. The true test of whether a finding is replicable is to replicate it; but as is observed *ad nauseum,* such replications are seldom actually undertaken. Hence, the scientific attitude is not to desire actual replication, *but such a description of a study that it could in theory be replicated.* If one desired, one could then perform the same steps that led to the prior observations. Hence, to report a study so that it is "replicable" means to report it with such clarity and explicitness that a second investigator could follow the identical steps to the identical conclusion. Thereby, science is guaranteed to be "intersubjective" rather than an endeavor subject to the whims and idiosyncracies of individual researchers. These values and standards are ingrained in contemporary scientists' training but too often are forgotten when the context changes slightly and the task is to integrate numerous empirical studies instead of to perform a single primary study. Thus do reviews become idiosyncratic, authoritarian, subjective—all those things that cut against the scientific grain.

The important point about the example in Table 1.1 is not that Unlenhuth, Luborsky, and May disagreed, but that they did not approach the problem of research integration with methods so explicit, unambiguous and operationally identified that an outsider could examine the same evidence and come to the same conclusion. By contrast, Miller (1977) approached the same research integration problem (viz., "drug-plus-psychotherapy" vs. "drug therapy") with an attitude like that of a researcher collecting and analyzing primary data: Concepts must be defined and measured, measurements must be checked for reliability, evidence must not be excluded on arbitrary or ad hoc grounds, multiple observations inform on residual error, statistical methods are an important adjunct to raw perception. He found that the combined effect of drug and psychotherapy was approximately .3 standard deviation (on outcome measures of psychological well-being) greater than the isolated effect of drug therapy (see Chapter 8 in Smith et al., 1980).

CHAPTER TWO

META-ANALYSIS OF RESEARCH

Primary analysis is the original analysis of data in a research study. It is what one typically imagines as the application of statistical methods.

Secondary analysis is the reanalysis of data for the purpose of answering the original research question with better statistical techniques, or answering new questions with old data. Secondary analysis is an important feature of the research and evaluation enterprise. Cook (1974) has written about its purposes and methods. Some of our best methodologists have pursued secondary analysis in such grand style that its importance has eclipsed that of the primary analysis.

But our topic is what we have come to call—not for want of a less imposing name—*meta-analysis* of research. The approach to research integration referred to as "meta-analysis" is nothing more than the attitude of data analysis applied to quantitative summaries of individual experiments. By recording the properties of studies and their findings in quantitative terms, the meta-analysis of research invites one who would integrate numerous and diverse findings to apply the full power of statistical methods to the task. Thus it is not a technique; rather it is a perspective that uses many techniques of measurement and statistical analysis.

CHARACTERISTICS OF META-ANALYSIS

The essential character of meta-analysis is that it is the statistical analysis of the summary findings of many empirical studies.

21

Meta-Analysis Is Quantitative

Meta-analysis is undeniably quantitative; and by and large it uses numbers and statistical methods in a practical way, namely, for organizing and extracting information from large masses of data that are nearly incomprehensible by other means. Numerosity creates many of the problems of research synthesis; naturally, numerical methods are employed in their solution.

Meta-Analysis Does Not Prejudge Research
Findings in Terms of Research Quality

The findings of studies are not ignored a priori or by imposing arbitrary and nonempirical criteria of research quality. In this respect, meta-analysis differs greatly from many other approaches to research integration. Typical narrative reviews attempt to deal with multiplicity by arbitrary exclusion. The dissertation literature might be excluded if it is believed that any worthwhile study would have been published. Huge numbers of studies may be excluded on methodological grounds: poor design, bad measurement, badly implemented treatment, and the like. Yet evidence is never given to support the assumption that these deficiencies of the studies influence their findings.

An important part of every meta-analysis with which we have been associated has been the recording of methodological weaknesses in the original studies and the examination of their relationship to study findings. Thus, the influence of study quality on findings has been regarded as an empirical a posteriori question, not an a priori matter of opinion or judgment used to exclude large numbers of studies from consideration.

Meta-Analysis Seeks General Conclusions

The most common criticism of meta-analysis is that it is illogical because it mixes findings from studies that are not the same; it mixes apples and oranges. The narrative review cannot escape this criticism simply because it is less systematic. There is typically little difference in the scope and complexity of literature integrated either by narrative review or meta-analysis. Implicit in the concern about comparing *different* studies is the belief that only studies that are the *same* in certain respects can be aggregated. The claim that only studies which are the same in *all* respects can be compared is self-contradictory; there is no need to compare them since they would obviously have the same findings within statistical error. The only studies which need to be synthesized or integrated are *different* studies. Generalizations will necessarily entail ignoring some distinctions that can be made among studies. Good generalizations will be arrived at by ignoring only those distinctions that make no important difference. But ignore we must; knowledge itself is possible only through the orderly discarding of information.

Yet it is intuitively clear that some differences among studies are so large or critical that no one is interested in their integration. What, for example, is to be made of study 1 which demonstrates the effectiveness of disulfiram in the treatment of alcoholism and of study 2 which demonstrates the benefits of motorcycle helmet laws? Not much, we suppose. But it hardly follows that the integration of study 1 on lysergide treatment of alcoholism and study 2 on "controlled drinking" is meaningless; one is understandably concerned with which treatment has a greater cure rate. Is the essential difference between the two examples that in the former case the *problems* addressed by the studies are different but the *problem* is the same in the latter example? "Problem" is no better defined than "study" or "findings" and invoking the word clarifies little. It is easy to imagine the Secretary for Health comparing 50 studies on alcoholism treatment with 50 studies on drug addiction treatment or 100 studies on the treatment of obesity. If the two former groups of studies are negative and the latter is positive, the Secretary may decide to fund only obesity treatment centers. From the Secretary's point of view, the *problem* is public health, not simply alcoholism *or* drug addiction treatment.

Meta-analysis is aimed at generalization and practical simplicity. It aims to derive a useful generalization that does not do violence to a more useful contingent or interactive conclusion. The world runs on generalizations and marginal utilities. Therein lie many of the difficulties that scientists and men of practical affairs encounter when they meet.

Our approach, meta-analysis, has been misunderstood—a circumstance for which we must accept that share of the responsibility due us. It has been characterized by some as "averaging effect sizes," which is a little like characterizing analysis of variance as "adding and multiplying." The sine qua non of what we call meta-analysis is the application of research methods to the characteristics and findings of research studies. By "research methods" is meant such considerations as are normally addressed in conceptualizing, designing, and analyzing empirical research: problem selection, hypothesis formulation, definition and measurement of constructs and variables, sampling, and data analysis (see Kerlinger, 1964, or many others).

The methods of meta-analysis have much in common with those of survey research, for in fact research review and integration is a process of surveying and analyzing in quantitative ways large populations of studies. Many of the issues faced in a meta-analysis are akin to the problems addressed in survey design and analysis (cf. Kish, 1965). The similarity between the two should not be taken as implying that meta-analysis shares with survey research the latter's limitations as regards the analysis of causal claims. Survey research continues to struggle with the problems of unknown third variables and ambiguous direction of causality. Meta-analysis, on the other hand, through no great accomplishment of its own, may very well be applied to the findings of a literature of controlled experimental studies, each of which has a valid claim on a causal conclusion.

DEVELOPMENT OF META-ANALYSIS

We do not wish to imply that a clear break can be discerned between earlier methods of research integration and meta-analysis. In fact, under the pressure of numbers, research reviewers have gradually of necessity adopted increasingly rigorous and quantitative methods of study integration in the past 30 years. For example, Underwood (1957) found 16 experiments on the link between memory and interference when he attempted to integrate the existing research. The standard designs and the near standard measurements common to the studies suggested a more quantitative amalgamation of the evidence than was typical in research reviewing at the time. By graphing the number of lists of items to be recalled in these experiments against the percent correct recall on the last list, Underwood obtained an orderly and convincing pattern describing the relationship (see Figure 2.1). By portraying multiple findings quantitatively and aggregating across some potentially irrelevant distinctions (e.g., lists of geometric forms vs. nonsense syllables; paired-associate vs. serial presentation, long lists vs. short lists), Underwood discovered a convincing and important finding not apparent in the disparate constituent studies. This is the essence of the meta-analysis approach.

Rosenthal (1976) integrated the findings of several hundred studies of the experimenter expectancy effect in behavioral research. The technique he used and his discussion of methodology were remarkably like

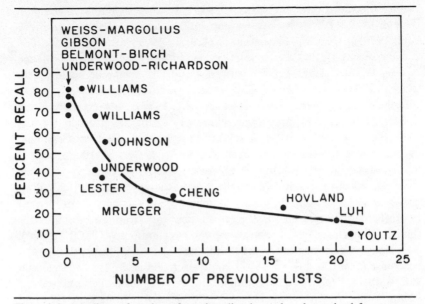

Figure 2.1 Recall as a function of previous lists learned as determined from a number of studies. (After Underwood, 1957)

those presented in Glass (1976), though the two efforts (born of similar necessities) proceeded independently. In 1974, Sudman and Bradburn synthesized hundreds of empirical studies of "response effects" in survey research. In the five years since our work has been publicized, the methods developed and recommended have been applied repeatedly and in diverse areas: treatment of stuttering (Andrews, 1979), modern versus traditional math instruction (Athappilly, 1980), treatment of migraine and tension headache (Blanchard et al., 1980), "process-oriented" science instruction (Bredderman, 1980), mainstreaming special education students (Carlberg, 1979), student ratings of instruction and student achievement (Cohen, 1980), neuropsychological assessment of children (Davidson, 1978), "inquiry-oriented" science teaching (El-Nemr, 1979), transcendental meditation (Ferguson, 1980), teaching style and pupil achievement (Glass et al., 1977; Gage, 1978), social-psychological environments and learning (Haertel et al., 1979), sex differences in decoding verbal cues (Hall, 1978), individualized mathematics instruction (Hartley, 1977), effects of tele-

vision on social behavior (Hearold, 1979), validity of employment tests
(Hunter et al., 1979), home environment and learning (Iverson and Walberg, 1979), psycholinguistic training (Kavale, 1979), treatment of hyperactivity (Kavale, 1980a), correlation of auditory perceptual skill and
reading (Kavale, 1980c), racial desegregation and academic achievement
(Krol, 1979), personalized college-level instruction (Kulik et al., 1979),
computer-based instruction (Kulik et al., 1980), advance organizers
(Luiten et al., 1979), drug therapy and psychological disorders (Miller,
1977; Smith et al., 1980), test validity in personnel selection (Pearlman,
1979), effects of direct versus open instruction (Peterson, 1978), patient
education programs in medicine (Posavac, 1980), teachers' questioning
style (Rousseau and Redfield, 1980), psychotherapy and medical utilization (Schlesinger et al., 1978), psychotherapy and recovery from medical
crisis (Schlesinger et al., 1980), aesthetics education and basic skills
(Smith, 1980a), sex bias in counseling and psychotherapy (Smith, 1980c),
class size and affective outcomes (Smith and Glass, 1980), psychotherapy
outcomes (Smith and Glass, 1977), motivation and achievement (Uguroglu
and Walberg, 1978), socioeconomic status and academic achievement
(White, 1980), relationship between attitude and achievement (Willson,
1980), and diagnostic/remedial instruction and science learning (Yeany
and Miller, 1980).

ILLUSTRATIONS OF META-ANALYSIS

Meta-analysis has been misunderstood and criticized, the criticisms
often gathering their force from the misunderstandings. But the objections
raised to meta-analysis are the subject of the final chapter. In the
remainder of this chapter, we wish instead to elaborate on the verbal
characterization of meta-analysis by describing briefly several applications
of the method.

Psychotherapy and Asthma

Twelve studies were located that tested the effects of psychotherapy on
asthma (see Schlesinger et al., 1978). Eleven studies used treatment and
control group designs; two designs were pretest versus posttest.

The summary of the data and findings appears as Table 2.1 which offers
the following items of information about each study: (1) Author(s); (2)
type of therapy; (3) average age of subjects; (4) number of hours of
therapy given; (5) the nature of the control group (no treatment, relaxa-

TABLE 2.1 Findings of 11 Studies of Psychological Treatment of Asthma

Study	Therapy Type	Age	Hours of Therapy	Control Group	Follow-up Time (weeks)	Dependent Variable	Δ
(a)	(b)	(c)	(d)	(e)	(f)	(g)	(h)
Moore (1965)	Reciprocal Inhibition	21 1/2 adults 1/2 children	4	Relax Training	0	Lung functioning No. Asthma attacks	1.41 .88
Sclare, et al. (1957)	Psycho-dynamic	30 (19-42)	28	Physical Treatment	0	Remission of symptoms	.66
Yorkstun et al. (1974)	Verbal Desensitization	42	3	Relax Training	0	Lung functioning	1.00
					96	Psychiatrist's rating of improvement	1.00
					96	Use of drugs.	1.52
Maher-Loughnan, et al. (1962)	Hypno-Therapy	25	20	No treatment	0	Symptoms, wheezing	.64
Citron, K. M. (1968)	Hypno-therapy	30	12	Relax Training	0	Symptoms, wheezing	.52
Groen & Pelser (1960)	Psycho-dynamic (group)	45	50	Medical treatment	24	Rated Improvement	1.36
Barendregt (1957)	Eclectic (4 dynamic)	42	100	Medical treatment	0	Increased hostility, decreased "oppression & damage; Rorschach"	.57
Ago, et al. (1976)	Eclectic (4-somatic 4-therapy)	34	20	Medical treatment	120	Remission of asthma symptoms	1.51

TABLE 2.1 (Continued) Findings of 11 Studies of Psychological Treatment of Asthma

Study	Therapy Type	Age	Hours of Therapy	Control Group	Follow-up Time (weeks)	Dependent Variable	Δ
(a)	(b)	(c)	(d)	(e)	(f)	(g)	(h)
Kahn (1977)	Counter-conditioning	12	15	No treatment	32	Use of drugs & medication	.29
					32	Hospitalization	.19
					32	Asthma attacks	.24
Kahn, et al. (1973)	Counter-conditioning	11	15	Medical treatment	40	No. of ER visits	.76
					40	Amount of drugs & medication	1.11
					40	No. of asthma attacks (one hospitalization in control group, none in therp.)	.66
Alexander et al.	Jacobson relaxation training	12	3	No treatment	0	Pulmonary functioning (peak expiratory flow)	.82
McLean, A. F. (1965)	Hypnotherapy	13	6	None (pretest vs. posttest)	12	Wheezing Score	1.23
Arnoff, G. M. et al.	Hypnotherapy	10	1/2	None (pretest vs. posttest)	0	Forced lung capacity	0.71
						Peak air flow rate	0.67
						Dyspnea	1.25

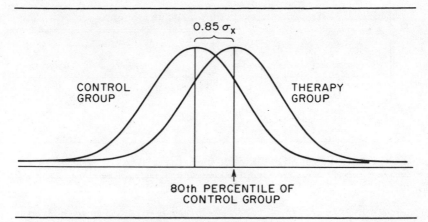

Figure 2.2   Average effect of psychotherapy on asthma outcome measures across 13 studies which included 22 outcome variables.

tion therapy, medical treatment); (6) the number of weeks elapsing between the end of therapy and measurement of the outcome variable; (7) the nature of the dependent (outcome) variable; (8) the effect (Δ) achieved in the study, that is, the treatment mean minus the control mean divided by the control group standard deviation, namely,

$$\Delta = \frac{\overline{X}_{Psych.} - \overline{X}_{Con.}}{s_{control}}.$$

The overall (i.e., summed across all studies) measure of impact of psychotherapy on asthma is depicted in Figure 2.2.

The average effect comparing therapy and control groups was .86 σ_x, the average subject who received psychotherapy was at .86 standard deviation above the mean of the untreated controls. (The standard deviation of the 22 effect size measures is $\sigma_\Delta = .400$; thus, the 95% confidence interval of the true average Δ is .86 ± [1.96 (.400)]/$\sqrt{22}$ = (.69, 1.03). It follows that the average therapy subject exceeds 80% of the untreated controls on the aggregate outcome variables.

There were six outcome measures in the 13 studies that assessed the use of medical services: use of medicine, hospitalization, and emergency room

TABLE 2.2   Effect Sizes Classified by Type of Therapy

	Type of Therapy			
	Behavioral	Psychodynamic	Hypnotherapy	Relaxation
n:	11	4	6	1
$\bar{\Delta}$. :	.82	1.03	.84	.82
σ_Δ :	.45	.48	.32	0

TABLE 2.3   Effect Sizes Classified by Patients' Age

	Age						
	10-15	16-20	21-25	26-30	31-35	36-40	41-45
Frequency:	11	0	3	2	1	0	5
$\bar{\Delta}$. :	.72	-	.98	.59	1.51	–	1.09

visits. The average effect size for these six outcomes was $\bar{\Delta}$. = .76. The two summary effect sizes—.86 for all out comes and .76 for direct medical services—imply an average effect size of .92 for the nonmedical outcomes. The effects are even substantial on the reduction of utilization of direct medical services, showing a reduction in utilization such that only 23% of the therapy subjects used as many medical services as half the control subjects. It is important to note, in this regard, that in 5 of the 11 experimental versus control group studies, the control group received medical treatment that was not given to the psychotherapy group.

The relationship between the effects of psychotherapy and some features of the therapy and the patients is examined in Tables 2.2 through 2.5. The differences among the effects of different types of therapy are not large, and in no case do they reach conventional levels of statistical significance. The linear correlation between age of patients (at the study level) and Δ is + .40, which is reasonably statistically significant.

The linear correlation of "hrs. of therapy" and Δ across the 22 outcome measures is −.15, not significantly different from zero. The follow-up times for measurement of effects for the 22 outcome measures were distributed as shown in Table 2.5. The linear correlation of "weeks

TABLE 2.4   Effect Sizes Classified by Duration of Therapy

| | | *Hours of Therapy* | | | |
1-5	*6-10*	*11-20*	*21-50*	*51-100*	
Freq. 9	1	9	2	1	$\bar{X}$. = 21.3 hrs.
$\bar{\Delta}$.: 1.03	1.23	.66	1.01	.57	

TABLE 2.5   Effect Sizes Classified by Follow-up Time

| | | *Weeks Post Therapy* | | | | | |
0	*12*	*24*	*32*	*40*	*96*	*120*	
Frequency: 11	1	1	13	3	2	1	$\bar{X}$. = 25.6 weeks
$\bar{\Delta}$.: .81	1.23	1.36	.24	.84	1.26	1.51	

post therapy" and $\bar{\Delta}$ is .34, not significantly different from zero at any respectable significance level. Psychotherapy (primarily behavioral therapies and hypnotherapy) shows impressively large effects on ameliorating the effects of asthma.

Psychotherapy and Alcoholism

In Table 2.6 data appear from 15 studies on the effects of psychotherapy on alcoholism. The 15 studies encompassed 20 different experimental comparisons (see Schlesinger et al., 1978). In successive columns the following information appear about each study:

(1) the investigator(s) and year of the study
(2) the type of therapy administered (e.g., behavioral modification, eclectic, psychodynamic)
(3) the number of hours of therapy administered
(4) the number of months after therapy at which outcomes were measured
(5) a definition of "success" for the outcome measure
(6) the percentage of "successes" in the therapy group
(7) the percentage of "successes" in the control group
(8) the differential success, Δ ; 6) minus 7), above.

TABLE 2.6 Results of Outcome Studies on Psychological Treatment of Alcoholism

a)	Type of Therapy b)	Hrs. of Therapy c)	Mos. post-therp. for follow-up d)	Outcomes			
				Type of Outcome e)	Percent Success in Therp. f)	Percent Success in control g)	Δ%
Vogler et al. (1970)	Beh. Mod.	15	8	Not relapsed into alcohol-ism	14/25 = 56%	5/12 = 42%	14%
Cadogan (1973)	Eclectic	18	6	Abstinence	18/20 = 90	4/20 = 20	70
Clancy et al. (1967)	Beh. Mod.	4	12	Abstinence	6/25 = 24	3/17 = 18	6
Gallant (1971)	Eclectic	50	0	Sobriety	17/140 = 12	3/70 = 4	8
Gallant et al. (1968)	Psychodynam.	50	0	Sobriety	2/21 = 10	1/21 = 5	5
Gallant et al. (1968)	Psychodynam.	60	0	Abstinence or nearly so	7/10 = 70	1/9 = 11	59
Hunt & Azrin (1973)	Eclectic	75	0	Abstinence	7/8 = 88	1/8 = 13	75
McCance & McCance (1969)	Psychodynam.	12	6	Abstinence or nearly so	20/31 = 65	23/51 = 45	20
	Psychodynam.	12	12	Abstinence	13/30 = 43	23/49 = 47	–4
	Beh. Mod.	6	6	Abstinence or nearly so	24/45 = 53	23/51 = 45	8
	Beh. Mod.	6	12	Abstinence or nearly so	24/45 = 53	23/49 = 47	6

TABLE 2.6   Results of Outcome Studies on Psychological Treatment of Alcoholism (continued)

a)	b) Type of Therapy	c) Hrs. of Therapy	d) Mos. post-therp. for follow-up	e) Type of Outcome	Outcomes f) Percent Success in Therp.	g) Percent Success in control	Δ%
Kissin et al. (1970)	Psychodynam.	20	6	Abstinence or nearly so	22/62 = 35%	2/44 = 5%	30%
	Psychodynam.	20	6	Abstinence or nearly so	5/33 = 15	2/41 = 5	10
Sobell & Sobell (1973)	Beh. Mod.	25	6	Full or part-time employ.	21/35 = 60	14/35 = 40	20
	Beh. Mod.	25	12	Full or part time employ.	21/35 = 60	16/35 = 46	14
Levinson & Sereny (1969)	Eclectic	30	12	Slight or much improv.	15/26 = 58	17/27 = 63	−5
Newton & Stein (1972)	Eclectic	15	6	Not readmitted to hosp. for alcohol.	10/15 = 67	11/16 = 69	−2
Newton & Stein (1972)	Implosive	15	6	" " " "	7/15 = 47	11/16 = 69	−22
Ashem & Donner (1968)	Beh. Mod.	5	6	Sobriety	6/15 = 40	0/8 = 0	40
Storm & Cutler (1970)	Sys. desen.	12	6	Some or marked improv.	10/15 = 67	39/62 = 63	4

33

TABLE 2.7   Characteristics of Studies on the Psychological
             Treatment of Alcoholism

*Experimental Comparisons
Classified by Type of Therapy*

Non-behavioral Therapy					*Behavioral Therapy*	
Freq: 11					9	

*Experimental Comparisons
Classified by Hours of Treatment*

Hours

	1-10	11-20	21-30	31-40	41-50	51-60	61-75
Freq:	4	9	3	0	2	1	1

*Experimental Comparisons
Classified by Follow-up Times*

Months

	0	1-3	4-6	7-9	10-12
Freq:	4	0	10	1	5

Summary tabulations of a few characteristics of the studies are presented in Table 2.7.   For the data in Table 2.6, interest centers primarily on the outcome measures. Since the "effect size" for these studies is expressed as a "success" rate, there are two ways of summarizing the outcomes: (1) the data can be pooled across all studies to calculate aggregate "success" rates for treatment and control groups or (2) the "success" rates for treatment and control groups can be averaged across the 20 experiments within the 15 studies.

By the first method of aggregation, one finds 651 patients treated with psychotherapy with 269 reported as "successes," for a success rate of 41%. The comparable figures for the control condition are 641 cases, 222 "successes" for a "success" rate of 35%. The 41% versus 35% difference is not very impressive; but it may not be very fair. Since each study is given a weight in the aggregate proportional to its sample size, a few studies like Gallant (1971) and McCance and McCance (1969) carry unreasonably large weight in determining these aggregates. Between them, these two studies account for nearly half of all the therapy cases.

Averaging success rates across studies seems preferable. Doing so yields "success" rates of 51% and 33% for psychotherapy and control conditions, respectively. These figures are probably more defensible than the 41% versus 35% figures. Even so, a "success" rate of about 33% for untreated controls is unusual and indicates that the experiments were probably conducted under favorable circumstances with other than chronic alcoholics. But even if the 33% base-rate figure is unrealistic, the 18% gap between treatment and control groups is not. One can conclude that *on the average 20 hours of psychotherapy produces 18 "successes" (sobriety 6 months after therapy) out of every 100 persons treated beyond those "successes" that would occur naturally.*

The percentage "success" rates can be transformed into a metric measure of effect by means of the probit transformation (see Chapter 5 below). A discrepancy from 51% to 33% success rate corresponds to a standardized measure of effect of + .96 standard deviation unit. Expression of the effect in this way would permit comparison of the effects across problem areas such as alcoholism, asthma, or surgery (Schlesinger et al., 1980).

The relationship of the differential success rate to follow-up time was also studied (see Figure 2.3). The difference in percentages of "successes" between treatment and control groups diminished across follow-up intervals. Immediately after therapy, there were 35% more successes in the therapy group than the control group; at 6 months after therapy this difference dropped to about 20%; at 12 months it was virtually 0%, that is, the rate of sobriety is virtually the same in the treatment and control groups, the treated patients having relapsed. Apparently, for the benefits of the therapy to be sustained, it must be readministered at periodic intervals.

Finally, the correlation across the 15 studies between the number of hours of therapy and the differential "success" rate was positive and reasonably large: + .49. More therapy was better than less.

School Class Size and Achievement

Some of the first empirical research in education, that of Rice in the 1890s, examined the association between class size and learning. The literature on class size and achievement had been reviewed repeatedly. The reviewers disagreed wildly. The problems with these previous reviews of the class size literature are several: (1) literature searches were haphazard

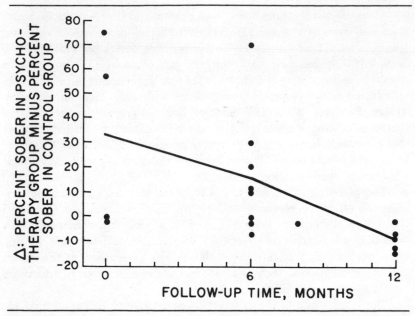

Figure 2.3 Effect of psychological treatment of alcoholism related to follow-up
time.

and often overly selective—dissertations were avoided, as a rule, and few
reviewers sought out large archives of pertinent data; (2) reviews were
typically narrative and discursive though the multiplicity of findings could
not be absorbed without quantitative methods of reviewing; (3) reviewers
used crude classifications of class sizes; and (4) they took statistical
significance of differences far too seriously.

For the meta-analysis, class size studies were sought in three places:
document retrieval and abstracting resources; previous reviews of the class
size literature, and the bibliographies of studies once found. The ERIC
system and *Dissertation Abstracts* were searched completely on the key
words "size," "class size," and "tutoring." The dissertation literature was
covered as far back as 1900, and the fugitive educational research literature was covered from the mid-1960s to 1978.

About 300 documents were obtained and read. Of them, 150 were
found to contain no usable data, that is, no data whatsoever were reported
on the comparison of small- and large-class achievement. About 70 studies

examined the relationship of class size to nonachievement outcomes (attitudes and interests) and classroom process variables (see Smith and Glass, 1980). Approximately 80 studies on the class size and achievement relationship were included in the meta-analysis.

It is difficult to estimate what portion of the existing literature was captured by this search. Even though 80 studies exceeded by 50% the most extensive reviews published to that time, perhaps less than half of all studies that exist on the topic were found. Some studies (credited to school districts) could not be located even after several phone calls and letters. Other studies were surely missed because of odd or nondescript titles. Fortunately, the ERIC system uses key words based on the contents of an article and not titles alone. Several studies found in the journal literature by branching off existing bibliographies had neither "size" nor "class size" in the title, evidence enough that several studies were missed because their titles lacked the key words. Another complication concerns the use of class size as an incidental variable in studies focused on other issues. There are probably many such studies, and only a few of the most visible ones were located.

The meta-analysis was to determine what the available research revealed about the relationship of class-size to achievement. Drawing boundaries around this topic was simple compared to the difficulties encountered in defining psychotherapy, for example. Conventional definitions of achievement seem scarcely to have changed over 80 years; and class size is relatively easily described and measured.

The quantification of characteristics of studies permitted the eventual statistical description of how properties of studies affect the principal findings. Such questions can be addressed as "How does the class size and achievement relationship vary as a function of age of pupils?" or "How does it vary between reading and math instruction?" The first step was to identify those properties of studies that might interact with the relationship between class size and achievement. There is no systematic logical procedure for taking this step. The major properties coded were as follows: (1) year of publication; (2) publication source (book, thesis, journal); (3) subject taught (reading, math, etc.); (4) duration of instruction (number of weeks); (5) number of pupils in the study (different from class size since there might be many classes); (6) number of teachers in the study; (7) pupil ability; (8) pupil ages; (9) types of experimental control (random assignments, matching, etc.); (10) achievement measurement (standardized test, ad hoc test, etc.); (11) quantification of outcomes (gain scores, analysis of covariance adjustment, etc.).

No matter how many class sizes were compared in a particular study, the results could be reduced to some number of pairs, a smaller class against a larger class. The mean difference between the performances of the pair was standardized in a manner similar to that illustrated earlier in the asthma study. Because the comparisons were not between a standard treatment and standard control condition, the effects were subscripted to indicate the sizes of the two classes compared. The effect measure is given by the formula:

$$\Delta_{S-L} = (\overline{X}_S - \overline{X}_L)/\hat{\sigma} \qquad [2.1]$$

where:

$\overline{X}_S$ is the estimated mean achievement of the *smaller* class which contains S pupils

$\overline{X}_L$ is the estimated mean achievement of the *larger* class which contains L pupils

$\hat{\sigma}$ is the estimated within-class standard deviation, assumed to be homogeneous across the two classes.

The effect size measure in Equation 2.1 provides a common expression of the magnitude of study outcomes for all types of outcome variable (school achievement, in this example). Where such basic descriptive measures as means and standard deviations were not included in a report, the effect size was usually estimated by transformations of common reported statistics (t, F, etc.) by methods outlined in Chapter 5.

In all, 77 different studies were read, coded, and analyzed. These studies yielded a total of 725 Δ's. The comparisons were based on data from a total of nearly 900,000 pupils spanning 70 years of research in more than a dozen countries. In Table 2.8 appears the frequency distribution of Δ's by year in which the study appeared. It is clear from Table 2.8 that class-size research was an active early topic in educational research, was largely abandoned for 30 years after 1930, and has been resurrected in the last 15 years. In Table 2.9, the comparisons are tabulated by the type of assignment of pupils to the different size classes. Each of the first three types of assignment represents reasonably good attempts at eliminating

TABLE 2.8   Class-Size Comparisons ($\underline{\Delta}$) by Year of Study

Year	No. of Δ's	%	Cumulative %
1900-1909	22	3.0%	3.0%
1910-1919	184	25.4%	28.4%
1920-1929	138	19.0%	47.4%
1930-1939	47	6.5%	53.9%
1940-1949	1	0.0%	53.9%
1950-1959	62	8.6%	62.5%
1960-1969	150	20.8%	83.3%
1970-1979	121	16.7%	100.0%
	725	100%	

TABLE 2.9   Class-Comparisons (Δ) by Assignment of Pupils to the Small and Large Classes

Type of Assignment	No. of Δ's	%
Random	110	15.2%
Matched	235	32.4%
"Repeated Measures"	18	2.5%
Uncontrolled	362	49.9%
	725	100.0%

gross inadequacies in design; these three conditions account for slightly more than half of all the comparisons. Even though half of the comparisons involved comparing naturally constituted and nonequivalent large and small classes, some of these were based on ex post facto statistical adjustments for preexisting differences. So the data are not half worthless; indeed, whether the experimental inadequacies influenced the findings is an empirical question—rather than an a priori judgment—which was examined in the data analyses. In Table 2.10 appears the joint distribution of smaller and larger class sizes on which the 725 Δ's are based. For example, 6 Δ's derive from comparisons of group sizes 1 and 3. (The table contains

TABLE 2.10   Joint Distribution of Smaller and Larger Class-sizes in the
              Comparisons Δ_{S-L}

		1	2	3	4-5	6-10	11-16	17-23	24-34	≥35	Total
						Larger Class-size					
	1	-	1	6	1	3	7	1	34	0	53
	2		-	0	1	0	0	1	0	0	2
	3			-	0	0	0	0	6	0	6
Smaller Class-size	4-5				-	0	0	1	2	0	3
	6-10					-	8	0	5	2	15
	11-16						-	19	44	27	90
	17-23							-	78	106	184
	24-34								-	197	197
	≥35									-	-
	Total	-	1	6	2	3	15	22	169	332	550

only 550 entries instead of 725, since comparisons would not be recorded
in this tabulation if S and L were contained within the same broad
category, for example, if $S = 18$ and $L = 22$.)

The simple statistical properties of the Δ's were interesting in themselves, even though their full import required more sophisticated analysis:

Properties of Distribution of Δ_{S-L}

(1) N = 725
(2) Mean = .088; Median = .050
(3) 40% of the Δ_{S-L} were negative; 60%, positive
(4) Standard deviation = .401
(5) Range: –1.98 to 2.54.

On the average, the 725 Δ_{S-L}'s were positive, that is, over all comparisons available—regardless of the class sizes compared—the results favored
the smaller class by about .1 of a standard deviation in achievement. This
finding is not too interesting, however, since it is an average across many
different sizes of classes compared. However, only 60% of the Δ's were
positive, that is, favored the smaller class in achievement. This is so even

though every effort was made to find studies spanning the full range of class sizes from individual tutorials to huge lectures. One suspects that the odds of observing a positive Δ_{S-L} in the class size range so often studied (15 to 40, say) were even smaller, perhaps as low as 55% to 45%.

In these rough summaries, one of the fundamental problems is revealed that has made the class size literature so difficult for reviewers. If the relationship one seeks has only 55-to-45 odds of appearing and one looks for it without all the tools of statistical analyses that can be mustered, the chances of finding it are slight. One need not wonder why narrative reviews of a dozen or two studies produced little but confusion.

To make sense of the class size and achievement relationship, one must account for the magnitude of the Δ's and their variance in terms of the sizes of the smaller and larger classes. What was needed was a continuous quantitative model that would relate class size C to achievement z. Class size and achievement might be expected to be related in something of an exponential or geometric fashion—reasoning that one pupil with one teacher learns some amount, two pupils learn less, three pupils learn still less, and so on. Furthermore, the drop in learning from one to two pupils might be expected to be larger than the drop from two to three, which in turn is probably larger than the drop from three to four, and so on. A logarithmic curve represents one such relationship:

$$z = \alpha - \beta \log_e C + \epsilon, \qquad [2.2]$$

where C denotes class size and is a unit variance normal variable. Since β could be zero or negative, the model in Equation 2.2 does not preclude the data showing that class size and achievement are unrelated or that larger classes learn more than smaller ones.

In Equation 2.2, α represents the achievement for a "class" of one person, since $\log_e 1 = 0$, and β represents the speed of decrease in achievement as class size increases. Equation 2.2 cannot be fitted to data directly because z is not measured on a common scale across studies. This problem was circumvented by calculating Δ_{S-L} for each comparison of a smaller and a larger class within a study. Then, from Equation 2.1 and 2.2 one has:

$$\begin{aligned}
\Delta_{S-L} &= (\alpha - \beta \log_e S + \epsilon_1) - (\alpha - \beta \log_e L + \epsilon_2) \\
&= \beta(\log_e L - \log_e S) + \epsilon_1 - \epsilon_2 \\
&= \beta \log_e (L/S) + \epsilon \qquad\qquad\qquad\qquad\qquad [2.3]
\end{aligned}$$

The model in Equation 2.3 was particularly simple and straightforward. The values of $\Delta_{S\text{-}L}$ were merely regressed onto the logarithm of the ratio of the larger to the smaller class size, forcing the least squares regression line through the origin.

The least-squares estimate of the β parameter was found to have the form:

$$\hat{\beta} = \frac{\Sigma(\Delta_{S\text{-}L})\,(\log_e L/S)}{\Sigma(\log_e L/S)^2}.$$

The model in Equation 2.2 was fitted to the data base as a whole and to many subdivisions of it. The strength of the relationship between class size and achievement did not vary (with one exception) with characteristics of the studies (e.g., age of pupils, ability, subject taught). The relationship was much stronger for studies in which pupils were randomly assigned to the classes of different sizes than for studies that used matched or uncontrolled assignment; thus, better controlled studies gave more positive results. Hence, the estimation of the relationship was restricted to the 100 or so Δ's that arose from the well-controlled experiments. After fitting the model in Equation 2.2 to the data, estimating β and transforming z to a percentile scale, the relationships in Figure 2.4 emerged. Assuming arbitrarily that the average pupil in a class of 40 scores at the 50th percentile in achievement, then student's improvement in achievement as class size is reduced is indicated by the upper curve in the figure. When taught in a class of 15, achievement rises to the 60th percentile; in a group of 10, to the 65th percentile; and taught alone (class size equals 1), to a score above the 80th percentile. The report of the meta-analysis concluded with these words:

A clear and strong relationship between class-size and achievement has emerged. The relationship is seen most clearly in well-controlled studies in which pupils were randomly assigned to classes of different sizes. Taking all findings of this meta-analysis into account, it is safe to say that between class-sizes of 40 pupils and one pupil lie more than 30 percentile ranks of achievement. The difference in achievement resulting from instruction in groups of 20 pupils and groups of 10 can be larger than 10 percentile ranks in the central regions of the distribution. There is little doubt that, other things equal, more is learned in smaller classes [Glass and Smith, 1979: 15].

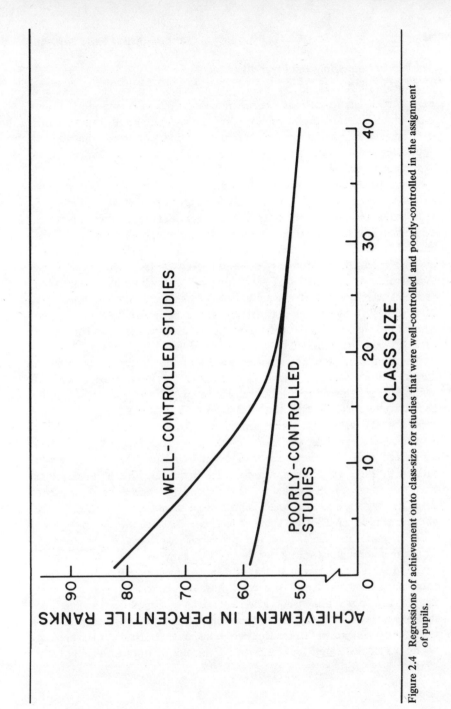

Figure 2.4 Regressions of achievement onto class-size for studies that were well-controlled and poorly-controlled in the assignment of pupils.

Sex Bias in Counseling and Psychotherapy

Smith (1980c) found 34 studies of possible bias of counselors and psychotherapists toward male versus female clients. A typical study examined experimentally the possibility that counselors and therapists varied their diagnoses, recommendations, and attitudes toward their client depending on the client's sex. The 34 studies contained 60 assessments of possible sex bias.

There was wide variation in the designs used, their adequacy, and the extent to which "client" individual differences were considered. However, each study was used in the meta-analysis regardless of its qualities. Thus, the reviewer's theoretical and methodological biases had minimal influence. The studies were rated for design quality so that the magnitude of sex bias produced by studies of different levels of design quality could be ascertained. A score of 3 was given for studies in which all experimental variables were controlled and the effects of client characteristics. A score of 2 was given to studies that merely had experimental variables under control. A score of 1 was assigned to studies in which experimental variables were uncontrolled or seriously confounded.

The transforming of the reported results of the studies into a common metric followed the method of Chapter 5 of this text. Each dependent variable from the studies was coverted into an "effect of sex bias" (ESB) according to the following formula: ESB $= (X_{Male} - X_{Female}) / \hat{o}$. In a study of the effect of client gender on therapist judgment of client prognosis, for example, the mean for the prognosis given to females was subtracted from the mean prognosis given to males. The difference was divided by the average standard deviation. Hence, an ESB of +1 indicates that the mean of the males on the dependent variable is 1 standard deviation higher than the mean of the females on that variable. In the above example, an ESB of 1 would indicate that the average male prognosis is more favorable than the prognosis for 84% of the females, assuming a normal distribution of the sex bias variable.

The ESB is standardized so that different measures can be viewed on a common, convenient metric and combined with others to form an overall picture of the sex bias effect. The dependent measures were arranged so that a positive ESB always meant bias against females or against nontraditional, nonconformist, or androgynous actions, decisions, or labels. A negative ESB indicated bias in favor of females or nonconforming, nonstereotypic goals.

Transformation of dependent measures into ESBs was simple when means and standard deviations were given. When t, F, or chi-square statistics were given, estimates of $\hat{\sigma}$ were found by backward solution of statistical formulas (see Chapter 5). Problems arose in the calculation of ESB when the researcher reported only significance levels of effects (when, for example, it was reported only that client sex produced no significant difference on the dependent variable). In this case, an ESB of zero was entered for that variable. (A check on this procedure was conducted after the meta-analysis was completed. Neither altering the procedure nor eliminating these findings from the summary changed the final $\overline{ESB}$ by more than a fraction.)

Another problem was encountered in studies that reported item-by-item significance tests on sex-role stereotyping measures. The item-level data were converted to ESBs, and the average $(\overline{ESB})$ for the item set was recorded for that study. Except for the few studies in which multiple item-level data were averaged, the practice was to record an $\overline{ESB}$ for each dependent measure that the researcher reported. (A later check on the effect of ESB calculated at the level of the dependent measure and at the level of the study showed no differences in the magnitude of effect.) Table 2.11 contains the ESBs calculated for the studies.

The ESB measures were accumulated by the domain under investigation (counseling or psychotherapy) and by the construct measured (attitudes, judgments, or behaviors) and for other variables of interest. The resulting summary statistics are contained in Table 2.12. The means, standard deviations, and the number of effects are presented, along with the standard error of effects, $\hat{\sigma}ESB / \sqrt{n}$. Presentation of the standard error of effects permits a rough-and-ready measure of the significance of difference of the means of two contrasting conditions (e.g., $\overline{ESB}$ for well-controlled studies vs. $\overline{ESB}$ for poorly controlled studies). A difference in means of less than two standard errors was deemed unreliable.

Table 2.12 contains the summary statistics for the sex-bias meta-analysis. The overall mean of ESBs is given along with the mean for each construct, domain, the source of the study, and the validity of the design. The results are clear: There is no evidence for the existence of counselor sex bias when the research results are taken as a whole. The average ESB is $-.04$, indicating that the counselor bias is near zero or even slightly in favor of women and nonstereotyped actions for women. The size of the sex-bias effect does not change from construct to construct. Attitudes,

(text continued on page 51)

TABLE 2.11 Author, Source, Domain, Type of Effect and Effect of Sex Bias (ESB) of Studies

	Source (Dissertation or Journal)	Domain (Psychotherapy or Counseling)	Construct (Attitude, Judgment or Behavior)	Validity	Type of Effect	ESB, Effect of Sex Bias
Aslin, (1974)	D	P	A	2	Sex stereotypes	.23
Broverman, et al. (1970)	J	P	A	2	Sex stereotypes of mentally healthy persons	.56
Friedersdorf (1969)	D	C	A	2	Sex stereotyped interests	0.00
Hayes and Wolleat (1978)	J	C	A	2	Sex stereotypes	–.31
Maslin and Davis, (1975)	J	C	A	2	Sex stereotypes	.56
Lesser (1974)	D	C	A	2	Acceptance of self-orientation	–1.03
Maxfield (1976)	D	P	A	3	Sex stereotypes	0.00
Neulinger (1968)	J	P	A	2	Sex stereotypes	.60
Smith (1972)	D	C	A	3	Sex stereotypes	.01
Wirt (1975)	D	C	A	3	"Evaluation" "Potency" "Activity:	–.68 .63 –.87

TABLE 2.11   Author, Source, Domain, Type of Effect and Effect of Sex Bias (ESB) of Studies (Continued)

	Source (Dissertation or Journal)	Domain (Psychotherapy or Counseling)	Construct (Attitude, Judgment or Behavior)	Validity	Type of Effect	ESB, Effect of Sex Bias
Abramowitz, et al. (1973)	J	C	J	3	Psychological adjustment	.14
Abramowitz, et al. (1976)	J	P	J	2	Prognosis	– .22
Abramowitz, et al. (1975)	J	C	J	2	Psychological adjustment	.01
Billingsly (1977)	J	P	J	3	Treatment goals	0.00
Borgers, et al., (1977)	J	C	J	2	Appropriateness of vocational choice	– .10
Coen (1974)	D	P	J	3	Desire to treat	– .46
					Degree of impairment	.06
					Prognosis	– .30
Donahue and Costar (1977)	J	C	J	1	Remoneration of vocational choice	.58
					Education required for vocational choice	.21
					Supervision required for vocational choice	.61
Freedman (1975)	D	P	J	2	Personality type	.15
					Degree of disturbance	– .26

TABLE 2.11 Author, Source, Domain, Type of Effect and Effect of Sex Bias (ESB) of Studies (Continued)

	Source (Dissertation or Journal)	Domain (Psychotherapy or Counseling)	Construct (Attitude, Judgment or Behavior)	Validity	Type of Effect	ESB, Effect of Sex Bias
Goldberg (1975)	D	P			Treatment type	-1.15
					Readiness for therapy	-.30
					Willingness to treat	-.42
			J	3	Conventionally of chosen occupation	0.00
Hill, et al. (1977)	J	C	J	3	Seriousness of problem	.22
					Ability to profit from counseling	-.17
					Attractiveness as client	.04
					Number of sessions needed	0.00
Lesser (1974)	D	C	J	2	Acceptance of self-orientation	-.03
Lewittes (1973)	J	P	J	2	Degree of pathology	0.00
Maxfield (1976)	D	P	J	3	Degree of disability	-.61
					Recommendation for counseling	
					Prognosis	-.54
					Recommendation for hospitalization	0.00
					Diagnosis	0.00

TABLE 2.11 Author, Source, Domain, Type of Effect and Effect of Sex Bias (ESB) of Studies (Continued)

	Source (Dissertation or Journal)	Domain (Psychotherapy or Counseling)	Construct (Attitude, Judgment or Behavior)	Validity	Type of Effect	ESB, Effect of Sex Bias
Price and Borgers (1977)	J	C	J	2	Appropriateness of course choice	.05
Smith (1972)	D	C	J	3	Need for further counseling	.24
Smith (1974)	J	C	J	3	Prediction of academic success	− .04
					Recommended occupation	.05
Thomas and Stewart (1971)	J	C	J	2	Acceptance	.08
					Appropriateness of career goal	.66
					Need for further counseling	.32
Hill (1975)	J	C	B	2	Counselor behaviors (empathy, etc. combined)	.11
Hill, *et al.* (1977)	J	C	B	3	Empathy	− .23
Libbey (1975)	D	P	B	3	Positive emotion	−1.13
					Specificity	− .52
					Confrontation	− .02

TABLE 2.11   Author, Source, Domain, Type of Effect and Effect of Sex Bias (ESB) of Studies (Continued)

	Source (Dissertation or Journal)	Domain (Psychotherapy or Counseling)	Construct (Attitude, Judgment or Behavior)	Validity	Type of Effect	ESB, Effect of Sex Bias
Petro and Hansen (1977)	J	C	B	2	Affective sensitivity	.29
Pietrofesa and Schlossberg (1971)	J	C	B	1	Sex-biased statements	1.68
Stengel (1976)	D	C	B	2	Empathy	0.00
					Warmth	0.00
					Genuineness	0.00
Wirt (1975)	D	C	B	3	Empathy	0.00
					Positive regard	– .21
					Genuineness	– .87

TABLE 2.12   Summary Data from Sex Bias Meta-Analysis—Mean, Standard Deviation and Number of Sex Bias Effects (ESB) and Standard Error of $\overline{ESB}$ ($\hat{\sigma}_{\overline{ESB}}$)

	$\overline{ESB}$	σ_{ESB}	n_{ESB}	$\hat{\sigma}_{\overline{ESB}}$
Construct				
Attitudes	−.03	.59	12	.17
Judgments	−.03	.35	35	.06
Behaviors	−.07	.66	13	.18
Domain				
Psychotherapy	−.18	.43	24	.09
Counseling	.05	.48	36	.08
Source				
Journals	.22	.41	28	.08
Dissertations	−.24	.46	32	.08
Design Validity				
High	−.18	.38	30	.07
Medium	−.01	.43	26	.08
Low	.77	.63	4	.32
Total	−.04	.47	60	

judgments, and behaviors all show about the same size of effect. Considered separately, the findings labelled *clinical stereotypes* produced an $\overline{ESB}$ of .24, which agrees with the conventional wisdom that clinicians hold negative stereotypes of women. When the standard error of average effects is used to evaluate this, one finds that the $\overline{ESB}$ for stereotypes is not reliably different from the $\overline{ESB}$ of the data as a whole.

The analysis of sex bias reported in journals as opposed to dissertations is extremely interesting. Journal articles showed bias *against* women. Dissertations showed the opposite. One is tempted to suppose that dissertations are more poorly designed and executed and therefore less likely to be published. That supposition is incorrect; the average rating of design quality was slightly *higher* for dissertations than for journals (2.57 and 2.16, respectively). The best designed studies—those in which experimental variables were well-controlled and provision was made to separate sex effects from personal characteristics—yielded results opposite to those of the sex-bias hypothesis. Studies with moderate validity—controlled vari-

TABLE 2.13   Interactions of Design Validity and Source of Study-Means, $\underline{n}$'s and Standard Errors of Effect of Sex Bias

	Source of Study	
Validity of Design	Journals	Dissertation
Low	$\overline{ESB}$ = .77	No Cases
	$\hat{\sigma}\overline{ESB}$ = .32	
	n_{ESB} = 4	
Medium	$\overline{ESB}$ = .19	−.23
	$\hat{\sigma}\overline{ESB}$ = .09	.13
	n_{ESB} = 14	12
High	$\overline{ESB}$ = .00	−.25
	$\hat{\sigma}\overline{ESB}$ = .05	.09
	n_{ESB} = 9	21

ables but no provision for gender and case distinctions—averaged zero on the ESB variable. Studies with poor controls or severe confounding of variables yielded the results most supportive of the sex-bias hypothesis.

Analysis of interactions failed to yield reliable results, with one exception. There was a statistically significant interaction between design quality and publication status, but not in the predicted direction. Table 2.13 contains the $\overline{ESB}$ and standard error of $\overline{ESB}$ for the Design Quality X Source of Publication interaction. Studies published in journals were more likely to show the effect of sex bias, regardless of the quality of their research design. Viewed another way, studies most likely to be submitted or accepted for publication tended to be those that demonstrated the sex-bias effect, their design quality notwithstanding.

DRUG THERAPY FOR PSYCHOLOGICAL DISORDERS

Miller (1977; Smith et al., 1980) sought to integrate a fragmented and widely scattered empirical literature on the effects of drug therapy on persons with debilitating psychological disorders. The conventional wisdom that had long pervaded the field both reflected and supported the political equilibrium that psychiatrists and psychologists had struck. Most mental health practitioners would have declared that verbal psychotherapy practiced by itself on the seriously disturbed (schizophrenic, psychotic) is a waste of time, but that combined with drug treatment (which is effective in isolation) the synergistic combination is much more beneficial than the sum of their separate contributions.

Miller found several thousand experimental studies that bore on the question of the relative efficacy of drug and psychotherapy effects. Most of these were clinical trials comparing drugs against placebos. From this huge literature, Miller sampled at random about 50 studies. The remainder of the literature that Miller reviewed comprised about 125 experiments that compared drugs and psychotherapy in various odd combinations (e.g., drug-plus-psychotherapy vs. drug vs. psychotherapy; or drug-plus-psychotherapy vs. placebo).

Miller calculated the standardized average difference on the dependent variable for each of the outcomes measured in the experimental comparisons. Nearly 550 effects were thus calculated. Summaries of the averages appear in Table 2.14. There one sees, for example, that in 55 comparisons of verbal psychotherapy with an untreated control group or placebo, the psychotherapy group averaged .30 standard deviation units higher on the outcome measure. In 94 comparisons of drug-plus-psychotherapy with psychotherapy alone, the former averaged .44 standard deviation units higher than the latter on the dependent variables. Table 2.14 also gives a parametric structure for the comparisons.

Consider now the problem of combining data in Table 2.14 to obtain estimates of the parameters. That the drug-plus-psychotherapy versus drug comparison, which estimates $\psi + \eta$, is a full one-tenth standard deviation larger than the .30 estimate of ψ from the first line of the table might lead one to believe that η is positive; but the comparison of the estimates of $\delta + \eta$ and δ (being .44 and .51, respectively) reverses this impression. Parameter estimation by inspection in this way is too arbitrary and confusing. Several comparisons in Table 2.14 contain information about the same parameters; it seems reasonable that every source of information about a parameter should be used in estimating it. A complete and standard method of combining the data in Table 2.14 into estimates of the parameters is needed. Such a method is suggested when one recognizes that the two middle columns of Table 2.14 constitute a system of linear equations, three of them independent and containing three unknows (ψ, δ and η). The method of least squares statistical estimation can be applied to obtain estimates of the separate and interactive effects of drug and

TABLE 2.14 Average Effect Sizes from Various Experimental Comparisons Made in the Experiments on Drug and Psychotherapy

Comparison	Parameter(s) Estimated	Average Δ	No. of Δ's
Psychotherapy vs. No-Treatment or Placebo	ψ	.30	55
Drug Therapy vs. No-Treatment or Placebo	δ	.51	351
Drug & Psychotherapy vs. Drug	$\psi + \eta$	.41	10
Drug & Psychotherapy vs. Psychotherapy	$\delta + \eta$	.44	94
Drug vs. Psychotherapy	$\delta - \psi$	.10	7
Drug & Psychotherapy vs. No-Treatment or Placebo	$\delta + \psi + \eta$	.65	49

NOTE: ψ denotes the separate or "main" effect of psychotherapy;
δ denotes the separate effect of drug therapy; and
η denotes their interaction.

psychotherapy. The estimates obtained by application of least squares methodology to the data in Table 2.14 are as follows:

$\hat{\psi}$, the separate effect of psychotherapy = .31
$\hat{\delta}$, the separate effect of drug therapy = .42
$\hat{\eta}$, the interactive effect of drug-plus-psychotherapy = .02

Each effect is expressed on a scale of standard deviation units. Thus, the data of Table 2.14 lead to the conclusion that with the groups of clients studied psychotherapy produces outcomes that are about one-third standard deviation superior to the outcomes for placebo or untreated control groups. The drug effect is only about a third greater than the psychotherapy effect. An effect of $.31s_x$ will move an average client from the middle of the control group distribution to about the 62nd percentile; an effect of .42 would move the average client to only about the 66th percentile. The effects of the two therapies were not greatly different. In addition, the drug therapies were conducted for only half the time it took to conduct the psychotherapies (2.6 months vs. 6.1 months). Any careful assessment of the relative value of drug and psychotherapy will take both effects and costs into account.

Arguments over the relative value of drug and psychotherapy will be simpler for the fact that the *interactive* effect of combining the two therapies is virtually zero ($\hat{\eta}$ = .02). This must not be misunderstood as implying that drug-plus-psychotherapy as a treatment is ineffective, far from it. The near zero interaction effect means that when drug and psychotherapy are combined, one can expect benefits equal roughly to the sum of the separate drug and psychotherapy effects (.31 + .42 = .73), not more or less.

CONCLUSION

The five summaries of meta-analyses presented in this chapter give an indication of the scope of the questions that can be addressed through a statistical integration of a body of empirical research. They also illustrate the ability of such an empirical integration to bring order to large and complex bodies of literature in which narrative reviewers have found confusion or have created an impression of order by radical selection and exclusion of studies.

In the chapters that follow, detailed advice is provided about the identification of a body of literature for review, the classification of study characteristics, the quantification of study findings, and the analysis of data thus generated. In the concluding chapter, various objections raised against meta-analysis are considered.

CHAPTER THREE

FINDING STUDIES

Reviewing and integrating a research literature begins with the identification of the literature—often a widely scattered, variegated landscape of articles, theses, project reports, and whatever. Jackson (1978) showed how this first step was occasionally taken rather uncertainly by reviewers. Of 36 reviews that Jackson analyzed, only one reviewer reported having searched the literature with the help of indexes like *Psychological Abstracts* or *Dissertation Abstracts;* only three reported searching bibliographies of previous reviews of the topic. Whether reviewers do not take such obvious steps in finding studies or take them but neglect to say so may be immaterial from their reader's point of view; in either case it is difficult to judge whether the studies being reviewed represent most of the existing evidence on the question or only an unrepresentative portion. Earlier we likened meta-analysis to survey research; thus, finding studies is comparable in importance to sampling frameworks and methods in survey design and analysis. Locating studies is the stage at which the most serious form of bias enters a meta-analysis, since it is difficult to assess the impact of a potential bias. The best protection against this source of bias is a thorough description of the procedures used to locate the studies that were found so that the reader can make an intelligent assessment of the representativeness and completeness of the data base for a meta-analysis.

As an example of the lengths to which one might sometimes have to go to feel confident of having done a thorough job of finding relevant studies,

consider Miller's experiences in reviewing an enormous literature on the
psychological effects of drug therapy.[1]

To draw conclusions about the entire realm of clinical drug research
on psychological disorders, a sample was taken from the large
number of existing drug therapy studies. An attempt was made to
draw a representative sample of all published clinical drug trials on
mentally ill humans reported in the English language literature
between 1954 and 1977.

The only design requirement for inclusion in the sample was that
studies employ a no-drug treatment or a placebo control group.
Though previous reviewers were admonished for inclusion requirements that were, in this author's opinion, too restrictive (e.g.,
including only double-blind placebo controlled studies), this somewhat arbitrary line was drawn because of a conviction that without a
control group, spontaneous symptom remission rampant in psychiatry would be recorded as a drug effect. Case studies, experiential
reports, pre-post designs, and drug versus drug studies were therefore
omitted.

To identify more clearly the domain from which to sample, further
restrictions were imposed on selection of potential studies. Studies
of patients whose primary diagnosis was somatic were excluded.
Thus omitted were studies of drugs used to treat patients for organic
brain syndrome, epilepsy, phenylketonuria, minimal brain damage,
or Down's Syndrome, and studies of patients with psychophysiologi-
cal disorders (asthma, backache, acne, ulcer, enuresis, angina, etc.).
This criterion did not exclude studies whose primary focus was
examination of neurotic or psychotic patients or patients with
character disorders whose somatization of symptoms led to physiological illness.

All studies of normal subjects and all studies that used *only* physiological outcomes (e.g., blood plasma levels of amines, EEG's, urinaly-
sis) were omitted. Lastly, studies of toxic psychosis (e.g., drug
induced psychosis) or model psychosis (e.g., using hallucinogens)
were not examined.

A Medical Literature and Retrieval System (MEDLARS) search from
the University of Colorado Medical Center computer search facility
generated all research meeting specified meeting specified criteria
catalogued between January 7, 1966, and January 30, 1977. [The
search specifications appear in Table 3.1] The facility catalogues all
studies from approximately 2,400 journals.

TABLE 3.1   Search Formulation–Psychopharmacologic
Research in Humans: Clinical Trials

1) Affective Disturbances F3.126.56	6) Psychoses F3.709.755
Anxiety	Depression, Reactive, Psychotic
Depersonalization	Folie a Deux
Depression	Paranoia
2) Aggression	Psychoses, Involutional
Torture	Involutional Paranoid State
Violence	Melancholic, Involutional
3) Neuroses	Paraphrenia
Depression	Psychoses, Manic-Depressive
Depression, Reactive	Schizophrenia
Depressive Neuroses	Schizophrenia, Catatonic
Hypochondriacs	Schizophrenia, Childhood
Hypochondriacal Neuroses	Autism, Early Infant
Munchausen Syndrome	Schizophrenia, Hebephrenia
Hysteria	Schizophrenia, Latent
Conversion Reaction	Schizophrenia, Paranoid
Globus Hysterious	7) Personality Disorders
Dissociative Reaction	Alcoholism
Duel Personality	Skid Row Alcoholic
Multiple Personalities	Antisocial Personality
Hysterical Neuroses	Sociosyntonic Personality
Neuroesthenia	Disorder
Neurocirculatory Asthenia	As If Personality
Neuroses Anxiety	Cyclothymic Personality
Anxiety, Castration	Hysterical Personality
Anxiety, Separation	Inadequate Personality
Homesickness	Obsessive-Compulsive
Neuroses, Obsessive-Compulsive	Personality
Kleptomania	Paranoia
Obsession	Paranoic Personality
Trichotillomania	Passive-Aggressive Personality
Neuroses, Post-Traumatic	Passive-Dependent
Neuroses, War	Personality
Phobias	Schizoid Personality
Agraphobia	Tension-Discharge Disorders
Claustrophobia	Impulse-Ridden Personality
Phobia Neuroses	8) 1 or 2 or 3 or 4 or 5 or 6 or 7
4) Compulsive Behavior F3.126.208	9) 8 and Drug Therapy
Firesetting Behavior	10) Clinical Research or Research
Gambling	Design
Risk Taking	11) 9 and 10
Obsessive Behavior	
Smoking	12) 11 and Placebos
5) Alcholism C21.613.53.270	13) 11 and (control or controlled)
Psychoses, Alcoholic	14) 12 or 13
Delirium Tremens	
Kersakoff's Syndrome	

Reprinted with the kind permission of Dr. T. I. Miller.

Studies could not be suppressed by design characteristics or outcome variables so though all listed studies met the inclusion requirements there was an unspecified number of studies listed that met the exculsion requirements as well (e.g., there were some uncontrolled studies and studies designed to assess only bio-chemical outcomes of drug administration). Approximately 1,100 studies were located by the MEDLARS search.

Several studies were selected at random from the MEDLARS printouts. As the referenced articles were located and read, it became clear that many studies lacked control groups. Titles containing no allusion to the existence of a control group (via such key words as "double-blind," "crossover," "controlled," or "placebo") portended studies lacking this crucial ingredient. Therefore, to reduce reference retrieval time by directing gathering efforts toward studies very likely to have control groups, articles with titles containing the above-mentioned key words became the primary focus of the random sample. Forty such studies were randomly chosen from the MEDLARS bibliography.

From the psychopharmacological literature prior to January 1, 1966, the period not covered by MEDLARS, a random sample of about fifty studies was taken from bibliographies of comprehensive review articles on the efficacy of drug treatment in psychiatric cases and from studies listed in *Psychological Abstracts* between 1954 and 1966 under the heading Therapy/Drugs. These review articles and the number of bibliographical references made in each are presented in Table 3.2. Shown as the last reference in Table 3.2 is the number of studies sampled from the 1954-1966 *Psychological Abstracts* that became part of the pool of pre-1966 references from which studies were sampled.

Once again the emphasis on title terminology that was likely to indicate the use of a control group was applied to selection of studies from these bibliographies.

The selection of the ninety or so articles (fifty articles from the 1954 to 1966 literature; forty articles from the 1967 to 1977 literature) was stratified so that approximately equal numbers would be represented in three major drug categories: antipsychotic, anti-anxiety, and antidepressant. Once these articles were assembled a few articles were added to assure that major well-known studies and very recently published articles (February and March, 1977) were

TABLE 3.2   Bibliographic References from Which Most Pre-1966 Studies
were Sampled

References	Topic	Number of Studies Listed in Bibliography
Azcarate (1975)	Anti-Agression	43
Davis (1965)	Anti-Depression	410
Davis et al. (1968)	Anti-Depression	369
Hollister, L. (1969)	All Drugs	120
Hollister, L. (1973)	All Drugs	241
Itil, T. (1975)	Anti-Agression	81
Klein and Davis (1969)	a) Mood Stabilizer	472
	b) Minor Tranquilizer	185
	c) Anti-Psychotic	420
Klerman and Cole (1965)	Anti-Depression	341
Morris and Beck (1974)	Anti-Depréssion	185
Sheard, M. (1975)	Anti-Agression	60
Psychological Abstracts	Therapy/Drugs	26
(1954-1966)		
	TOTAL	2,963

Reprinted with the kind permission of Dr. T. I. Miller.

not overlooked. Ninety-six articles or books studying the effects of
drug therapy were thus collected, read and coded [Miller, 1977:
31-36].

Miller's example has been reported here, in rather more detail than may
seem kind to the reader, to make a point. Documenting the methods used
in finding research literature takes more space than custom traditionally
allocates to describing one's search. How one searches determines what
one finds; and what one finds is the basis of the conclusions of one's
integration of studies. Searches should be more carefully done and docu-
mented than is customary.

THE LANDSCAPE OF LITERATURE

Scholarly, empirical literature in the social sciences and applied fields can be found in either primary or secondary sources. By primary sources is meant the archival periodical literature—"the journals," hundreds, perhaps thousands, of them from all over the world. Dissertations and theses are also regarded as primary sources, as well as "fugitive" literatures of government reports, papers from scholarly meetings, reports to foundations, public agencies, and the like.

Secondary sources cite, review, and organize the material of the primary sources; they include review periodicals (e.g., *Psychological Bulletin, Review of Educational Research, Sociological Review*), periodical reviews (*Encyclopedia of the Social Sciences, Encyclopedia of Educational Research*), and various abstract and citation archives such as these:

> Abstracts in Anthropology
> Child Development Abstracts and Bibliography
> Current Index to Journals in Education
> Dissertation Abstracts International
> Education Index
> Government Reports Announcements & Index
> Index Medicus
> Index of Economic Articles
> Interagency Panel Information System
> International Bibliography of Economics
> International Bibliography of Political Science
> International Political Science Abstracts
> Journal of Economic Literature
> Library of Congress Catalog
> National Clearinghouse for Mental Health Information
> National Institute for Mental Health Grants and Contracts Information System
> National Technical Information Service
> Psychological Abstracts
> Research in Education
> Smithsonian Science Information Exchange
> Sociological Abstracts.

Some systems are computerized and quite sophisticated. For example, the Educational Resources Information Center (ERIC) operated by the

National Institute of Education is a remarkable service that not only indexes and abstracts the published literature in education (see *Current Index to Journals in Education*) but the fugitive literature as well (see *Resources in Education*). More significantly, ERIC is a system organized around a thesaurus of topic descriptors assigned by experienced staffs of readers of the documents; this feature represents a significant advance over indexes that depend on author-selected descriptors or the key words of titles.

Secondary sources can thus facilitate the identification of the primary sources that will be the subject of the review. These primary sources, however, can supplement the search since their bibliographies will contain many relevant articles, some of which will be fugitive documents that might well not have appeared in the secondary sources. For early literature there is no other source as Miller's example illustrated. Our purpose is not to provide either an exhaustive listing of the sources from which a reviewer might most effectively identify the items in a body of literature or to describe the characteristics of various indexes. The technology of information storage and retrieval is advancing so rapidly that whatever detail we might give here is likely soon to be out of date. The potential reviewer must first determine the current stage of development of all systems that could be put to good use.

RELIABILITY OF LITERATURE SEARCHES

No matter how ambitious and sophisticated are one's efforts to find *all* empirical research on a topic, the aspiration to find everything must be inevitably frustrated. There is simply too much literature in too many strange places to find it all. But reviewers can do a better job than they typically have done. The arbitrary exclusion of vast amounts of literature (e.g., excluding all dissertations or all fugitive manuscripts in ERIC) is unsound and bespeaks more faintness of heart than intelligence of judgment. Nevertheless, even the most conscientious efforts fall short of perfection. There is less reliability in searching for research studies than would be tolerable in survey research, for example; but it is an especially intransigent sort of unreliability for which we have no facile solutions.

We tested the reliability of four large research indexes by computerized search on descriptors for "group homes for delinquents." The four indexes were ERIC, *Psychological Abstracts, Dissertation Abstracts*, and *Council for Exceptional Children Abstracts.* A total of 27 different studies were found. But they were distributed according to the cross-classification in Table 3.3. For example, of 8 studies on the topic found in the ERIC system, 2 were also listed in *Psychological Abstracts*, and 3 also appeared in the *CEC Abstracts*. Of the 8 ERIC studies, 5 did not appear in any of the other three indexes. The greatest proportion of redundancy appears to be between *Psychological Abstracts* and *CEC Abstracts* on this topic. Table 3.3 gives one pause. Perhaps the social and behavioral sciences need indexes of indexes.

PUBLICATION BIAS AND META-ANALYSIS

The goal of the meta-analyst should be to provide an accurate, impartial, quantitative description of the findings in a population of studies on a particular topic. This may be done by exhausting the population or sampling representatively from it. No survey would be considered valid if a sizable subset (or stratum) of the population was not represented in the cumulative results. Neither should a meta-analysis be considered complete if a subset of its population is omitted. One very important subset of evidence is the subset of unpublished studies. To omit dissertations and fugitive research is to assume that the direction and magnitude of effect is the same in published and unpublished works.

The most radical criticism of the assumption of equivalence is the old saw that the published literature only represents the 5% of false positives in a population of studies wherein the null hypothesis is true. That is, the published stratum and the unpublished stratum have opposite average effects, and a meta-analysis containing only published studies would be wholly unrepresentative of the population. Rosenthal (1979) effectively countered this attack by mathematical demonstration of the numbers of studies which would have been languishing in file drawers to make up the 95% null results. The existence of such huge numbers is considered implausible.

The results of meta-analyses which did represent both published and unpublished literature provide direct evidence on the assumption of equivalence. Table 3.4 contains the results of 11 such meta-analyses. *In every one of the nine instances in which the comparison can be made, the average experimental effects from studies published in journals is larger than the corresponding effect estimated from theses and dissertations.* If one integrates only "published" (meaning journal published) studies, the impression of support for the favored hypothesis will be artificially

TABLE 3.3 Numbers of Listings from Different Data Bases

Search on: (Achievement (w) Place) and (Teaching (w) Family) (group homes for delinquents)

	ERIC	PSYCHOLOGICAL ABSTRACTS	DISSERTATION ABSTRACTS	CEC ABSTRACTS
ERIC	8	2	–	3
PSYCHOLOGICAL ABSTRACTS	2	22	2	9
DISSERTATION ABSTRACTS	–	2	4	–
CEC ABSTRACTS	3	9	–	18
UNIQUE	5	11	2	9

TABLE 3.4 Relationship Between Source of Publication and Findings in 11 Meta-Analyses of Experimental Literatures

Investigator(s)	Topic		Source of Publication			
			Journal	Book	Thesis	Unpubl.
Kavale (1979)	Psycholinguistic training	n.:	13		16	5
		$\bar{\Delta}$.:	.50		.30	.37
Hartly (1977)	Computer-based instruc.	n.:	34		13	34
		$\bar{\Delta}$.:	.36		.28	.54
	Tutoring	n.:	9		47	17
		$\bar{\Delta}$.:	.77		.40	1.05
Rosenthal (1976)	Experimenter bias	n.:	25		50	
		$\bar{\Delta}$.:	1.02		.74	
Smith (1980c)	Sex bias in psychotherapy	n.:	28		32	
		$\bar{\Delta}$.:	.22		−.24	
Smith (1980a)	Effects of aesthetics educ. on basic skills	n.:	29		164	56
		$\bar{\Delta}$.:	1.08		.48	.50
Carlberg (1979)	Spec. ed. room placement vs. reg. room placement	n.:	146	17	45	114
		$\bar{\Delta}$.:	−.09	−.01	−.16	−.14
	Resource room plac. vs. reg. room place	n.:	33	6		
		$\bar{\Delta}$.:	.32	−.09		
Miller (1977)	Drug therapy of psych. disorders	n.:	336	21		
		$\bar{\Delta}$.:	.49	.56		
Hearold (1979)	Effects of TV on anti-social behav.	n.:	262	120	96	13
		$\bar{\Delta}$.:	.40	.14	.18	.23
Subtotals		n.:	1025	177	473	268
		$\bar{\Delta}$.:	.38	.18	.30	.27
Smith, Glass & Miller (1980)	Psychotherapy	n.:	1179	42	483	61
		$\bar{\Delta}$.:	.87	.80	.66	1.96
Totals		n.:	2204	219	956	329
		$\bar{\Delta}$.:	.64	.30	.48	.58

enhanced over what would be seen if the entire literature were integrated (i.e., journals, books, and dissertations). The bias in the journal literature relative to the bias in the dissertation literature is not inconsiderable. The mean effect size for journals is .64 as compared with .48 for the dissertation literature; hence, the bias is of the order of $[(.64 - .48)/.48]$ 100% = 33%. Thus, findings reported in journals are, on the average, one-third standard deviation more disposed toward the favored hypotheses of the investigators than findings reported in theses or dissertations.

In the meta-analysis of sex bias in counseling and psychotherapy (Smith, 1980c), not only the magnitude but also the direction of effect was different in published and unpublished studies. A positive effect size indicated the biasing effect of counselor attitudes, judgments, and behaviors against female clients or against nonstereotyped roles for females. The effect size from published studies was .22, demonstrating counselor bias against females. The effect size from unpublished studies was - .24 demonstrating counselor bias *in favor* of females.

White (1976) also produced evidence of a selective publication effect in his meta-analysis of the relationship between socioeconomic status and achievement. The average of 165 correlations published in books was .31; 38 r's in journals averaged .25, and 286 dissertation correlations between achievement and socioeconomic status showed an average of .20. This trend, toward weaker relationships in dissertations than in journals, agrees with the trend established above for various experimental literatures.

From these data it is appropriate to conclude that failing to represent unpublished studies in a meta-analysis may produce misleading generalizations. To omit dissertations because of their assumed lack of rigor is also unwarranted. Only after the studies have been quantified and their results transformed to effect size measures can it be determined whether published studies on a topic were more rigorously designed than were unpublished studies and whether rigor of design related to magnitude of effect. In the psychotherapy meta-analysis (Smith et al., 1980), there was no reliable difference in the rigor of design of published versus unpublished studies. In the sex bias meta-analysis (Smith, 1980c), the published studies that showed bias against females actually had *less rigorous* designs than did studies (either published or unpublished) which showed no bias against females.

To make these decisions a priori may inject arbitrariness and bias into the conclusions. If meta-analysis offers any improvement over traditional methods of reviewing research, it is precisely in the area of removing these sources of arbitrariness to arrive at an impartial and representative view of "what the research says."

NOTE

1. Quoted here with the kind permission of Dr. T. I. Miller.

CHAPTER FOUR

DESCRIBING, CLASSIFYING AND
CODING RESEARCH STUDIES

In meta-analysis, primary research reports constitute the data for statistical integration of a literature. Both the characteristics of the primary studies and their findings are quantified so that the statistical integration can be performed. Quantification of study findings is the topic of Chapter 5. In this chapter our concern is the quantitative description of the characteristics of studies; this quantification usually involves measurement in its metric aspects (e.g., in what year was this study done? What is the sample size on which r_{xy} is based?) as well as its nominal or coding function (were initial differences corrected by analysis of covariance? Yes = 1, No = 2). Since meta-analysis entails the measurement of study characteristics and findings, many concerns that apply to measurement generally apply to measurement as used in meta-analysis.

Consider the example in Table 4.1. There are recorded the characteristics and findings of about 20 correlational studies of the relationship between teachers' "indirect" teaching style (nonauthoritarian, encouraging discussion instead of lecturing) and pupils' learning. For example, in Study # 13 (Torrance and Parent, 1966), the indirectness of 10 teachers' styles was correlated with their pupils' mathematics achievement for a yearlong course at the high school level; the data were reported in the form of a Spearman rank-order correlation coefficient, which is itself the best estimate of the Pearson r. The reported correlation of teacher indirectness and pupil achievement was +.32, pupils learned more mathematics from more indirect teachers.

On the face of the problem, there are five variables or characteristics descriptive of each study : the number of teachers studied (the sample size, in effect), the duration of the period of instruction, the subject tested, the grade level of the pupils, and the form of the originally reported findings (r's, F's, etc.). In addition, of course, there is an estimate of the correlation on the Pearson r scale, either provided directly in the report or estimated from the results that were reported.

If one probes deeper, even more characteristics of studies than the five indicated are apparent or can be inferred from the research reports. For example, the year in which the study was reported appears in Table 4.1 and could be an interesting property of studies in a field subject to fads and trends. The identity of the researcher is known, and sometimes other characteristics can be inferred from such knowledge, for example, whether this researcher has done several studies or only one; whether he has taken a public position on what this research ought to show; whether he is related to other researchers as mentor to student or as colleague to colleague. Moreover, variables that appear simple and straightforward reveal unexpected complications after a closer look. Take, for instance, "grade level" in Table 4.1. If students and teachers are spread among several grades (across fourth, fifth, and sixth but averaging grade five, say), it may be necessary to code both the average or modal grade of pupils represented and the range of grades as separate characteristics of the studies.

The point of measuring and coding of study characteristics is to relate the properties of the studies to the study findings. For example, by comparing the r's for studies done at the elementary (K-6) and secondary (7-12) levels in Table 4.1, we can see that the correlation between teacher indirectness and pupils' learning is higher ($r = .30$, based on 8 studies) at the secondary level than at the elementary level ($r = .16$, based on 10 studies), perhaps because young pupils need more direction or perhaps because lecturing style is less relevant in earlier grades (Glass et al., 1977).

We hope that the example of a meta-analysis of teacher indirectness helped make the point that the measurement of study characteristics and findings requires thought and care in the definition of properties of studies and their quantification.

GENERAL CONSIDERATIONS

Measurement of study characteristics can be evaluated in terms of both its validity and reliability, as can any instance of measurement.

TABLE 4.1 Results of Studies on the Relationship Between Teacher Indirectness and Pupil Achievement (After Gage, 1978)

Study	No. of Teachers	Duration of Teaching	Learning Tested — Subject	Grade Level	Reported Statistics	Equivalent Value in Terms of r_{xy}
1. Flanders (1970)	15	2 semesters	Language skills	2	r = −.073	−.073
			Number skills			
2. Flanders (1970)	16	2 weeks	Social studies	4	r = .308	.308
3. Flanders (1970)	30	2 semesters	Composite MAT	6	r = .224	.224
4. Flanders (1970)	15	2 weeks	Social Studies	7	r = .481	.481
5. Flanders (1970)	16	2 weeks	Mathematics	8	r = .428	.428
6. Cook (1967)	8	2 semesters	Discussion–Lab Work	10		.09
						.07
7. Furst (1967)	15	4 one-hour lessons	Economics	10, 12	$F_{1,13} = 7.15$	.11
						.26
8. Medley-Mitzel (1959)	49	2 semesters	Reading	3-6	r = .20	.20
9. Powell (1968)	9	2 semesters	Composite SRA	3	F=5.85 F=10.68	.23
			Reading		F=1.30 df=1,164	.11
			Arithmetic			.31
10. Snider (1966)	17 (10 in analysis)	2 semesters	Science	12	Mann-Whitney U: U = 18 U = 12	.29
					U = 13 U = 14	.00
						.00
						.06
11. Weber (1968)	26	3 years	Creative Thinking	4	F = 10.58 df = 1,176	.30
			Verbal Fluency			

TABLE 4.1   Results of Studies on the Relationship Between Teacher Indirectness and Pupil Achievement (After Gage, 1978) (continued)

Study	No. of Teachers	Duration of Teaching	Learning Tested Subject	Grade Level	Reported Statistics	Equivalent Value in Terms of r_{xy}
12. Thompson & Bowers (1968)	15	2 semesters	Word Meaning Social Studies	4	$F \leq 1$, $F = 2.0$ $df = 1,13$	.34 .46
13. Torrance-Parent (1966)	10	2 semesters	Mathematics	7-12	rho = .32	.32
14. Allen (1970	18	2 semesters	Arithmetic	1	$p = .83$; $p = .83$; $p = .79$	-.23 -.23 -.19
15. Soar (1966)	55	2 semesters	Vocabulary; Reading Arithmetic (Concepts) Arithmetic (Problems) Arithmetic (Total)	3-6	$r = .068$ $r = .021$ $r = .034$ $r = .083$ $r = .081$	.068 .021 .034 .083 .081
16. Soar et al. (1971)	35	6 months	Reading Readiness	K	$r = .00$	.00
17. Hunter (1968)	20 11	2 semesters	Reading, Spelling & Arithmetic	1 ages 8-14	$r = .30$ $r = .62$	.30 .62
18. LaShier (1965)	10	6 weeks	Biology	8	$\tau = .60$	.60
19. Pinney (1969)	32	2 45-minute lessons	Social Studies & English	8-9	$F = 4.2$ $df = 1,30$	.22

Validity

The validity of measurements of study properties is a very broad topic. Most things that bear on the meaning of a coded or measured characteristic are matters of validity. These considerations include such things as clarity of definitions, adequacy of reported information, the degree of inference a coder must make in determining from the written report what characterized the research, and the like. Some problems of validity can be corrected by greater care in reading and coding studies: making definitions sharper and more detailed, splitting broad concepts into more refined ones. Other problems of validity cannot easily be corrected: One might have to infer that in a particular study the assignment of subjects to experimental conditions was nonrandom because random assignment was not specified and there were significant differences on most pretest variables. There probably are no useful general technical guidelines for making study measurement more valid. Examples will have to substitute for principles.

Consider a somewhat extreme example of measurement of study characteristics that was pursued with more than normal care for the sake of the validity of the measurement. Smith and Glass (1977) performed a meta-analysis of nearly 400 controlled experiments on psychotherapy outcomes. One characteristic of studies that was of principal interest was the type of psychotherapy being evaluated (e.g., Rogerian, Adlerian, behavioral). Even the simple labelling of the psychotherapy in a single study grew unexpectedly difficult at times. Could a psychotherapy described as "nondirective reflection of feeling plus empathic understanding" be properly coded as Rogerian in the absence of the investigator's having labelled it Rogerian or otherwise referred to Carl Rogers? Yes, it probably was safe to do so. But what of tougher cases? Suppose an investigator reported a study comparing "psychotherapy" against a wait-list control group, but rather than naming the specific type of psychotherapy, merely referred to the therapists' attempts "to interpret clients' defense mechanisms and help them gain insight into the causes of their difficulties." Is it safe to assume that the therapy was psychoanalytic psychotherapy and code it as such in the meta-analysis? Or would it be more prudent to classify the therapy as "eclectic insight therapy?" There is no general answer since questions at this level would be resolved by particular considerations of the purposes of the meta-analysis. The examples merely illustrate the complexities of defining and recognizing qualities of studies from written reports and the inadequate descriptions of treatments provided in many reports.

In this work on psychotherapy outcomes, complexities of measurement (or classification) were encountered again at a more general level. More than 20 specific types of psychotherapy appeared in the nearly 400 experiments. These 20 were fairly easily grouped into 10 more general types of psychotherapy: Rogerian, Gestalt, Rational-emotive, Transactional Analysis, Adlerian, Freudian, Psychoanalytic Psychotherapy, Behavioral Modification, Systematic Desensitization, and Implosion. It was deemed worthwhile to attempt to group these 10 psychotherapies into a small number of still more general classes so as to address additional questions in the meta-analysis. But questions remained about how this grouping might best be done. On the basis of what evidence or what process of judgment would therapies, A, B, and C be deemed to belong to Therapy Class I and therapies D and E to Therapy Class II? In a general sense, the question was one of measurement validity, even if measurement in this instance was only classification and coding. Perhaps the least valid grouping of therapies into homogeneous classes would have been based on the reviewers' own unexplained judgment of which therapies were similar to which others. Instead, the help of about 25 clinicians and counselors was enlisted. For about 10 hours, the theory and techniques of each of the 10 psychotherapies were studied and discussed. Then the therapists gave their rankings of the similarities among the psychotherapies using the method of multidimensional scaling (Shepard, 1962). A graphic representation of the therapists' perceptions of the similarities among the 10 psychotherapies (see Figure 4.1) was the result. In the three-dimensional space in Figure 4.1, the distance between two therapies (represented by black circles) is inversely related to the similarity between the therapies in the perceptual space of the judges (therapists). The four amoebalike figures in Figure 4.1 connect therapies that are near each other in the space. Thus, Rogerian and Gestalt therapies form a class of psychotherapies, as do Rational-emotive and Transactional Analysis. In this manner, four classes of psychotherapies were derived, and they were derived so as to reduce the influence of arbitrariness and idiosyncrasy—thus, one hopes they represent a more valid classification (measurement) of studies than might otherwise have been done.

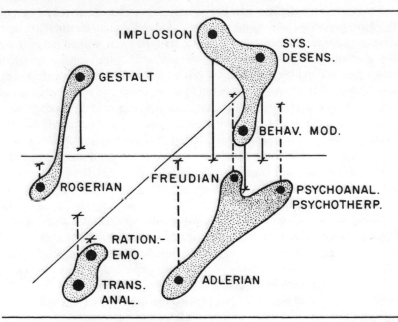

Figure 4.1   Multidimensional scaling of ten types of psychotherapy by 25 clinicians and counselors.

Reliability

Reliability in the generic sense of the word refers to consistency of measurement. Inconsistencies can occur if the phenomenon observed (e.g., individual or group behavior) is unstable, if the method of judging the behavior (e.g., interview, observation, questionnaire) varies, or if the judges are inconsistent because of disagreements among themselves or across time.

The measurement problem in meta-analysis is the problem of measuring (quantifying, classifying, coding) the characteristics and findings of studies based on written reports. The principal source of measurement unreliability in meta-analyses, therefore, arises from different readers (coders) not seeing or judging characteristics of a study in the same way. Judge consistency or rater agreement is the most important consideration for our purposes. The report itself is stable.

There is no total remedy for the inconsistency that arises among different coders of the same research study. Explicit instructions, specificity in defining characteristics, and *Gruendlichkeit* will all help reduce the problem somewhat, but there are limits to what can be specified before the fact and how much detail can be imposed on coders before they quit. The guidelines we propose are (1) good sense and reasonable care at the outset, (2) assessment of the extent of disagreement by having multiple judges read a set of common studies, and (3) correction of flagrant inconsistencies discovered at step 2. Step 2 is the important one; all but the simplest meta-analyses should be subjected to an assessment of the reliability (in the rater agreement sense of the word) of the coding procedures.

An example may help clarify this recommendation. In assessing the comparative effects of drug versus psychotherapy, Smith et al. (1980) developed an extensive coding system for describing the characteristics and findings of 151 experiments collected from the literature of psychopharmacology. To test the reliability of the coding, two judges were enlisted to code five studies. One judge coded two studies, and one coded three. The judges were unfamiliar with the psychopharmacological literature, but well-practiced in general coding and effect-size calculation common in meta-analysis.

Each judge received a drug-only study and a study of drug-plus-psychotherapy. The studies were chosen at random from all studies under 10 pages in length. This restriction of length was adopted to reduce the time necessary for the judges to devote to the task. A brief list of coding conventions was given to each judge, with a request to code only the effect size for one or two dependent variables if there were many from which to choose.

There were 162 ratings recorded by the two judges over the five studies (not including the effect sizes themselves) and matched with an equal number of ratings by a third judge. Of these, 122 (75%) were identical and another 13 (8%) were within one or two scale points for five-point rating scales or continuous variables such as patient age, duration of treatment, and the like. Of the ratings, 17% were placed into the wrong category or were off by more than two scale points. These incorrect codings included such inconsistencies as the rating of an outcome measure as hospital adjustment rather than work adjustment or as somatic symptoms instead of anxiety. The codings of the two judges did not differ substantially from the codings of the third.

TABLE 4.2 Effect sizes for two judges compared to those of a third judge

	Study	Δ for judge 1 or 2	Δ for judge no. 3	Size of error
Judge 1	Study 1	0.50	0.54	0.04
	Study 2	0.64	0.67	0.03
Judge 2	Study 3	−1.15	−0.95	0.20
	Study 4	0.87	0.85	0.02
	Study 5	1.58	1.58	0.00
	Study 6	1.08	0.93	0.15
		$\bar{\Delta} = 0.59$	$\bar{\Delta} = 0.60$	Average: 0.07

Agreement between each judge's calculation of effect sizes and an earlier independent calculation was substantial. A sixth study was added exclusively to give another test to the replicability of effect-size calculation. This study was chosen to represent a relatively complex case for calculation. Calculated by the second judge, it is reported last in Table 4.2.

The effect sizes referred to in Table 4.2 are mean differences divided by standard deviations, a measure of experimental outcome already encountered several times in this text. It may strike the reader as curious that in only one of six instances in Table 4.2 did the two judges make calculations of effect size that agreed through two decimal places. Be assured that the discrepancies (none terribly large and on the average quite small, viz., .07) do not seem surprising at all to us. As will be seen in Chapter 5, although the definition of Δ is very simple, its calculation in particular instances can be extremely complex, frequently calling on complicated judgments about how to aggregate sources of variation, about when to make simplifying assumptions and when not to, and often entailing arduous chains of calculations in which accuracy may be compromised by rounding off a six-digit answer to four digits at some intermediate stage.

CHARACTERISTICS OF STUDIES

The characteristics of studies that are most important in a meta-analysis (apart from the findings, of course) can be roughly classified as either *substantive* or *methodological*. Substantive features are those characteristics of studies that are specific to the problem studied, for example, in a meta-analysis of drug treatment of hyperactivity the substantive characteristics might include: (1) the type of drug administered (caffeine, amphetamines, etc.); (2) the size of the dose; (3) the age of the subjects; (4) the presence or absence of checks for ingestion; and so on. The methodological characteristics of studies are more general; they may be nearly the same for all meta-analyses of a general type, such as experimental studies, correlational studies, or surveys. They include a virtual table of contents of research methods books: (1) sample size; (2) test reliability; (3) randomization versus matching versus nonequivalent groups; (4) degree of subject loss; (5) single-blind, double-blind or unblinded; and the like.

The purpose underlying coding the substantive and methodological characteristics of studies is the same: one wants to learn whether the

TABLE 4.3   Class Size Coding Sheet

IDENTIFICATION:
  1) Study ID#: _____-_____ . 2) Authors: _____. 3) Year: _____
  4) Source of data: ___Journal ___Book ___Thesis ___Unpublished report
  5) Classification of study: ___Class size   ___Ability grouping   ___Tutoring
                              ___Psychol. experiment ___Secondary analysis
  6) Country of origin: _____ .

INSTRUCTION:
  1) Subject taught: ___Reading ___Math ___Language ___Other: _____
  2) Duration of instruction: ___hrs. ___weeks
  3) Supplemental vs. integral: ___Instruction supplemented other large group instruction.
                                ___Instruction constituted entire teaching of the subject.
  4) Adaptation of instruction to class size:
       Type of instruction in smaller class: _____

       Type of instruction in larger class: _____

	Smaller Class	Larger Class
5) No. of pupils:	_____	_____
6) No. of instructional groups:	_____	_____
7) No. of instructors:	_____	_____
8) Pupil/instructor ratio:	_____	_____
9) Accuracy of estimate of ratio:	Lo Av Hi	Lo Av Hi

  10) Instructor type: ___Teachers ___Adult aides of tutors ___Both
  11) Sex of teacher: ___M ___F
  12) Years teaching experience: ___years

CLASSROOM DEMOGRAPHICS:
  1) Pupil ability: ___IQ < 90 ___90 < IQ < 110 ___IQ > 110
  2) Percent pupils female: ___%
  3) Ages: 4 5 6 7 8 9 10 11 12 13 14 15 16 17 18
  4) Average age: ___years

TABLE 4.3   Class Size Coding Sheet (continued)

STUDY CONDITIONS:
1) Study setting: ____Regular classroom ____Experimental setting
2) Assignment of Ss to groups: ____Random ____Matched ____"Repeated measures"
   ____Uncontrolled
3) Assignment of instructors to groups: ____Random ____Matched ____"Repeated measures"
   ____Uncontrolled
4) Percent attrition: Small class: ____% Large class: ____%

OUTCOME VARIABLE:
1) Type of Outcome Variable:
   ____Standardized achievement test: _____
   ____Ad hoc achievement test: _____
   ____Pupil attitude: _____
   ____Teaching behavior: _____
   ____Pupil-teacher interaction: _____
   ____Teacher attitude or satisfaction: _____
2) Quantification of Outcome:
   ____Gain scores (simple)
   ____Residualized gain scores
   ____Uncorrected dependent variable
3) Congruence of instruction and outcome measure: Low Average High
4) Follow-up time: ____weeks from the end of instruction to the measurement of outcomes
5) Standardized mean difference (Small-Large): _____

findings differ depending on certain of the characteristics of the studies. A meta-analysis seeks a full, meaningful statistical description of the findings of a collection of studies, and this goal typically entails not only a description of the findings in general but also a description of how the findings vary from one type of study to the next. An example might clarify the use of both substantive and methodological study characteristics in this respect.

Coding in a Meta-Analysis of School Class-Size and Achievement

In a meta-analysis of the relationship between school class size and pupil achievement, nearly 30 substantive and methodological features of each study were coded including the findings, namely, the standardized average difference in achievement between the larger, L, and the smaller, S, class (details in Chapter 2)—a facsimile of the coding sheet used for the classification is reproduced as Table 4.3. Substantive features of studies were classified using the items Instruction # 1-# 12, Classroom Demographics # 1-# 4, Outcome Variable # 1, # 4. Methodological features were classified using the items Identification # 3-# 6, Study Conditions # 1-# 4, Outcome Variable # 2, # 3 (and to some extent # 1). The quantification of the Outcome Variable was item # 5. The data from over 700 comparisons of pupil achievement in smaller and larger classes were integrated into an aggregate curve descriptive of the relationship as revealed by the empirical research literature. But the analyses did not stop there. Many persons feel that the nature of the relationship between class size and learning may vary depending on what subject is taught (mathematics learning may flourish in small classes, but not physical education, for example) or the age of the learners. To check for these possibilities, the class size and achievement relationship was analyzed separately for various subdivisions of the data. For example, all studies involving pupils in grades kindergarten through six were separated from those involving pupils in secondary school. Statistical curves describing the relationship of achievement and class size were then derived using the data from these two sets of the studies. The two curves were nearly the same (within statistical error) so that there was no evidence that the relationship between class size and achievement depended on the age groups of pupils. In fact, none of the substantive classifications revealed variations in the relationship.

One methodological characteristic of the studies, however, was strongly related to the conclusions. Over 100 comparisons of achievement in smaller and larger classes came from studies in which preexisting differences between classes were controlled by random assignment to the two classes; the remaining comparisons came from studies in which poor controls were exercised (e.g., naturally occurring smaller and larger classes were compared). The studies were thus distinguished with respect to a characteristic of research method. When the statistical curves were derived for these two parts of the data, quite a different picture emerged from what was seen when elementary-grade and secondary-grade studies were compared. The graphs of the two curves appear in Figure 4.2. Not only what was said about the class size and achievement relationship but also what was concluded about the trustworthiness of research on the question were affected by the discovery that the study findings varied as a function of methodological characteristics of the studies themselves.

Coding for a Meta-Analysis of Psychotherapy Experiments

For the meta-analysis of psychotherapy outcome experiments (Smith et al., 1980), a long list of substantive and methodological characteristics for describing the research literature was developed. The numeric coding of each study extended across nearly three computer cards—211 digits of coding in all. A facsimile of the coding sheet appears as Appendix A to this

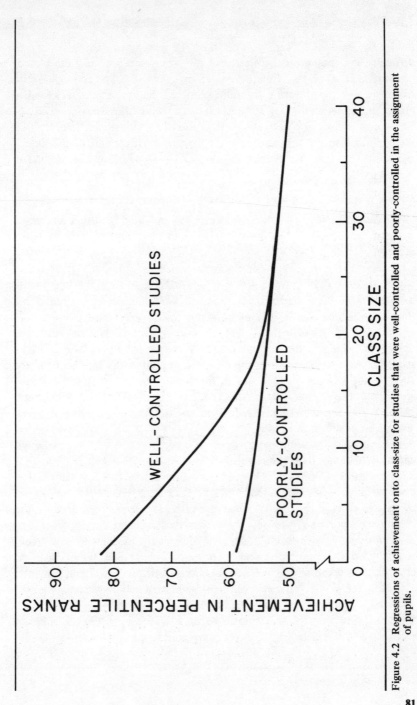

Figure 4.2 Regressions of achievement onto class-size for studies that were well-controlled and poorly-controlled in the assignment of pupils.

book. The task of filling out this sheet for a study presented a range of difficulty depending on the clarity of the research report and the experimenter's adherence to standard research practices. A list of coding conventions was developed during the pilot phase of the project and was used to guide the classification of studies when characteristics were ambiguous. These conventions for both substantive and methodological characteristics are explained in the following paragraphs and illustrated in the coding of the study by Krumboltz and Thoresen (1964) which is reproduced in Appendix B.

Methodological Coding for Psychotherapy Outcome Experiments

Publication date. The date was recorded as stated on the manuscript. For studies that were published more than once, the earliest date was recorded.

Publication form. The study was classified according to the form in which it appeared: journal article, book, thesis, or unpublished manuscript. If more than one form was used, such as a thesis later published in a journal, the study was designated in its most accessible form.

Blinding of experimenter. This study characteristic represents the degree of blinding that prevailed in the assessment of outcomes in the study. If the experimenter or the outcome evaluator was kept uninformed about whether each subject was in the control or the treated group, the study was classified as "single blind." If no information was provided that showed that the experimenter or evaluator was kept uninformed about group composition, the study was categorized as either "experimenter did the therapy" or "experimenter knew the composition of the groups but did not personally treat the client."

Solicitation of Clients. The use of volunteers in therapy studies has been sufficient cause for some previous reviewers to disallow these studies as tests of therapeutic effect. Yet in the case of most analogue studies, the volunteers reported symptoms, then requested and were given psychological treatment. It is possible that they differ only in degree from "real" clients who independently seek treatment. The studies were classified according to whether (1) the subjects were solicited for therapy by the experimenter (usually by offering treatment to psychology students who obtained extreme scores on anxiety measures); (2) the subjects came to the treatment program in response to an advertisement; (3) the subjects recognized the existence of a problem and sought treatment; (4) the subjects were referred for treatment; or (5) the subjects were committed to the treatment, without choice.

Assignment to groups. Random assignment of persons to groups insures, within probability limits, that the two groups are initially comparable and that differences between them on the posttest are attributable either to chance (with probability equal to the significance level) or to the treatment and no other source of influence. Matching pairs of subjects is the next best method, although using it presumes that all sources of influence on therapy are known and can be used as matching variables. Moreover, it renders significance levels meaningless when calculated in the usual ways. Ex post facto matching and covariance adjustments are less satisfactory allocation methods. Studies were classified according to the assignment of both clients and therapists to groups.

Experimental mortality. The percent mortality was coded separately for treated and untreated groups. These figures were occasionally difficult to ascertain and involved comparing degrees of freedom in posttest analyses with the numbers of subjects originally allocated to groups. A study might also have different rates of mortality at the times of the posttest and the follow-up. These different mortality percents were noted separately.

Internal Validity. The internal validity of a study was judged on the basis of the assignment of subjects to treatment and the extent of experimental mortality in the study. To be judged high on the internal validity scale, a study had to have used random assignment of subjects to groups and have a rate of mortality less than 15% and equivalent between the two groups. If mortality was higher or nonequivalent, internal validity was still rated high if the experimenter included the scores of the terminators in the posttest statistics or established the initial equivalence of terminators and nonterminators. Medium internal validity ratings were given to (1) studies with randomization but high or differential mortality; (2) studies with "failed" randomization procedures (e.g., where the experimenter began by randomizing, but then resorted to other allocation methods, such as taking the last 10 clients and putting them into the control group) with low mortality; and (3) extremely well-designed matching studies. Low validity studies were those whose matching procedures were quite weak or nonexistent (e.g., where intact convenience samples were used) or where mortality was severely disproportionate. Occasionally, statistical or measurement irregularities decreased the value assigned to internal validity, such as when an otherwise well-designed study employed different testing times for treated and untreated groups.

Allegiance of the experimenter. Faith in the therapy on the part of the therapist has been mentioned as a cause of positive therapeutic effects. From the tone and substance of the research report, it was usually possible to determine whether the experimenter was partial to the treatment evaluated. For example, when the report contained enthusiastic endorsements of the therapy, this variable was coded as positive. Where a second therapy was clearly a foil for the favored therapy, this variable was coded as negative. Placebo treatments were always coded as negative.

Reactivity of outcome measure. Highly *reactive* instruments are those which reveal or closely parallel the obvious goals or valued outcomes of the experimenter, which are under control of the therapist who has an acknowledged interest in achieving predetermined goals, or which are subject to the client's need and ability to alter his scores to show more or less change than actually took place. Relatively nonreactive measures are not so easily influenced in any direction by any of the parties involved. Usng this definition of reactivity, it was possible to define a five-point scale with the low end anchored at unreactive measures, such as physiological measures of stress (e.g., Palmar Sweat Index), and the high end anchored by "therapist judgments of client improvement." Points on the scale are further illustrated in the following table:

Conventions for assigning values of reactivity to tests and ratings

Reactivity value	Tests and ratings of therapy outcome
1 (lowest)	Physiological measures (PSI, Pulse, GSR), grade point average
2	Blinded ratings and decisions–blind projuctive test ratings, blind ratings of symptoms, blind discharge from hospital
3	Standardized measures of traits having minimal connection with treatment or therapist (MMPI, Rotter I-E)
4	Experimenter-constructed inventories (nonblind), rating of symptoms (nonblind), any client self-report to experimenter, blind administration of Behavioral Approach Tests
5 (highest)	Therapist rating of improvement or symptoms, projective tests (nonblind), behavior in the presence of therapist or nonblind evaluator (e.g., Behavioral Approach Test), instruments that have a direct and obvious relationship with treatment (e.g., where desensitization hieratchy items were taken directly from measuring instrument)

Methodological codings of studies such as those provided by the categories above would be relevant for many different meta-analyses since they reflect important considerations of research design. Whether variations among studies on dimensions such as these make a difference in their results is an empirical question. In the psychotherapy meta-analysis (Smith et al., 1980), they did not. In the class size meta-analysis (Glass and Smith, 1979; Smith and Glass, 1980), they did.

Substantive Coding for Psychotherapy Outcome Experiments

Professional affiliation of experimenter. The study was classified according to the affiliation of the experimenter, as either psychology, education, psychiatry, social work, or "other." This classification was determined by the institutional and departmental identification on the manuscript or by membership in a visible scholarly organization.

Client-therapist similarity. The socioeconomic and ethnic similarity between client and therapist is also thought to influence the outcome of therapy. The cultures of the therapists and the client are regarded as similar if they share languages, value systems, and educational backgrounds. The healthier the client, the more he resembles the therapist. The highest value (4) was used for studies of white, middle-class, well-educated, and mildly or moderately distressed clients. The lowest value (1) was used when the typical therapist treated lower class minority or severely disturbed clients.

Client diagnosis. The diagnostic label that the experimenter used was recorded and classified into 12 categories: (1) neurotic or true (complex) phobic, (2) simple (monosymptomatic) phobic, (3) psychotic, (4) normal, (5) character disordered, (6) delinquent or felon, (7) habituee (e.g., alcohol, tobacco, drug addiction), (8) emotional-somatic disordered, (9) handicapped (physically or mentally), (10) depressive, (11) mixed diagnoses, and (12) unknown.

Hospitalization. The duration of previous hospitalization, as stated or implied by the author, was another indication of the severity of client distress.

Intelligence. The intelligence of the group was rated as "below average" for IQ scores less than 95, "average" for IQ scores between 95 and 105, and "above average" for IQ scores above 105. The source of information about client intelligence was also recorded. In 4% of the studies, IQ was reported by the experimenter. In 61% of the studies, IQ could be inferred roughly from the client's placement in an institution such as a college or a treatment facility for the mentally retarded. In 35% of the cases, client intelligence could not be assessed from the report.

Therapy modality. Each study was coded for the modality in which the therapy was delivered—individual, group, family, mixed modalities, automated, or "other."

Treatment location. Each study was coded according to the location in which the therapy was delivered—school, hospital, mental health center, other clinic, private practice, college facility, prison, residential facility, or "other."

Therapy duration. The duration of therapy, both in number of hours and weeks, was recorded. The rate (hours per week) of therapy was computed from these two variables.

Therapist experience. The therapists' experience was recorded. Because reports frequently omitted this information, the following conventions were developed for translating relevant bits of information into years of therapist experience:

Therapist Status	*Years Experience*
Undergraduates or other untrained assistants	= 0 year
MA candidates	= 1 year
MA-level counselor or therapist	= 2 years
Ph. D. candidate or psychiatric resident	= 3 years
Ph. D.-level therapist	= 5 years
Well-known, Ph. D.-level therapist	= 7+ years

Outcome measurements. The specific outcome was recorded and grouped into 1 of 12 outcome types: (1) fear or anxiety measures; (2) measures of self-esteem; (3) tests and ratings of global adjustment; (4) life indicators of adjustment; (5) personality traits; (6) measures of emotional-somatic disorders; (7) measures of addiction; (8) sociopathic behaviors; (9) social behaviors; (10) measures of work or school achievement; (11) measures of vocational or personal development; and (12) physiological measures of stress. The table below contains the outcome measures that were grouped within two outcome types (life indicators of adjustment and social behaviors):

Outcome labels grouped into two outcome types

	Outcome type
Life indicators of adjustment	*Social behaviors*
Number of times hospitalized	Interpersonal maturity
Length of hospitalizations	Interpersonal interaction
Time out of hospital	Social relations
Employment	Assert
Time out of hospital	Social relations
Employment	Asswet
Time out od	
Time out of hospital	Social relations
Employment	Assertiveness
Discharge from hospital	IPAT sociability scale
Completion of tour of duty	Acceptance of others
Recidivism	FIRO-B
	Dating behavior measures
	Problem behavior in school social setting
	Social effectiveness
	Social distress
	Sociometric status
	Social distance scale
	Social adjustment

Treatment. To determine whether the therapeutic effect produced in a study was related to the type of treatment used, a system for categorizing treatments was developed. There were 18 types of psychotherapy (including placebo) distinguished.

(1) Psychodynamic therapies were those employing concepts such as unconscious motivation, transference relationship, defense mechanisms, structural elements of personality (id, ego, superego), ego development, and analysis.

(2) Dynamic-eclectic therapies are based on dynamic personality theories, but employ a wider range of techniques than the more orthodox Freudian theory.

(3) Adlerian therapy is based on the notion of never-ending strivings of the personality to escape from a sense of inferiority. Striving for superiority alienates people from love, logic, community life, and social responsibility.

(4) Hypnotherapy (Wolberg, Erickson) is one type of therapy that uses hypnosis as a tool for increasing relaxation and suggestibility and weakening ego defenses. Hypnotherapy is closed related to psychodynamic theory, suggesting that such neurotic states as anxiety, hysteria, and compulsions are susceptible to this treatment.

(5) Client-centered or nondirective psychotherapy is associated with Rogers, Truax, Carkhuff, Gendlin, and Axline, among others. The key concepts of this therapy include the necessary conditions of therapist congruence, empathy, and unconditional positive regard for the client.

(6) Gestalt therapy was developed by Perls and, like Rogerian therapy, is humanistic and phenomenological in philosophy. The healthy person can readily bring into awareness all parts of his personality and apprehend them as an integrated whole. Therapy is a process of heightening awareness through immediate here-and-now emotional and physical experiences and exercises and integrating alienated elements in the person.

(7) Rational-emotive psychotherapy was developed by Ellis and rests on a cognitive theory of human personality and therapeutic intervention. Irrational beliefs are common for people in distress and pervasive in our society. They include the notion that one must be universally loved, or that failure at a task is utterly catastrophic. The therapist confronts the irrational reactions and teaches the client to confront them himself. The objective of therapy is to replace the irrational, self-defeating cognitions with logical and empirically valid cognitions.

(8) Other cognitive therapies comprise a family of therapeutic theories related to Ellis's rational-emotive psychotherapy in that the place of cognitive process—faulty beliefs, irrational ideas, logically inconsistent concepts—is central. These therapies are often active, didactic, directive, sometimes bordering on being hortatory. The therapists confront logical inconsistencies, interpret faulty generalizations and self-defeating behaviors, assign tasks, and generally use suggestion and persuasion to get the client to give up his self-defeating belief system.

(9) Transactional analysis is primarily associated with Eric Berne, who developed a personality theory based on three ego states—the parent, adult, and child—and the interrelationship of these ego states within a person and between persons. All beliefs, cognitions, and behaviors are under the control of these ego states. Therapy consists of on-going (usually group) diagnosis and interpretation of the structural elements of communication and interaction, with the goal of improved reality testing and complementary transactions.

(10) Reality therapy is identified with William Glasser and is based on the idea that persons who deny reality are unsuccessful and distressed. Reality is achieved by the fulfillment of the basic needs—to love and be loved and to feel self-worth (success identity). The therapist establishes a personal relationship with the client; attends to present behavior rather than historical events or feelings; interprets behavior in light of the theory; and encourages the formation of value judgments about correct behavior and a plan for changing behavior, rejecting excuses for a failure to change, and the development of self-discipline.

(11) Systematic desensitization is a therapy based on scientific behaviorism, primarily associated with Wolpe. In this therapy, anxieties are eliminated by the contiguous pairing of an aversive stimulus with a strong anxiety-competing or anxiety-antagonistic response. The usual procedure is to teach the client deep muscle relaxation (a response antagonistic to anxiety) and then introduce anxiety-provoking stimuli, arranged in hierarchies, in connection with the relaxation until the client can confront and overcome the anxiety directly.

(12) Implosive therapy, developed by Stampfl, operates on many problems similar to those addressed by systematic desensitization and is based on classical conditioning models. The therapist directs the client's imagery so that he is forced to imagine the worst possible manifestation of his fear, and the connection between conditioned stimulus and conditioned response is extinguished.

(13) Operant-respondent behavior therapies are a family of treatment programs in which the scientific laws of learning (according to Skinner) are invoked. The client is viewed as a recipient of reinforcement or conditioning.

(14) Cognitive behavior therapies are a family of therapies in which laws of learning are applied to cognitive processes. Unlike the strictly operant or respondent theories, in cognitive-behavioral therapies, the client

is more of an active agent in his own therapy, occasionally even administering the treatment himself (e.g., self-control desensitization). Modeling treatments are included in this family of therapies because the client must identify with the model and adopt the behavior for which the model (but not the client) is reinforced.

(15) Eclectic-behavioral therapy is a collection of treatments that employs behavioral principles in training programs designed to affect a variety of emotions and behaviors. Assertiveness training is the principal therapy.

(16) Vocational-personal development counseling involves providing skills and knowledge to clients to facilitate adaptive development. Frequently, a trait and factor approach is used with aptitude and personality testing, diagnosis, prescription, and interaction with the client to facilitate the development of personal, social, education, and vocational skills.

(17) "Undifferentiated counseling" refers to therapy or counseling that lacks descriptive information and references that would identify it with proponents of theory. It is usually practiced in schools, but sometimes is used as a foil against which a more highly valued therapy can be compared. That is cannot be attributed to any single theorist or group of writers is indicative of its lack of theoretical explication.

(18) Placebo treatments were often included in an experimental study of therapeutic effectiveness. Placebos were used to test the effects of client expectancies, therapist attention, and other nonspecific and informal therapeutic effects. The placebo treatments tested in the meta-analysis were the following: relaxation training, attention control, relaxation and suggestion, relaxation and visualization of scienes in an anxiety hierarchy, group discussion, reading and discussing a play, informational meetings, pseudo-desensitization placebo, written information about the phobic object, bibliotherapy, high expectancy placebo, visualization of reinforcing scenes, minimal contact counseling, T-scope therapy, pseudo-treatment control, and lectures.

A scale was developed to indicate the degree of confidence in classifying therapy labels into therapy types. The greater the number of concepts, descriptions, and proponents named by the experimenter and associated with a major school of thought, the higher the value assigned to this scale. The highest value (5) was given to a study when the major proponent of a theory actually participated in the study or when the therapy sessions were recorded and rated for their fit with the theory. The low point of the scale (1) was given to studies when the experimenter provided almost no key concepts or references.

The coding of the substantive characteristics presented here will not be as readily generalized to other meta-analyses as will the methodological characteristics in the previous section. For enhancing one's understanding of a body of literature and the field it represents, however, substantive issues are usually more important than methodological ones. As it happened with the class size research (Glass and Smith, 1979; Smith and Glass, 1980), the substantive distinctions did not alter the general conclusion, thus confirming its general validity. In the psychotherapy meta-analysis (Smith et al., 1980), the substantive distinctions produced some important differences, though not always those that were most expected.

CHAPTER FIVE

MEASURING STUDY FINDINGS

All quantitative, empirical studies aim to assess some particular phenomenon. In the case of experiments, that phenomenon is an effect of an independent variable on some dependent variables which are measured by differences between means, perhaps more than one such difference from a single experiment. In the case of correlational studies, the phenomenon of principal interest is the relationship between two variables, its strength and direction, usually expressed on a scale derived from Pearson's notion of product-moments. In case of surveys, the phenomenon is usually a simple rate or incidence figure, for example, 37% of people live in multiple-family dwellings. Meta-analysis provides for the statistical integration of empirical studies of a common phenomenon. The findings of all the studies must be expressed on some common scale for this integration to be feasible. The findings are the dependent variable in the statistical analysis. The independent variables in the analysis are the substantive and methodological characteristics of the studies discussed in Chapter 4.

In this chapter, our concern is with the quantification of the findings of empirical research. Study findings can be expressed directly in cases where a simple statistical expression of results is common to all studies. The differential success rate of psychotherapy and control conditions in the treatment of alcoholism (see Chapter 2) is an example of findings expressed as a difference between two percentages. In this chapter, we are concerned with more complex cases where scales and methods of reporting findings vary from study to study. We consider first those methods that make use of findings reported in the form of statistical significance test statistics or their associated probabilities. At this first level, studies are classified only as "statistically significant" or "nonsignificant." This primitive translation of complex findings into crude categories proves to have some unexpected drawbacks; but in modified forms, it may yet prove to have some advantages in a few special instances. Then we shall discuss at length the properties and uses of $\Delta_{E\text{-}C}$, the standardized mean difference for describing experimental effects. A special aspect of this problem is the measurement of experimental effects, Δ, for dichotomously measured outcome variables. A brief section is devoted to the measurement of findings in correlational studies.

USING SIGNIFICANCE TESTS

Vote-Counting Procedures

The most commonly used method of integrating research studies is what Light and Smith (1971) referred to as the *voting method*. There exists a virtually huge number of such reviews, and no purpose would be served by citing examples here. Light and Smith characterized the voting method in these words:

> All studies which have data on a dependent variable and a specific independent variable of interest are examined. Three possible outcomes are defined. The relationship between the independent variable and the dependent variable is either significantly positive, significantly negative, or there is no significant relationship in either direction. The number of studies falling into each of these three categories is then simply tallied. If a plurality of studies falls into any one of these three categories, with fewer falling into the other two, the modal category is declared the winner. This modal categorization is then assumed to give the best estimate of the direction of the true relationship between the independent and dependent variable [1971: 443].

Light and Smith pointed out that the voting method of study integration disregards sample size. Large samples more frequently produce "statistically significant" findings than do small samples. Suppose that nine small-sample studies yield not quite significant results, and the tenth large-sample result is significant. The vote is one "for" and nine "against," a conclusion quite at odds with one's best instincts. So much the worse for the voting method. Precisely what weight to assign to each study in an aggregation is an extremely complex question, one that is not answered adequately by suggestions to pool the raw data (which are rarely available) or to give each study equal weight, regardless of sample size. If one is aggregating arithmetic means, a weighting of results from each study according to $\sqrt{n}$ might make sense, reasoning from an admittedly weak analogy between integrating study findings and combining independent random samples from a population. The problems of proper integration of statistical findings are not simply problems of sample size; if pursued for long, they lead back to the ambiguities of the concept of a "study."

Some of the complications of sample size can be avoided post hoc if the sample size, n, of studies is shown to be not systematically related to the magnitude of the findings of the studies. Smith and Glass (1977) found for over 800 measures of the experimental effect of psychotherapy versus a control condition that the effect size had a linear correlation of only - .10 with n and essentially no curvilinear correlation. Smaller size studies tended to show slightly larger effects, but the relationship was so weak that it is doubtful that any weighting of findings would make any difference in the aggregation. This type of analysis does not indicate which weights to use when sample size proves to be related to findings, but it can indicate when the problem might be safely ignored.

A serious deficiency of the voting method of research integration is that it discards good descriptive information. To know that televised instruction beats traditional classroom instruction in 25 of 30 studies—if, in fact, it does—is not to know whether television wins by a nose or in a walkaway. One ought to integrate measures of the *strength* of the study findings. Unfortunately, researchers commonly believe that significance levels are more informative than they are. Tallies of statistical significance or insignificance tell little about the strength or importance of a relationship, an observation made with tedious regularity in contemporary research literature.

An example will demonstrate that the aggregation of even simple statistical information can create unexpected difficulties. There exists a paradox attributed to E. H. Simpson by Colin Blyth (1972) which has a counterpart in aggregating research results. Imagine that researcher A is conducting a study of the effect of amphetamines on hyperactivity in sixth-grade children. (It is alleged that amphetamines act as depressants on prepubescent children.) In A's study, 110 hyperactive children receive the amphetamine, and 70 receive a placebo. After six weeks' treatment, each child is rated as either "improved" or "worse." The following findings are obtained:

Study A

	Amphetamine	Placebo	
Improved	50	30	80
Worse	60	40	100
	110	70	180

The improvement rate for the amphetamines exceeds that for the placebo: .45 versus .43.

Suppose researcher B is studying the same problem at a different site and obtains the following results:

Study B

	Amphetamine	Placebo	
Improved	60	90	150
Worse	30	50	80
	90	140	230

Again, the improvement rate for amphetamines is superior to that for the placebo: .67 versus .64.

By the voting method of aggregation, the score would be 2-0 in favor of amphetamines. However, an aggregation of the raw data produces the opposite conclusion:

Studies A & B Combined

	Amphetamine	Placebo	
Improved	110	120	230
Worse	90	90	180
	200	210	410

The improvement rate for placebo now exceeds that for amphetamines: .55 for amphetamines versus .57 for placebo.

Which method of aggregation is correct? Obviously they cannot both be correct, since they lead to contradictory conclusions. In pondering this paradox and its implications for research integration, it is helpful to note that (1) the paradox has nothing whatever to do with statistical significance, (2) the sizes of the differences in rates could be made as large or small as one wished by juggling the figures, (3) the basic problem is related to the problems of unbalanced experimental designs (Simpson's paradox could not occur if amphetamine and placebo groups were of equal size within each study), and (4) the practical consequences of the paradox are not negligible it occurred, for example, in a study of sex bias in graduate school admissions (see Bickel et al., 1975).

Hedges and Olkin (1980) discovered some intriguing and unexpected deficiencies in the vote-counting method of integrating studies. They assumed that J studies each with sample size n are performed to compare an experimental (E) and a control (C) condition. In each study, the same effect size, $\Delta = (\mu_E - \mu_C) / \sigma_C$, is estimated. The findings of each study are evaluated by a two-tailed t test of mean differences at the .05 level of significance. Each result is classified into one of three categories: negative significant, positive significant, or statistically insignificant. The decision rule is that the overall result is regarded as supporting the hypothesis (that μ_E is greater than μ_C) if a plurality (i.e., greater than one-third) of the studies fall into the "positive significant" category.

Hedges and Olkin assumed normally distributed variables and then calculated the probabilities for various sample sizes and numbers of studies, J, that more than a third of the studies would fall in the "positive significant" category. In Table 5.1 appear these probabilities subtracted from one; thus, the tabulated probability is the probability of *failing* to detect an effect size, Δ, of a given size by the "one-third plurality" rule. Consider, for example, the case of 15 studies in each of which Δ is estimated from n = 50 cases and the true effect size being estimated equals .40, a fairly large effect. Hedges and Olkin's table shows that the probability of *not* deciding that there is a positive effect using the vote-counting strategy is .770, that is, the probability of error is greater than three-quarters. What is even more remarkable is that for $\Delta < .40$, the probability of making the error indicated *increases* as the number of studies integrated increases. Clearly, there is much that is unacceptable in research integration by means of vote counting.

TABLE 5.1 Probability that a Standard Vote Count Fails to Detect an Effect for Various Sample, Effect and Cluster Sizes.*

Number, J, of studies to be integrated	Sample size, n, per study	Effect size $\Delta \equiv (\mu_E - \mu_C)/\sigma_C$							
		.1	.2	.3	.4	.5	.6	.7	.8
10	10	1.00	.999	.998	.994	.985	.968	.935	.880
10	20	1.00	.998	.990	.966	.906	.987	.606	.395
10	30	.999	.995	.975	.906	.947	.502	.252	.089
10	40	.999	.991	.950	.813	.547	.254	.073	.012
10	50	.999	.986	.914	.694	.358	.105	.016	.001
15	10	1.00	1.00	1.00	.999	.997	.991	.975	.939
15	20	1.00	1.00	.999	.991	.958	.862	.672	.419
15	30	1.00	.999	.994	.958	.824	.549	.244	.064
15	40	1.00	.999	.983	.885	.604	.246	.049	.004
15	50	.999	.997	.962	.770	.373	.080	.006	.000
20	10	1.00	1.00	1.00	.999	.997	.989	.966	.914
20	20	1.00	1.00	.998	.988	.941	.800	.545	.265
20	30	1.00	1.00	.993	.941	.747	.400	.118	.016
20	40	1.00	.999	.978	.834	.463	.119	.011	.000
20	50	1.00	.997	.948	.672	.222	.023	.001	.000
25	10	1.00	1.00	1.00	1.00	.999	.997	.986	.954
25	20	1.00	1.00	1.00	.996	.971	.863	.610	.291
25	30	1.00	1.00	.998	.972	.815	.448	.120	.013
25	40	1.00	1.00	.992	.892	.519	.121	.008	.000
50	10	1.00	1.00	1.00	1.00	1.00	1.00	.998	.986
50	20	1.00	1.00	1.00	1.00	.994	.915	.589	.174
50	30	1.00	1.00	1.00	.994	.862	.363	.035	.000
50	40	1.00	1.00	.999	.942	.461	.036	.000	.000
50	50	1.00	1.00	.995	.773	.124	.001	.000	.000

*(Each of the J replicated studies has a common sample size, n. A two-tailed t-test is used to test mean differences at the .05 level of significance. An effect is detected if the proportion of positive significant results exceeds one-third.)

Integrating Significance Tests

Some researchers have set forward as the principal problem of research integration the combining of significance levels into a joint test of a null hypothesis. The aggregation problem is seen as the problem of determining whether several individual studies, many of which showed no statistically significant results, constitute in the aggregate sufficient evidence to reject the null hypothesis at a high level of significance. The chi-square method of K. Pearson and E. S. Pearson via Jones and Fiske (1953) is usually employed. If k independent studies yield significance levels, $p_1, p_2 \ldots,$ p_k, then under the common null hypothesis tested in each study

$$-2 \sum_{i=1}^{k} \log_e p_i \sim \chi^2_{2k}.$$

This approach seems defensible and more powerful than a binomial test—testing whether the probability of "positive" findings is different from .5—where statistical hypothesis testing is a genuine concern. For most problems of meta-analysis, however, the number of studies will be so large and will encompass so many hundreds of subjects that null hypotheses will be rejected routinely.

If the Pearson χ^2 test of combined results begins to play an increasingly important role in research integration, methodologists will need to scrutinize its assumptions and properties. It is probably quite sensitive to nonindependence of studies (cf. Jones and Fiske, 1953).

Furthermore, the extreme tails of statistical distributions are exotic places about which more would have to be learned. For example, violation of normality assumptions has little effect on 95th and 99th percentiles of t and F distributions, but conceivably it could change a p of .001, under normality, to a p of .0001, which is a disturbance in natural logarithms from -6.91 to -9.21.

Rosenthal (1978) recently evaluated nine different methods that have been used at one time or another to aggregate statistical significance measures from many studies. These methods include addition of logs of p levels mentioned above as well as adding probabilities (Edginton, 1972a), adding t's (Winer, 1971), Stouffer's method of adding Z's (Mosteller and Bush, 1954), adding weighted Z's (Mosteller and Bush, 1954), testing the average p level (Edgington, 1972b), testing the average Z (Mosteller and Bush, 1954), and counting (vote method) and blocking (see Rosenthal, 1978: 190). Rosenthal's summary of the advantages and limitations of the various methods appears as Table 5.2.

STANDARDIZED MEAN DIFFERENCES

Definition and Interpretation of Effect Size

Describing findings of experimental studies so that results can be aggregated and their variability studied presents several technical problems.

TABLE 5.2* Advantages and Limitations of Nine Methods of Combining Probabilities

Methods	Advantages	Limitations	Applicable when
Adding logs	Well established	Cumulates poorly support opposite conclusions	N of studies is small ($\leqslant 5$)
Adding ps	Good power	Inapplicable when N of studies (or ps) is large, unless complex corrections are introduced	N of studies is small ($\Sigma p \leqslant 1.0$)
Adding ts	Unaffected by N of studies, given minimum df per study	Inapplicable when ts are based on very few df	Studies are not based on too few df
Adding Zs	Routinely applicable, simple	Assumes unit variance when under some conditions Type I or Type II errors may be increased	Anytime
Adding weighted Zs	Routinely applicable, permits weighting	Assumes unit variance when under some conditions Type I or Type II errors may be increased	Whenever weighted is desired

TABLE 5.2* Advantages and Limitations of Nine Methods of Combining Probabilities (continued)

Methods	Advantages	Limitations	Applicable when
Testing mean p	Simple	N of studies should not be less than four.	N of studies $\geqslant 4$
Testing mean Z	No assumption of unit variance	Low power when N of studies is small.	N of studies $\geqslant 5$
Counting	Simple and robust	Large N of studies is needed; may be low in power.	N of studies is large
Blocking	Displays all means for inspection, thus facilitating search for moderator variables	Laborious when N is large; insufficient data may be available.	N of studies is not too large

*After Rosenthal (1978).

The findings of comparative experiments are probably best expressed as standardized mean differences between pairs of treatment conditions. It will seldom be satisfactory to express experimental findings as a measure of association between *several* levels of an independent variable and a metric dependent variable. Such association measures (e.g., ω^2) are descriptive of a complete, somewhat arbitrary set of experimental conditions an investigator chooses to investigate in a single study. For example, if one wished to determine the comparative effects of computer-assisted and traditional foreign language instruction, then it is irrelevant that a televised instruction condition was also present in a study, and one would not want a quantitative measure of effect to be influenced by the irrelevant condition (Glass and Hakstian, 1969).

In what follows, reference will be made to the comparison of a particular experimental condition with a control group. Of course, there may be no "control" group in a traditional sense, and one could imagine that two different experimental conditions are compared. The most informative and straightforward measure of experimental *effect size* is the mean difference between experimental and control groups divided by within-group standard deviation:

$$\hat{\Delta} = (\overline{X}_E - \overline{X}_C) / s_x. \qquad [5.1]$$

Suppose that four experiments were performed in which either nialonide or iproniazid was compared with a placebo for efficacy in relieving depression. Three of the experiments measured outcomes with the Minnesota Multiphasic Personality Inventory (MMPI) D scale; the fourth study used the Beck Depression Inventory. Suppose the following results were obtained. (The data are hypothetical, but the findings are close to those reported in Smith et al., 1980.)

Study	Comparison	Test	Means	St. dev.	$\Delta A\text{-}B$
1	Nialomide vs. Placebo	MMPI	70.10-70.50	9.50	-.04
2	Nialomide vs. Placebo	MMPI	61.45-62.31	11.25	-.08
3	Iproniazid vs. Placebo	MMPI	60.21-65.15	7.80	-.63
4	Iproniazid vs. Placebo	Beck	110.75-121.45	20.50	-.52

In the above data, the average effect of nialomide is -.06, that is, .06 standard deviation superior to a placebo; the average effect of iproniazid is -.58, more than a half standard deviation.

The meaning of Δ is readily comprehended and, assuming some distribution form, can be translated into notions of overlapping distributions of scores and comparable percentiles. For example, suppose that a study of the effect of ritalin versus placebo on reducing hyperactivity reveals a $\hat{\Delta}$ of -1.00. One knows immediately that the average child on ritalin shows hyperactivity one standard deviation below that of the average child on placebo; thus, assuming normality, only 16% of the placebo children are less hyperactive than the average child on the drug, and so on. Such interpretations can be aided by visual representations such as that in Figure 2.2.

Some effect sizes are meaningful without comparison to anything else. The message of a zero effect size is categorically clear; and negative effect sizes are likewise meaningful in and of themselves. Another way to interpret the magnitude of an effect size is to compare it with known and familiar effects. Sometimes this comparison can be done within a single meta-analysis. For example, Hartley (1977) integrated experimental studies of the effects of computer-assisted instruction (CAI) and tutoring on mathematics learning. In each experiment, one of these two methods was compared with traditional classroom instruction. The average effect size for comparisons of tutoring and traditional instruction was about .50, favoring tutoring; the average CAI versus traditional effect size was .35. Thus, tutoring was nearly half again more beneficial than CAI for math learning.

In other circumstances, effect sizes can take on added meaning by referring them to the effects of well-known interventions. For example, grade-equivalent scales are commonly used in education to report pupils' achievement. A pupil whose achievement is reported as 8.5 grade-equivalent units in reading has scored sufficiently well on an achievement test to equal the average score earned by pupils in the fifth month of the eighth grade. By definition, the average pupil will gain 10 months of achievement in a school year, for example, the average third-grade pupil will score 3.0 in early September and 4.0 by the end of the year. It is also known, as an empirical—not a definitional—fact that the standard deviation of most achievement tests in elementary school is 1.0 grade-equivalent units; hence the effect size of one year's instruction at the elementary school level is about +1, for example,

$$\Delta = (4.0 - 3.0) / 1.0 = +1.$$

Suppose one considers an innovative teaching device, for example, computers, and determines through many studies that its effect size (computer teaching versus traditional teaching) is approximately .25 when pupils are taught by computer for an entire school year. What can one make of this? The effect size of .25 is one-fourth as great as the effect of instruction itself (.25 versus 1.00). Hence, computers benefit instruction by the equivalent of one-fourth school year of teaching effort. If this .25 standard deviation advantage accrued each year, then pupils taught by computer would learn as much in four years as pupils taught traditionally would learn in five, and so on.

Consider another example of an attempt to enhance the meaning of an effect size. Adult men and women differ in height at the average by about 3 inches; the standard deviation of heights within the two sexes is about 2 inches. Thus, the effect of gender on adult height is approximately

$$\Delta = 3/2 = 1.50.$$

As experience with expressing findings on an effect-size metric accumulates, particular magnitudes of effect will gain meaning by reference to what is typical in similar circumstances. If antianxiety drugs are known to produce effects of about one-half standard deviation on scales of self-reported anxiety when compared with inert placebos, then trials of a new drug that show a 1.25 effect size reveal it to be a remarkable achievement. (It is surprising that reporting study results in terms of inferential test statistics has been so common when one realizes that they reveal nothing about effect magnitudes and reveal most about sample sizes.)

Above all else, this is clear about magnitudes of effect: *There is no wisdom whatsoever in attempting to associate regions of the effect-size metric with descriptive adjectives such as "small," "moderate," "large," and the like.* Dissociated from a context of decision and comparative value, there is no inherent value to an effect size of 3.5 or .2. Depending what benefits can be achieved at what cost, an effect size of 2.0 might be "poor" and one of .1 might be "good." After decades of confusion, researchers are finally ceasing to speak of regions of the correlation coefficient scale as low, medium, or high. The same error should not be repeated in the case of the effect-size metric.

Interpretations of effect sizes, Δ_{E-C}, in terms of percentiles (e.g., if $\Delta = +1.00$, then the average person in the experimental group has a score that exceeds 84% of the persons' scores in the control group) depend, of course, on assumptions about the shapes of the distributions of the variable in the two groups. Normality is a convenient and unobjectionable assumption in many instances, but its convenience should not blind one to the fact that it is an assumption that may occasionally be false. Kraemer and Andrews (1980) have called attention to this problem. Suppose, for example, that the scores in the experimental and control groups are distributed according to the exponential distribution (Hastings and Peacock, 1974: 56-59) with the following parameters:

Group	Distribution	Mean	St. dev.
Experimental	$P(X_E) = a_1 e^{-a_1 X}$	$1/a_1$	$1/a_1$
Control	$P(X_C) = a_2 e^{-a_2 X}$	$1/a_2$	$1/a_2$

Now the effect size Δ_{E-C} equal to

$$(\overline{X}_E - \overline{X}_C)/ s_c$$

will estimate, in the case of exponential distributions,

$$\Delta = (1/a_1 - 1/a_2) / 1/a_2$$

$$= (a_2 - a_1) / a_1 \qquad [5.2]$$

Suppose that a particular experiment yields summary statistics as follows:

$$\overline{X}_E = 18, s_E = 16;$$

$$\overline{X}_C = 10, s_C = 8.$$

The value of Δ equals $(18-10)/8 = +1$. If it is assumed that the two distributions are normal, then the Δ of +1 has the usual interpretation: The average person in the experimental group exceeds 84% of the persons in the control group. Suppose, however, that the average experimental group person's score is expressed as a percentile in the control group, assuming exponential distributions in each group. Then the percentile rank of $X = 18$ in an exponential distribution with parameter $a_2 = 10$ is given by

$$\int_0^{18} P(x)dx = \int_0^{18} 10\ e^{-10X}\ d_x = .834.$$

Thus, assuming exponential distributions within experimental and control groups gives essentially the same interpretation of a Δ of $+1$ as the assumption of normal distributions (.83 versus .84). This example is not meant to suggest that the exponential distribution is in any sense interchangeable as an assumption with the normal distribution. The assumption of distribution shapes may be important and it should be checked when possible and the most reasonable assumption made.

Choice of Standard Deviation

The choice of the standard deviation with which to scale the differences between group means to determine Δ is crucial. Various choices can result in substantial differences in effect size.

The definition of Δ appears uncomplicated, but heterogeneous group variances cause difficulties. Suppose that experimental and control groups have means and standard deviations as follows:

	Experimental	*Control*
Means	$\overline{X}_E = 52$	$\overline{X}_C = 50$
Standard deviations	$s_E = 2$	$s_C = 10$

The measure of experimental effect could be calculated either by use of s_E or s_C or some combination of the two.

Basis of Standardization	$\hat{\Delta}$
(a) s_E	1.00
(b) s_C	.20
(c) $(s_E + s_C)/2$	.33

The average standard deviation (c) probably should be eliminated as a mere mindless statistical reaction to a perplexing choice. But both the remaining 1.00 and .20 are *correct*; neither can be ruled out as false. It is true, in fact, that the experimental group mean is one standard deviation above the control group mean in terms of the experimental group standard deviation; and, assuming normality, the average subject in the control group is superior to only 16% of the members of the experimental group. However, the control group mean is only one-fifth standard deviation below the mean of the experimental group when measured in control group standard deviations; thus, the average experimental group subject exceeds 58% of the subjects in the control group. These facts are not contradictory; they are two distinct features of a finding which cannot be expressed by one number. In a meta-analysis of psychotherapy experiments, the problem of heterogeneous standard deviations was resolved from a quite different direction. Suppose that methods A, B, and Control are compared in a single experiment, with the following results:

	Method A	Method B	Control
Means	50	50	48
Standard deviations	10	1	4

If effect sizes are calculated using the standard deviations of the "method," then Δ_A equals .20 and Δ_B equals 2.00—a misleading difference, considering the equality of the method means on the dependent variable. Standardization of mean differences by the control group standard deviation at least has the advantage of assigning equal effect sizes to equal means. This seems reason enough to resolve the choice in favor of the control group standard deviation, at least when there are more than two treatment conditions and only one control condition.

Problems of Pooled Estimates of Standard Deviation

In many studies where the emphasis in reporting is on inferential statistics, only pooled information is available about the within-group variances. Since the statistical tests used in these cases depend on an assumption of homogeneity of within-group variances, the test statistics frequently obscure whatever differences in variance might have existed.

When the results of an experiment are expressed as a t statistic which is reported along with n_E and n_C but without means and variances, one can calculate an effect size, Δ, via the formula:

$$\Delta_p = t(1/n_E + 1/n_C)^{1/2}, \hspace{3cm} [5.3]$$

where the variance estimate in the t statistic is:

$$s_p^2 = [(n_E-1) s_E^2 + (n_C-1) s_C^2] / (n_E + n_C - 2).$$

The subscript p indicates that Δ is based on a "pooling" of variances. Suppose, to the contrary, that the sample variances are unequal, and that one wishes Δ_C, the mean difference, standardized by the control group (group C, for example) standard deviation. Assuming $n_E = n_C$, the ratio of $\hat{\Delta}_C$ to $\hat{\Delta}_p$ can be derived:

$$\Delta_C / \Delta_p = \left\{ [1 + (s_E^2 / s_C^2)] / 2 \right\}^{1/2}. \qquad [5.4]$$

In Figure 5.1, the ratio of Δ_C to Δ_p is graphed as a function of s_E^2/s_C^2. As can be seen in Figure 5.1, Δ_C is exactly equal to the surrogate, but accessible, value Δ_p when variances are equal. The bias in the approximation is negative and no greater than about 25% when control group variance is less than experimental group variance; however, the bias can grow beyond any bounds when the inequality in the variances is reversed. This indicates that the approximation of Δ_C via a t statistic (or an F ratio, as well) could be unsafe if the sample variance of the experimental group substantially exceeds that for the control group.

A psychological experiment performed by Hekmat (1973) illustrates the problems of this section and concerns of earlier sections about choice of the control group standard deviation and nonnormality. Hekmat compared three methods of treating a phobia against an untreated control group. Ten persons constituted each of the four groups. A Behavior Avoidance Test (BAT) and a Fear Survey Schedule were administered to each of the 40 persons before and after the treatment. The means and standard deviations for the four groups on the two measures appear in Table 5.3. Notice the wide discrepancies among posttest standard deviations: on the BAT, the standard deviation for the systematic desensitization group is more than five times as great as that for the control group. If the effect size, Δ, comparing the systematic desensitization group against the control group is calculated by dividing by the experimental group standard deviation, its value is

$$\Delta = (5.0 - 17.8) / 3.39 = -3.78.$$

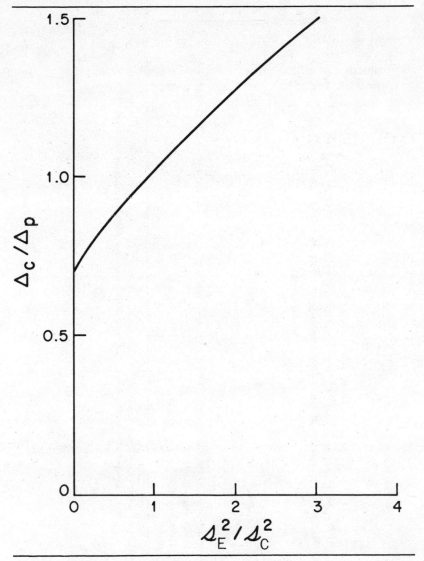

Figure 5.1 Relationship of control vs. experimental group variance ratio to bias in effect-size approximation.

TABLE 5.3   Means and Standard Deviations for the Behavioral Avoidance Test, Fear Survey Schedule

| Group | Behavior avoidance test | | | Fear Survey Schedule | |
| | Post-conditioning score | | | Post-conditioning score | |
	n	$\overline{X}$	s	$\overline{X}$	s
Systematic desensitization	10	5.0	3.39	2.7	.67
Semantic desensitization	10	4.5	3.17	2.5	.84
Implosive therapy	10	18.6	96	4.9	.31
Control	10	17.8	.63	4.4	.52

NOTE: On the Fear Survey Schedule, the pleasant pole scored 1, the unpleasant 7. The maximum phobia score was 5 which indicates "very much fear," and minimum score was 1 which indicates "no fear."

If, on the other hand, the control group standard deviation is used, the value of the effect size is

$$\Delta = (5.0 - 17.8) / .63 = -20.32.$$

An effect size of 20 standard deviations is an absurd figure.

Suppose that Hekmat had only reported t statistics instead of means and standard deviations. The t statistic for the comparison of the systematic desensitization and control groups would equal

$$t = (5.0 - 17.8) / \sqrt{(2/10)(11.889/2)} = -11.74.$$

Converting this t statistic to an effect size, assuming homogeneous variances, as is necessary, gives a Δ of -5.25.

Effect sizes that bounce around from 20 to 3 to 5 to whatever else depending on one or another assumption indicate that something is fundamentally wrong. In the case of Hekmat's data, the problem lies with the measurement scales. They undoubtedly would show, upon inspection of distributions of the data, severe ceiling and floor effects with resulting asymmetry and nonnormality.

Estimation of Δ

Given that

$$\Delta_{A-B} = (\mu_A - \mu_B) / \sigma_x, \qquad [5.5]$$

and assuming for the moment an understanding of which of many possible choices of σ_x is implied, the intuitively reasonable estimator of Δ is

$$\hat{\Delta}_{A-B} = (\overline{X}_A - \overline{X}_B) / s_x \qquad [5.6]$$

where the sample means are conventionally defined and s_x is the square root of the *unbiased* estimator of σ_x^2. Hedges (1979) showed the error of intuition with regard to Equation 5.6, and he derived the maximum likelihood estimator of Δ assuming normality and a single sample estimate of σ_x.

Hedges (1979) examined the statistical properties of

$$\hat{\Delta}_{E-C} = (\overline{X}_E - \overline{X}_C) / s_C$$

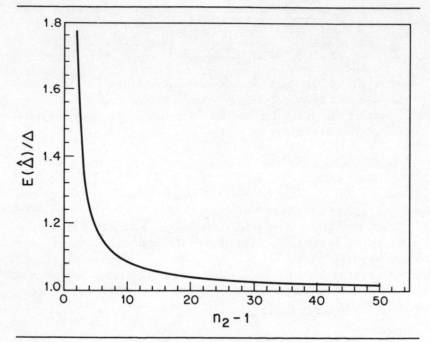

Figure 5.2   Ratio of the expected value of the estimated effect size to the parameter
value as a function of the control group sample size, n_2.

as an estimator of

$$\Delta_{E-C} = (\mu_E - \mu_C) / \sigma_C.$$

He was able to show that

$\hat{\Delta}_{E-C} [n_1 n_2 / (n_1 + n_2)]^{1/2}$ is distributed as a noncentral t variate with
noncentrality parameter

$$\Delta_{E-C} [n_1 n_2 / (n_1 + n_2)]^{1/2}$$

and degrees of freedom equal to $n_2 - 1$ where n_1 and n_2 are the sizes of the
samples for the experimental and control groups,respectively. Of course,
this finding rests on the assumption that X is normally distributed for both
the experimental and control groups. It followed as a consequence of this
theorem that the expected value of Δ_{E-C} is given by

TABLE 5.4   Value of $K(n_2 - 1)$ for n_2 to be used in obtaining unbiased estimates of Δ

$n_2 - 1$	K	$n_2 - 1$	K	$n_2 - 1$	K
2	0.56419	21	0.96378	40	0.98111
3	0.72360	22	0.96545	41	0.98158
4	0.79788	23	0.96697	42	0.98202
5	0.84075	24	0.96837	43	0.98244
6	0.86863	25	0.96965	44	0.98284
7	0.88820	26	0.97083	45	0.98322
8	0.90270	27	0.97192	46	0.98359
9	0.91387	28	0.97293	47	0.98394
10	0.92275	29	0.97387	48	0.98428
11	0.92996	30	0.97475	49	0.98460
12	0.93594	31	0.97558	50	0.98491
13	0.94098	32	0.97635		
14	0.94529	33	0.97707		
15	0.94901	34	0.97775		
16	0.95225	35	0.97839		
17	0.95511	36	0.97900		
18	0.95765	37	0.97957		
19	0.95991	38	0.98011		
20	0.96194	39	0.98062		

$$E(\hat{\Delta}) = \Delta [K(n_2 - 1)]^{-1},$$

where

$$K(n_2 - 1) = \frac{\Gamma[(n_2 - 1)/2]}{\sqrt{(n_2 - 1)/2}\,\Gamma(n_2 - 2\,/2)} \qquad [5.7]$$

Hence, $\hat{\Delta}$ is biased as an estimator of Δ. The degree of bias is a function of the ratio of two gamma distributions as can be seen above.[1] In Figure 5.2 (from Hedges, 1979), the bias in $\hat{\Delta}$ as an estimator of Δ is depicted by graphing the ratio $E(\hat{\Delta})/\Delta$ against n_2-1. As can be seen there, $\hat{\Delta}$ is positively biased for small n; beyond sample size n_2 of 20, the bias is 10% of less.

Clearly, an unbiased estimate of Δ could be obtained by multiplying $\hat{\Delta}$ by the correction factor $K(n_2-1)$. Hedges (1979: 11) provided a table of values of $K(n_2-1)$ which is reproduced as Table 5.4 in slightly modified form with his kind permission.

Hedges (1979) pointed out an unexpected and important property of effect sizes as estimators. Suppose that one obtains a series of observations of effect sizes, $\hat{\Delta}_i$, each of which estimates the same parameter value Δ. Assume further than for J such estimates, an aggregate estimate is obtained by averaging; thus

$$\Delta \text{ is estimated by } \sum_1^J \hat{\Delta}_i / J.$$

Denote this latter estimator by G, as did Hedges. He showed:

> G is *not* a consistent estimator of Δ as $J \rightarrow \infty$. That is, even though the number of experiments combined increases, the estimator does not necessarily approximate the true value Δ more closely. In fact, the estimates can differ from Δ by a considerable amount depending on the sample sizes. To see this, consider the example of a collection of experiments with five subjects per group. The estimator $\hat{\Delta}$ has a bias which results in overestimation of Δ by approximately 25 percent when four degrees of freedom are used to estimate σ. Each estimator $\hat{\Delta}_i$ has the same bias, therefore G is biased by the same amount as each $\hat{\Delta}_i$, $i = 1, \ldots, J$. As J increases, the bias is unchanged, but the variance of G tends to zero. Thus as the number of studies increases, the estimator G estimates the wrong quantity more precisely [Hedges, 1979: 8-9; notation altered slightly].

The inconsistency in G as an estimator of Δ can be corrected by using Hedges's earlier result, namely, correct each estimate $\hat{\Delta}_i$ by $K(n_2-1)$ before averaging.

Metric for Mean Differences

Final status scores. When subjects are randomly assigned to treatment and control groups, means can be obtained on a criterion measure Y as $\bar{Y}_E$ and $\bar{Y}_C$. The mean difference[2] can be scaled to an effect size by the control group standard deviation, s_y. Final status, as the scale of the criterion measure, has several advantages over derived measures such as raw and residual gain scores and covariance-adjusted final-status scores. First, it is experientially more relevant and, therefore, provides results more readily interpretable, particularly by lay audiences to whom a meta-analysis might be addressed. Second, the variance of the derived gain measures contains confounded "measurement error" which can significantly bias results.

Where there are nonrandom preexperiment differences between treatment and control groups, the use of a posttreatment status scale will also be biased. It is with such biases that the derived gain measures were designed to deal. That they do not deal with them adequately is one problem; that they express the group comparisons on a scale different from that used in randomized studies with only a final-status measure is a further problem for meta-analysis. If the final-status scale is to be preferred, then procedures must be found for converting results of studies using other scales to the final-status scale while minimizing the biases due to preexperiment differences.

Coping with preexperiment group differences. The three derived scores typically used to attempt to render groups comparable in experiments where there are nonrandom group differences are (1) gain scores, (2) residual scores, and (3) covariance-adjusted final-status scores. A gain score is the simple difference between the final status measure and the preexperiment status score on the same scale. For person i in the control group it is given by

$$G_{Ci} = Y_{Ci} - X_{Ci}. \qquad [5.8]$$

The difference between experimental and control group mean gains, therefore, is

$$\bar{G}_E - \bar{G}_C = (\bar{Y}_E - \bar{Y}_C) - (\bar{X}_E - \bar{X}_C). \qquad [5.9]$$

When the preexperiment status is measured on a scale different from the measure of final status, a simple gain score makes no sense. An alternative expression frequently used is the residual from the line of regression of Y on X:

$$g_{Ci} = Y_{Ci} - \left[\bar{Y} \ldots + b_{y \cdot x} (X_{Ci} - \bar{X} \ldots)\right]$$
$$= (Y_{Ci} - \bar{Y} \ldots) - b_{y \cdot x} (X_{Ci} - \bar{X} \ldots), \qquad [5.10]$$

where $b_{y \cdot x}$ is the pooled within-groups estimate of the regression of final status, Y, on initial status, X. The difference between experimental and control group mean residual scores, therefore, is

$$\bar{g}_E - \bar{g}_C = (\bar{Y}_E - \bar{Y}_C) - b_{y \cdot x} (\bar{X}_E - \bar{X}_C). \qquad [5.11]$$

Covariance adjustments of the final status scores take the form of Equation 5.10, hence the difference between experimental and control group covariance-adjusted means will also be given by Equation 5.11. Using the usual notation for the covariance adjusted mean, then,

$$\overline{Y}_E' - \overline{Y}_C' = \overline{g}_E - \overline{g}_C.$$

The use of gain scores, residual scores, and covariance adjustments when there are preexperiment group differences is an attempt to make non-equivalent groups more comparable. In a meta-analysis there is a different problem of comparability. If there are no pretreatment differences, then mean differences computed between groups will be the same whatever the scale. That is:

$$(\overline{Y}_E - \overline{Y}_C) = (\overline{G}_E - \overline{G}_C) = (\overline{g}_E - \overline{g}_C) = (\overline{Y}_E' - \overline{Y}_C') \qquad [5.12]$$

The choice of scales will influence the estimate s_y, of course, even where it does not affect the mean difference. Where there are pretreatment mean differences, then it is inappropriate to use $(\overline{Y}_E - \overline{Y}_C)$; but the question of which of the others to use remains. Some studies to be included in a meta-analysis may contain results with gain scores, others with residual or covariance-adjusted scores. Gain scores have the advantage over residual and covariance-adjusted scores of being on a scale of the same units as the final-status scores. Consistency is important. Results on one scale can be converted to the other using:

$$(\overline{G}_E - \overline{G}_C) = (\overline{g}_E - \overline{g}_C) - (1 - b_{y \cdot x})(\overline{X}_E - \overline{X}_C). \qquad [5.13]$$

Mean differences used for the computation of effect sizes will then all be either $(\overline{Y}_E - \overline{Y}_C)$ or on a scale with the same units as the final-status scale. A major practical problem is that the above conversion formula cannot be solved unless both $b_{y \cdot x}$ and $\overline{X}_E - \overline{X}_C$ are known. When they are not, differences on the residual scale will have to be used, and this use should be coded as a methodological feature of the meta-analysis to allow an investigation of whether the set of such effects is discrepant.

Metric for Standard Deviation

The choice of the standard deviation with which to scale the differences between group means is crucial. Variations in choice can result in substantial differences in effect size. Recording the choice made in each case can allow the investigation of any systematic interaction between the choice and the effect size computed; but, unless the relationship is simple, other important relationships with effect size may be obscured. The choice of a standardizing metric is hardly trivial. Consider an experimental study in which pretests and posttests were administered and in which no pretest mean differences existed. Suppose further that the pretest-posttest correlation is .75, the posttest mean difference is 5 points and the posttest standard deviation is 10. The effect size, Δ_y, in terms of the final-status measure is:

$$\Delta_y = 5/10 = .50.$$

As will be seen below, the standard deviation of residual scores in this instance is $10\sqrt{1-.75^2} = 6.61$. Hence, the effect size in terms of the metric of residual scores is:

$$\Delta_r = 5/6.61 = .76.$$

Obviously the choice of metric makes quite a difference in the calculated effect. Neither calculation is wrong; they merely reflect alternative expressions of the general phenomenon of the experimental results. Although there are no rigid rules about which metric is best, the final-status measure has the advantage of being a phenomenon more readily perceived and experienced than change or gain; hence, the expression of results on its metric may be more meaningful. In addition, there are several ways to measure change or gain that are equally good or bad (Cronbach and Furby, 1970). "Simple gain," "residual gain," "estimated true gain," and others each has a different variance and would give a different value of Δ. It seems better to avoid them all and standardize group mean differences in terms of final status.

Conversion from gain scores. With gain score defined by Equation 5.8, the variance of the gain scores can be shown to be

$$\sigma_G^2 = \sigma_y^2 + \sigma_x^2 - 2\rho_{xy}\,\sigma_x\sigma_y, \qquad [5.14]$$

which, if it can be assumed that $\sigma_x = \sigma_y$, reduces to:

$$\sigma_G^2 = \sigma_y^2[2(1-\rho_{xy})]. \qquad [5.15]$$

If the control group standard deviation is provided in terms of raw gain scores as s_G, its standard deviation on the final scores can be obtained from

$$s_y = s_G/\sqrt{2(1-r_{xy})}.$$ [5.16]

In many studies reporting in terms of raw gain scores, no information is provided about the correlation between the two status measures. It is also important to note that the correlation required is r_{xy} for the control group or, at least, a pooled within-groups estimate of it. If the correlation is not provided, a reasonable guess can probably be made if something is known about the tests involved. For standardized tests, a published test-retest reliability might be appropriate if based on a time lag similar to that in the study.

Conversion from residual scores. With residual status scores defined by Equation 5.10, the variance of the residual scores can be shown to be

$$\sigma_g^2 = \sigma_y^2(1-\rho_{xy}^2)$$ [5.17]

without any necessary assumption about equality of σ_x and σ_y.

If the control group standard deviation is provided in terms of residual scores as s_g, its standard deviation on the final-status scores can be obtained from

$$s_y = s_g/\sqrt{1-r_{xy}^2}.$$ [5.18]

Information about the correlation between scores on the two status measures is more likely to be provided in studies using residual scores than in studies using raw gain scores. The correlation required is the pooled within-group correlation not the control group correlation. Since the residuals are calculated using a pooled estimate of slope, and not separate group estimates, it is with the pooled estimate of correlation that the unreduced standard deviation can be recovered. If the control group standard deviation on residual scores, s_g, is available it should be used rather that a pooled estimate.

Conversion from covariance-adjusted scores. One effect of covariance adjustments is to reduce the within-group standard deviation in a manner similar to that described for residual scores. If the standard deviation for the control group on the residual scores is given, the standard deviation for the final-status scores can be estimated using Equation 5.18.

If only the covariance-adjusted pooled within-group mean square, MS_w', is known, a pooled estimate of the within-group standard deviation on final-status scores can be obtained from

$$s_y = \sqrt{\frac{MS'_w}{(1 - r^2_{xy})} \frac{(df_w - 1)}{(df_w - 2)}} .$$ [5.19]

Retrieval From Factorial Designs

Many experimental comparisons of a treatment and a control condition use more complex designs than the simple comparison of two groups. Some introduce other factors into a higher order analysis of variance design to examine interactions. In the process these designs create a new definition of within-cell variance. Others introduce stratification of subjects (matching of pairs being an extreme example) to reduce the error variance and obtain a more powerful significance test. The use of repeated measures designs in which subjects are matched with themselves is intended to achieve even more power by the same means.

In reports of studies of this type, only the pooled information in analysis of variance tables is usually provided. Means must be found to retrieve an appropriate estimate of the full control group standard deviation. If a higher order analysis of variance is used to explore interactions between the treatment and other factors, that information should not be lost but should instead be coded into the meta-analysis. It is just such interactions that meta-analysis may reveal between studies. Any results which reveal such interactions within studies should be preserved in the data for the meta-analysis. For example, a study to compare treatment and control conditions (Factor A) may stratify the sample of subjects into males and females (Factor B) to study the interaction of the treatment with the subject's sex. For an effect size based on the difference between the overall treatment and control means $(\overline{Y}_{E.} - \overline{Y}_{C..})$, the appropriate standard deviation would be that for the total control group. A pooled estimate of this would be given by

$$\hat{s}_y = \sqrt{\frac{(SS_B + SS_{AB} + SS_w)}{(df_B + df_{AB} + df_w)}} .$$ [5.20]

An effect size for males alone would be based on the mean difference $(\overline{Y}_{EM.} - \overline{Y}_{CM.})$. The appropriate standard deviation would be the one for the control group males for which a pooled estimate would be given by

$$\hat{s}_y = \sqrt{MS_w} .$$ [5.21]

If subjects in a study are stratified on a continuous variable which is correlated with the final status measure, the within-groups sum of squares from the corresponding unstratified design can be partitioned into

$$S_{w(A)} = SS_B + SS_{AB} + SS_{w(AB)} , \qquad [5.22]$$

as for the case where B is a factor of theoretical interest. Although this design also allows a more powerful test of the treatment effect, there is usually no substantive interest in the between-levels variation or the Treatment X Level interaction. The control group standard deviation should be obtained as the pooled estimate in Equation 5.22.

If the stratification is achieved by matching pairs, there will be no $SS_{w(AB)}$ term. Only the terms SS_B and SS_{AB} will exist to be pooled. Where the matched pairs data are analyzed by a dependent groups t test, the standard error of the mean difference between pairs is

$$\sigma_{\bar{d}} = \sqrt{(\sigma_E^2 + \sigma_C^2 - 2\rho_{EC}\sigma_E\sigma_C)/n}, \qquad [5.23]$$

where σ_E and σ_C are the standard deviations of the experimental and control groups, ρ_{EC} is the correlation between pairs and n is the number of pairs. If the standard deviations for experimental and control conditions are assumed to be homogeneous, then Equation 5.23 becomes

$$\sigma_{\bar{d}} = \sqrt{(2\sigma_y^2/n)(1-\rho_{EC})}. \qquad [5.24]$$

If the standard error of the mean difference between pairs is reported, the control group standard deviation on the final-status measure can be estimated as

$$s_y = s_{\bar{d}} \sqrt{[2(1-r_{EC})]} . \qquad [5.25]$$

Since the correlation between pairs, r_{EC}, will probably not be reported, it must be estimated. The matching will have been done on some variable X measured before the experiment. The partial correlation of scores on the outcome measure Y between members of pairs, controlling for the common X score for members of each pair, will be

$$\rho_{Y_E Y_C \cdot X} = \frac{\rho_{Y_E Y_C} - \rho_{Y_E X}\rho_{Y_C X}}{\sqrt{(1 - \rho_{Y_{EX}}^2)(1 - \rho_{Y_{CX}}^2)}} . \qquad [5.26]$$

If the correlation between X and Y is the same for each group, that is, ρ_{XY}, then:

$$\rho_{EC \cdot X} = (\rho_{EC} - \rho_{XY}^2)/(1 - \rho_{XY}^2) \qquad [5.27]$$

and, therefore,

$$\rho_{EC} = \rho_{XY}^2 + (1 - \rho_{XY}^2)\rho_{EC \cdot X} \cdot \qquad [5.28]$$

If all that members of a pair have in common can be accounted for by their common scores on the matching variable, then the partial correlation between their scores on any other variable, partialing out their scores on the matching variable, should be zero. A reasonable estimate of the correlation between pairs on the final-status measure then would be

$$\hat{r}_{EC} = r_{XY}^2. \qquad [5.29]$$

If r_{xy} (within group) is not provided in the report, a reasonable guess can be made if something is known about the tests involved. In some studies stratification on a continuous variable may be used to introduce a factor in which there is theoretical interest. For example, in research on ability grouping some studies test only overall mean performances of students taught in homogeneous groups and students taught in heterogeneous groups. Other studies examine, as well, the possibility of differential effectiveness, presenting and testing the significance of differences between homogeneously and heterogeneously grouped students at various levels of ability. Effect sizes can be estimated for both the overall mean differences and the mean differences at different ability levels. The question is, however, which standard deviation should be used to scale the mean differences at specific ability levels—the total control group standard deviation (or a pooled estimate of it) or the standard deviation for the subtest of the control group at that level (or a pooled estimate of it).

The choice will depend on both the interpretation to be made of the effect sizes and the extent of aggregation of effect sizes. If mean effect sizes over all levels are to be computed, or if effect sizes for various ability levels are to be compared, they should be scaled in terms of the standard deviation of the whole control group. If, from the analysis, it emerges that there are different effect sizes for different ability levels, new effect size estimates based on the control group for each particular level can be calculated. These effect sizes will be indices of the efficacy of treatment at a particular ability level with reference to the distribution of the scores of the relevant untreated groups at that level.

If a study presents data for only a part of the total distribution, it will be necessary to estimate the standard deviation for the whole control population from the available standard deviation for a truncated section of it. Otherwise the effect sizes calculated will vary according to the homogeneity of the truncated portion used. For this estimation, information will be required about the correlation between the variable on which the range is restricted (e.g., IQ) and the final-status measure and about the degree of restriction of the subgroup on this variable.

If the standard deviations on the initial status measure for the restricted group and the full range are s_x^* and s_x, respectively, and if the standard deviation on the final status measure is denoted by s_Y^* and the correlation between the variables is denoted by r_{xy}, then the standard deviation on the final-status score for the full range will be

$$s_Y = s_Y^* / \sqrt{1 - r_{xy}^2 (1 - r_x^{*2} / s_x^2)}.$$

Where the treatment and control conditions are such that they can both be applied to the same sample, repeated measures designs are sometimes used to avoid intersubject variability between groups. In the simplest case, where treatment is one factor (A) and subjects the other (S), the error term for testing the significance of the difference between the treatment group means is the A X S interaction mean square. An estimate of the appropriate control group standard deviation can be obtained if the sums of squares for S and A X S are pooled. Similar approaches to pooling can be used for mixed model designs in which subjects are nested under some additional factors but crossed with treatments. For example, in a study with subjects crossed with treatments A but nested under gender B, the sources of variation will be A,B,S(B),AB,AS(B). For the effect size based on the difference between overall treatment and control means $(\overline{Y}_{T..} - \overline{Y}_{C..})$, the appropriate standard deviation would be that for the total control group for which a pooled estimate would be given by

$$\hat{s}_Y = \frac{[SS_B + SS_{S(B)} + SS_{AB} + SS_{AS(B)}]}{\sqrt{[df_B + df_{S(B)} + df_{AB} + df_{AS(B)}]}}.$$

for an effect size based on males alone, the mean difference would be $(\overline{Y}_{TM.} - \overline{Y}_{CM.})$ and the relevant pooled estimate of the standard deviation would be

$$\hat{s}_Y = \sqrt{MS_{S(B)}}.$$

Studies Without Control Groups

Using individual studies that lack control groups. Suppose that in a meta-analysis of experimental evaluations of science curricula that typical studies involve the comparison of a new curriculum (e.g., Science Curriculum Improvement Study, SCIS, or Science: A Process Approach, SAPA) against traditional science curricula (group lecture, teacher-centered, and oriented toward knowledge acquisition rather than developing inquiry skills). From such studies, effect sizes comparing SCIS or SAPA against Traditional could be calculated in the usual way, for example,

$$\hat{\Delta} = (\overline{X}_{SAPA} - \overline{X}_T) / s_T,$$

where the Traditional curriculum is thought of as a "control" condition.

Experiments will exist in which SCIS is compared to SAPA and no Traditional comparison is involved. To create an effect size for the difference between these two experimental conditions, the standard deviation of the missing control group is required rather than that for either of the experimental conditions. An estimate of the control group standard deviation can be obtained, however. If all studies in which SCIS is compared with traditional are taken, the observed control group standard deviations, s_C, can be regressed on the observed SCIS group standard deviations (s_{SC}) to give:

$$\hat{s}_C = b_0 + b_1 s_{SC}. \qquad [5.30]$$

A similar regression can be established for s_C and s_{SA} from those studies comparing SAPA with Traditional. Nonlinear regressions are possible, of course. From a study comparing only treatments SCIS and SAPA, the observed standard deviations s_{SC} and s_{SA} can be substituted into their separate regression equations to provide two estimates of s_C. These two estimates could be pooled to provide the standard deviation with which to scale the mean difference $(\overline{X}_A - \overline{X}_B)$.

It makes no sense to pool in the same analyses some effect sizes based on SCIS versus Traditional comparisons, some based on SAPA versus Traditional comparisons, and a third group based on SCIS versus SAPA comparisons. For if SCIS and SAPA are both superior curricula, their large and positive effects should not be lumped with comparisons between themselves which would be small. The problem can be resolved by means of *control referencing* of the effect sizes. Each effect size based on a direct comparison of SCIS and SAPA can be broken into two effect sizes that reference the curriculum against a hypothetical control group (in this case, the Traditional curriculum).

Assume that there exists some number of effect sizes calculated from comparisons of SCIS and Traditional curricula; denote the average of these effects by $\overline{\Delta}_{SC}$. Likewise, denote the average of all effect sizes gotten by comparing SAPA and Traditional by $\overline{\Delta}_{SA}$. A single study in which SCIS and SAPA are compared without a Traditional group yields one effect size, Δ_{SC-SA}. We wish to break Δ_{SC-SA} into two effects, Δ^*_{SC} and Δ^*_{SA}, that estimate the effect sizes that would have been obtained in this study if a Traditional group had been included.

Two reasonable conditions may be imposed on Δ^*_{SC} and Δ^*_{SA}, the control-referenced effect sizes:

(a) $\Delta_{SC-SA} = \Delta^*_{SC} - \Delta^*_{SA}$, and   [5.31]

(b) $\Delta^*_{SC} - \overline{\Delta}_{SC} = \overline{\Delta}_{SA} - \Delta^*_{SA}$.   [5.32]

These conditions imply (a) that the observed difference from the direct comparison is preserved in the control-referenced comparison and (b) that the error (the deviation of a control-referenced effect from the average of all similar non-control-referenced effects) is equally shared between the two referenced effects. These two conditions establish a pair of independent linear equations in two unknowns that can be solved for the two control-referenced effects:

$$\Delta^*_{SC} = (\Delta_{SC-SA} + \overline{\Delta}_{SC} + \overline{\Delta}_{SA}) /2, \text{ and}$$

$$\Delta^*_{SA} = \Delta^*_{SC} - \Delta_{SC-SA}.   [5.33]$$

Consider this illustration. In 100 comparisons of SCIS and Traditional curricula, the average effect size for the dependent variable "interest in science" is .76. For 200 comparisons of SAPA and Traditional, the average is .48. An experiment in which SCIS and SAPA were compared showed an effect size on "interest in science" of $\Delta_{SC-SA} = .30$. The two control-referenced effects, then, are given by

$$\Delta_{SC}^* = (.30 + .76 + .48)/2 = .77, \text{ and}$$

$$\Delta_{SA}^* = .77 - .30 = .47.$$

Calculating effect sizes when there is no common control condition. Experiments with quantitive independent variables (time, size, and so on) often have no untreated "control" condition. (A general approach to integrating effects from experiments with quantitative independent variables is described in Chapter 6.) For studies of drug dosage, amount of instruction, and so on, a control condition of no treatment can be defined and included. For studies of an independent variable such as class size, one investigator's control can be another's treatment. But each study involves some number of comparisons of a small condition (S) and a large condition (L) and yields two means, $\overline{X}_S$ and $\overline{X}_L$, and two standard deviations s_S and s_L.

If the standard deviations vary with the value of the independent variable, then some value of that variable can be chosen as a reference point and its standard deviation used for converting all treatment mean differences to effect sizes. The problem is to find a way of converting from the observed s_S and s_L on the variable used in a given study to an estimate of s_R, the standard deviation for the reference group on that variable.

From all studies, the ratio of the observed standard deviations can be regressed on the values of the quantitative independent variable used in the comparison, namely, small (S) and large (L). The resulting regression function will be:

$$(s_S/s_L) = b_0 + b_1 S + b_2 L. \qquad [5.33]$$

If a standard deviation s_S is observed in a particular study for condition S, the standard deviation for the reference condition R could be estimated, if $R > S$, as:

$$\hat{s}_R = s_S/(b_0 + b_1 S + b_2 R). \qquad [5.34]$$

A second estimate s_R can be obtained from the observed s_L in the same study. The mean of the two estimates could be used. (If $R < S$ or $R > L$, the regression equation can still be used but with substitutions appropriately reversed.) All of the observed mean differences can then be scaled to effect sizes for the corresponding differences in the value of the independent variable as:

$$\Delta_{S-L} = (\overline{X}_S - \overline{X}_L)/\hat{s}_R \qquad [5.35]$$

Calculating Effect Sizes From Significance Tests

Although the notion of an effect size is simple, there can be real difficulties in recovering effect size estimates from some research reports. Many research reports do not contain means and standard deviations for experimental and control conditions. Where there are more than two experimental conditions and means are not reported, there is little hope of recovering any effect sizes from the report. Where there are only two groups, effect sizes can usually be recovered directly from parametric test statistics. Where only information about probability levels is provided for the test statistics, it is still possible in some cases to arrive at a reasonable estimate of effect size. Where nonparametric statistics are used, the chances are diminished though still reasonable in some cases.

Transforming parametric statistics into effect sizes. If the result of a comparison of experimental and control conditions is reported as a t statistic, the corresponding effect size is provided directly as

$$\hat{\Delta}_{E-C} = t\sqrt{(1/n_E) + (1/n_C)}. \qquad [5.36]$$

When the n's in the two groups are equal, the effect size is simply the value of the t statistic multiplied by the square root of the ratio of 2 to n, the common sample size. That is,

$$\hat{\Delta} = t\sqrt{2/n} \qquad [5.37]$$

where n is the sample size of the two equal-size groups.

Suppose, for example, that when two samples of 10 cases each were compared with a t test, a t statistic of 4.26 resulted. The corresponding effect size would be given by

$$\hat{\Delta} = 4.26\sqrt{2/10}$$

$$= 4.26\,(.447) = 1.91.$$

If the t statistic is reported as t_G for a comparison of groups on gain scores the appropriate change in metric to that of the final-status scale is achieved if the effect size is estimated as

$$\hat{\Delta}_{E-C} = t_G \sqrt{2(1-r_{xy})(1/n_E + 1/n_C)} \qquad [5.38]$$

If the comparison is based on residual scores, the effect size can be calculated from the test statistic t_g by

$$\hat{\Delta}_{E-C} = t_g \sqrt{(1 - r_{xy}^2)(1/n_E + 1/n_C)} - (1-b_{y \cdot x})(\overline{X}_E - \overline{X}_C)/s \qquad [5.39]$$

from which the second term on the right would have to be deleted if the regression coefficient $b_{y \cdot x}$ and the pretest means are not provided. The effect of deleting this term is to leave the mean difference from which the effect size is derived in the residual score metric instead of that of the final-status scale.

If the comparison between two groups is reported as an F statistic, the effect size can be obtained from

$$\hat{\Delta}_{E-C} = 2 \sqrt{\frac{F'(1-r_{xy}^2)}{(n_E + n_C)} \frac{(df_w - 1)}{(df_w - 2)}} \qquad [5.40]$$

The estimate obtained from Equation 5.40 will not be the same as that obtained from Equation 5.39 without the second term on the right even though both methods are based on residuals. The t_g in Equation 5.39 is derived from group mean residuals. The analysis of covariance F' in Equation 5.40, on the other hand, is derived from an adjusted sum of squares between groups which is not exactly the same as the sum of squares between adjusted (i.e., residual) group means. There is no way, therefore, of making precisely equivalent transformations to effect size estimates when some studies report covariance-adjusted F statistics and others report t statistics from an analysis of residuals.

Where a matched pairs analysis is used for experimental and control group comparisons, the dependent groups t statistic, t_d, can be converted to an effect size estimate using

$$\hat{\Delta}_{E-C} = t_d \sqrt{2/[n(1-r_{xy}^2)]}, \qquad [5.41]$$

which is equivalent, for the case where $n_E = n_C$ to the simplified form of Equation 5.39, the adjustment for residual scores. Matching is equivalent to partialing out of the final-status scores all that is predictable from the matching variable.

One difficulty which occurs when effect sizes are computed from significance tests is that, when the mean difference is not significant, it is sometimes not indicated whether the experimental or control group mean was larger. Thus, although an appropriate estimate of the magnitude of a small effect size might be derived, it may not be clear what sign is to be attached to it. If no inference can be drawn from the text, the effect size cannot be included.

When more than one experimental condition is compared with a control condition, effect sizes can be derived from an overall F statistic for each of the experimental conditions only if the group means are provided. Assuming homogeneous variance for all groups, the appropriate estimate of s_C^2 will be MS_w which, if the MS (between) is calculated from the group means, can be obtained from

$$MS_w = MS_B/F. \qquad [5.42]$$

When group means and some multiple comparisons statistics, such as Tukey's q or Dunn's statistics, are available, suitable estimates of effect size can similarly be obtained.

In all cases where effect size estimates are derived from parametric test statistics of the types discussed, the effect sizes are scaled by a pooled estimate of group variance. If the group variances are, in fact, not homogeneous, then the earlier cautions highlighted in Figure 5.1 must be noted.

Transforming significance levels into effect sizes. In some reports of studies, although a significance test was calculated, it is reported only that the calculation was based on n cases and that its level of significance (i.e., tail area under the null hypothesis) was p. How can one transform this meager information into a measure of effect size or correlation? Provided that the p value was reported exactly and not rounded to coarse approximations such as $.05 > p > .01$ (in which case some very crude conventions must be adopted), the transformation is straightforward. If, for example, it is reported that a two group t test with $n_E = n_C = 6$ was significant at the $p = .02$ level (two-tailed test), then it is a simple matter of looking up the value of t in a t table:

$$_{.99}t_{10} = 2.76.$$

Thus, one knows n_1, n_2, and the value of the t test; hence, one can proceed to Δ via the conventional steps derived and illustrated elsewhere:

$$\hat{\Delta} = t \sqrt{1/n_E + 1/n_C}$$
$$= 2.76 \sqrt{1/6 + 1/6}$$
$$= 1.59.$$

The reasoning and methods are similar for all of the other test statistics for which we have derived transformations to r or Δ.

A slight complication may arise at this point. Some investigators attempting an integrative analysis have routinely transformed any p value into its corresponding unit normal deviate z, then into a Δ or r. The transformation via z introduces small errors into the resulting estimates; when the particular test statistic on which p is based is known, then it is more accurate to transform via that statistic. For example, in the illustration above with p = .02 and $n_E = n_C = 6$, the transformation via z (which essentially ignores the "degrees of freedom" problem) gives the following estimate of Δ:

$$_{.99}z = 2.326$$
$$\hat{\Delta} = z \sqrt{1/n_E + 1/n_C}$$
$$\hat{\Delta} = 2.326 \sqrt{1/6 + 1/6}$$
$$\hat{\Delta} = 1.34.$$

The earlier estimate equaled 1.59; the error introduced by transforming via z instead of t is over 15% of the value of $\hat{\Delta}$.

Aside from this minor complication, the transformation of p values, given n, into Δ or r is rather obvious, and it proceeds by means of conventional statistical tables of significance levels and formulas previously developed for transforming test statistics.

One commonly encountered method of reporting results presents unique difficulties. Reports sometimes give only the sample sizes and an indication of whether a mean difference was statistically significant at a customary level. A conservative approximation to the Δ can be derived by setting a t ratio equal to the critical value corresponding to the reported significance level and solving for $(\overline{X}_E - \overline{X}_C)/s_X$, under the assumption of equal within-group variances. For example, suppose that a report contains only the information that the mean of the n_E experimental subjects exceeded the mean of the n_C control subjects at the .05 level of significance. At the very least, then,

$$t = \frac{\overline{X}_E - \overline{X}_C}{\sqrt{s_x^2(1/n_E + 1/n_C)}} = 1.96.$$

Clearly,

$$\hat{\Delta} = \frac{\overline{X}_E - \overline{X}_C}{s_x} = 1.96\sqrt{1/n_E + 1/n_C}$$

gives a conservative estimate of the experimental effect.

Transforming nonparametric statistics into effect sizes. When nonparametric statistical tests are used in the report of a study, there are particular difficulties in deriving effect size estimates. In many cases it is impossible.

Suppose that a study involved the test of a null hypothesis about equivalent locations of two distributions, and a Mann-Whitney U test was performed and reported. The U test competes with a normal distribution t test of means in these circumstances; the U test was once popular because it was believed to be safer when parametric assumptions were violated. The safety proved largely illusory, and today the t test is the method of choice. But many studies reported U-test results, and it is necessary to consider how information about Δ, say, can be retrieved from them.

No simple transformation of U into Δ is possible since the U test and most other nonparametric tests do not test simple hypotheses about population means. However, one could substitute for the reported U statistic the value of t that has the equivalent level of significance. For example, with $n_E = n_C = 10$, a U = 23 has a two-tailed significance level of p = .05. The corresponding t is $._{975}t_{18} = 2.10$. From this t statistic a $\hat{\Delta}$ is found in the conventional manner:

$$\hat{\Delta} = t\sqrt{1/n_E + 1/n_C}$$

$$\hat{\Delta} = .94.$$

The above series of transformations appear sensible and adequate, but one refinement may be possible. Nonparametric tests are known to have less power than parametric counterparts where the latter exist. Thus, a U statistic significant at the p = .05 level probably corresponds to a t statistic that is significant at the .03 or .02 level. For example, it is known that in many circumstances the power of the U test is about 95% as large as the power of the t test, a situation illustrated in Figure 5.3.

The area to the right of C under the curve H_1:t is p_t, the power of the t test against the particular alternative hypothesis illustrated. The area above C under H_1:f(U) is p_u, the power of the U test. It is generally true that $p_u/p_t = 3/\pi$ as $n \to \infty$ (Mood, 1954). Now suppose that p_u is approximately .94 in a particular situation. Then the corresponding power of t is $p_u(\pi/3) = .94(1.0472) = .984$. For large n_1 and n_2, the values of U (appropriately standardized) and t that cut off 94% and 98.4% of the area under roughly normal curves are 1.55 and 2.14. Hence, the small 5% difference in power gives rise to quite large differences in test statistics and, hence, in approximations of Δ 's. The prevalence and importance of these differences depend on the relative powers of *various* nonparametric and parametric tests.

Calculating effect sizes from ordinal information about means. For several reasons and in several ways it may occur that the findings of a comparative study exist only in the form of a report whether one mean (median or whatever) is higher or lower than another. This most basic report of a finding can arise from (1) very rudimentary reporting in a brief article, (2) the desire to avoid making dubious assumptions, or (3) incomplete data which obviate the calculation of a metric measure of effect or correlation. Thus, a data analyst attempting to integrate the findings of many studies may have in hand data of the following type: in 75 comparisons of treatments E and C, E exceeded C 45 times on the outcome measure, and C exceeded E the other 30 times. The key to converting these rudimentary results into metric measures of effects or correlation lies in traditional methods of psychometric scaling. In particular, if one can assume normality, then Thurstone's "law of comparative judgment" can be applied directly and the proportion of times E exceeds C can be translated directly into a measure of standardized mean difference between E and C (see Torgerson, 1958: 159ff.). This procedure was applied in connection with a meta-analysis of research on the relationship of class-size to achievement (Glass and Smith, 1979). Only the post-1960 studies were included in the scaling analysis. The regression analyses show that studies done prior to 1960 showed little relationship between class size and achievement (probably because of poor design, poor measures, and because genuinely small classes—fewer than a dozen pupils, say—were

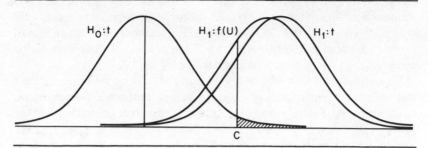

Figure 5.3 Illustration of relative power of parametric and non-parametric tests.

seldom studied). The post-1960 studies produced 246 values of Δ_{S-L}, for which one need only note whether Δ is positive or negative. In addition, there were a small number of studies that yielded only comparisons of the sizes of the achievement means for the small and large classes, but no metric information from which Δ might be calculated. The findings from these studies could be included in the scaling analyses even though they could not be included in the regression analyses. The total number of paired comparisons was 559.

The class size dimension was broken into five categories in an attempt to obtain an even distribution of comparisons. These categories were as follows: 1-11 pupils, 12-22, 23-32, 33-42, and 43 or more pupils. The actual average class sizes falling into these categories were as follows: 2, 18, 28, 38, and 84 pupils. These averages will be used to represent the categories. Thus, a comparison of achievement means for classes of sizes 4 and 30, for example, will be spoken of as a comparison of classes of size 2 and 28.

The following frequency matrix was obtained by counting direction of superiority in the paired comparisons:

Paired Comparison Frequency Matrix

Average Class Size

	2	18	28	38	84
2	–	7 of 8	45 of 46	3 of 3	
18	1 of 8	–	111 of 160	124 of 157	2 of 3
28	1 of 46	49 of 160	–	109 of 167	5 of 9

(Matrix continued on next page.)

38	0 of 3	33 of 157	58 or 167	–	1 of 6
84		1 of 3	4 of 9	5 of 6	–

This matrix is read as follows: Each entry represents the number of times the row class size had a higher achievement mean than the column class size. For example, there were 46 comparisons of class size 2 and class size 28; in 45 of them, achievement was superior in the class of 2.

It was decided at this point that some comparisons were so infrequently represented that including them in the scaling analysis might greatly overweight their unstable estimates. It was decided arbitrarily to include only those cells with more than a half-dozen comparisons. Thus, the following three cells (three on each side of the diagonal) were eliminated: row 1 column 4; row 2 column 4; row 4 column 5. The resulting frequency matrix was then transformed to a proportions matrix, π, for example, 111 of 160 = .69 and then to an X matrix where X_{ij} is the unit normal deviate below which lies π_{ij} proportion of the normal curve. The π and X matrices are combined in the following:

Class size

	2	18	28	38	84
2	–	π = .88 X = 1.18	.98 2.05		
18	.12 –1.18	–	.69 .50	.79 .81	
28	.02 –2.05	.31 –.50	–	.65 .39	.56 .15
38		.21 –.81	.35 –.39	–	
84			.44 –.15		–

The solution for scale values follows Gulliksen's (1956) least squares solution for incomplete data. A vector Z is formed by summing the columns of X: $-Z^T$ = (3.23, .13, –2.01, –1.20, –.15). A matrix M of order 5 × 5 is formed such that a – 1 is entered in each off-diagonal cell in

X that is not empty, a zero is entered for each empty cell, and the diagonal entry is the number of nonempty cells in the corresponding column of X. The last scale value, corresponding to class size 84, is arbitrarily set equal to zero, and the last row and column of M are deleted. The reduced matrices, M_1 and Z_1, are combined to form the normal equations of the least squares solution for S_1, the scale values:

$$S_1 = M_1^{-1} Z_1.$$

The estimates and their solution are as follows:

$$S_1 = \begin{bmatrix} 2 & -1 & -1 & 0 \\ -1 & 3 & -1 & -1 \\ -1 & -1 & 4 & -1 \\ 0 & -1 & -1 & 2 \end{bmatrix}^{-1} \begin{bmatrix} 3.23 \\ .13 \\ -2.01 \\ -1.20 \end{bmatrix}$$

$$S_1 = \begin{bmatrix} 1.625 & 1.250 & 1.000 & 1.125 \\ 1.250 & 1.500 & 1.000 & 1.250 \\ 1.000 & 1.000 & 1.000 & 1.000 \\ 1.125 & 1.250 & 1.000 & 1.625 \end{bmatrix} \begin{bmatrix} 3.23 \\ .13 \\ -2.01 \\ -1.20 \end{bmatrix}$$

$$S^T = (2.60, .72, .59, .39, 0)$$

The graph of the scaled relationship between class size and achievement appears as Figure 5.4. The scale values on the ordinate of the graph are arbitrary. The quadratic equation which best fits the five points by the least squares criterion is as follows:

$$s = 2.78912 - .09318(\text{Size}) + .000715(\text{Size})^2.$$

The multiple R^2 is .99. The following estimates of achievement (on an arbitrary scale) for various class-sizes were obtained from the regression curve:

Class Size	Estimated Scale Value for Achievement
1	2.70
10	1.93
20	1.21
30	.64
40	.21
50	-.08
60	-.23

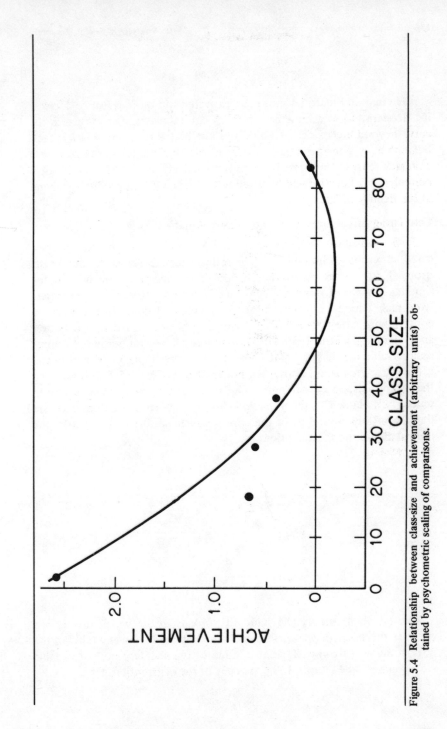

Figure 5.4 Relationship between class-size and achievement (arbitrary units) obtained by psychometric scaling of comparisons.

70   −.23
80   −.09

The curve in Figure 5.4 shows the expected and quite plausible decreasing deceleration in achievement as class size increases. The upturn in the curve beyond a class size of 60 should not be taken as an empirical fact, but rather as a mathematical artifact of having fit the five points with a quadratic curve. Undoubtedly a polynomial curve of higher order or a nonpolynomial curve could be fitted to the data without producing a bend in the vicinity of 60.

Calculating Effect Sizes for Dichotomous Variables

Probit transformation. Experimental outcomes are frequently measured in crude dichotomies where refined metric scales do not exist: dropped out versus persisted in school, remained sober versus resumed drinking, convicted versus not convicted of a crime. It seems inappropriate with such data to calculate means and standard deviations and take a conventional ratio. One approach to this problem is to attempt to recover an underlying metric information. Suppose that with respect to some unobservable metric (e.g., motivation to stay in school), the experimental and control groups are distributed normally as in Figure 5.5. It is assumed that there exists a cut-off point, C_X, such that if motivation to stay in school falls below C_X, the pupil will drop out. What can be observed are the proportions p_e and p_c of the groups which fall below C_X. Under the normal distributions assumption,

$$p_e = \int_{-\infty}^{z_e} \frac{1}{\sqrt{2\pi}} \, e^{-z^2/2} \, dz. \qquad [5.43]$$

where

$$z_e = \frac{X - \overline{X}_E}{s_e}.$$

Clearly, Z_e is simply the standard normal deviate which divides the curve at the $100 p_e$th percentile and can be obtained from any table of the normal curve. Likewise, Z_c is that value of the standard normal variable which cuts off the bottom $100 p_c$ percent of the distribution. Since,

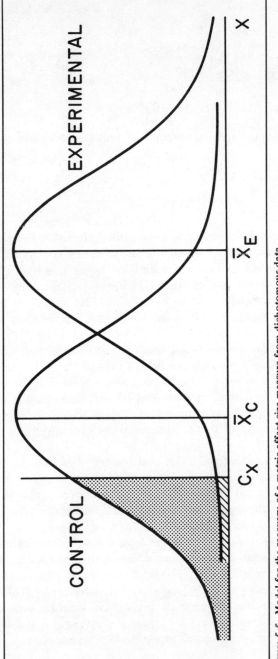

Figure 5.5 Model for the recovery of a metric effect-size measure from dichotomous data.

$$z_e = (C_x - \overline{X}_E)/s_e$$

and

$$z_c = (C_x - \overline{X}_C) / s_c,$$

it can be shown under the assumption of homogeneous variances that

$$z_c - z_e = \frac{\overline{X}_E - \overline{X}_C}{s_x} = \Delta.$$

Thus, effect size measures on hypothetical metric variables can be obtained simply by differencing the standard normal deviates corresponding to the percentages observed in the experimental and control groups. The reasoning followed here is essentially the same as that which underlines *probit analysis* in biometrics (see Finney, 1971). Where the unobservable metric distributions ought to be assumed skewed in an expected direction, the methods of *logit transformation* will be more appropriate (Ashton, 1972).

The transformation of dichotomous information to metric information via probits or logits makes it possible to expand greatly the data base of a meta-analysis. Frequently, studies on a single topic will encompass both metric and dichotomous measurement of outcomes. Having to integrate findings separately by type of outcome measurement is inconvenient as well as less than the broadest, most comprehensive integration of research possible.

Table 5.5 provides for the rapid calculation of Δ given p_e and p_c. For example, suppose that $p_e = .60$ and $p_c = .40$; from the table, the value of Δ is found to be .50. Suppose, as a second illustration, that $p_e = .35$ and $p_c = .70$. Then the sign of the effect size will be reversed after referencing Table 5.5 with .70 for columns and .35 for rows: $-.91$.

Several minor technical problems have arisen in connection with this technique: (1) what should be done when the distributions underlying the dichotomies are not normal?; (2) what if the two distributions (that giving rise to p_e and that yielding p_c) have different variances?; (3) how does the probit transformation compare to treating the dichotomy as an ordered metric and simply calculating $\Delta = (p_e - p_c)/ \sqrt{p_c(1-p_c)}$?; and (4) how can a probit transformation be carried out when p equals either zero or one?

TABLE 5.5   Probit Transformation of Difference In Proportions to Effect Size

p_e

p_c	.05	.10	.15	.20	.25	.30	.35	.40	.45	.50	.55	.60	.65	.70	.75	.80	.85	.90	.95
.05	0	.36	.60	.80	.97	1.12	1.25	1.39	1.51	1.64	1.77	1.89	2.03	2.16	2.31	2.48	2.68	2.92	3.28
.10		0	.24	.44	.61	.76	.89	1.03	1.15	1.28	1.41	1.53	1.67	1.80	1.95	2.12	2.32	2.56	2.92
.15			0	.20	.37	.52	.65	.79	.91	1.04	1.17	1.29	1.43	1.56	1.71	1.88	2.08	2.32	2.68
.20				0	.17	.32	.45	.59	.71	.84	.97	1.09	1.23	1.36	1.51	1.68	1.88	2.12	2.48
.25					0	.15	.28	.42	.54	.67	.80	.92	1.06	1.19	1.34	1.51	1.71	1.95	2.31
.30						0	.13	.27	.39	.52	.65	.77	.91	1.04	1.19	1.36	1.56	1.80	2.16
.35							0	.14	.26	.39	.52	.64	.78	.91	1.06	1.23	1.43	1.67	2.03
.40								0	.12	.25	.38	.50	.64	.77	.92	1.09	1.29	1.53	1.89
.45									0	.13	.26	.38	.52	.66	.80	.97	1.17	1.41	1.77
.50										0	.13	.25	.39	.52	.67	.84	1.04	1.28	1.64
.55											0	.12	.26	.39	.54	.71	.91	1.15	1.51
.60												0	.14	.27	.42	.59	.79	1.03	1.39
.65													0	.13	.28	.45	.66	.89	1.25
.70														0	.15	.32	.52	.76	1.12
.75															0	.17	.37	.61	.97
.80																0	.20	.44	.80
.85																	0	.24	.60
.90																		0	.36
.95																			0

Problem of nonnormality. We have examined alternative underlying distributions that could serve as a basis of a transformation method like probits. Two distributions seem particularly useful: (1) the logistic distribution and (2) the beta distribution. Their probability density distributions are as follows:

(1)   Logistic: $P(x) = \left\{ \operatorname{sech}^2 [(x-a)/2k] \right\}/4k$

(2)   Beta: $P(x) = [x^{v-1}(1-x)^{w-1}]/B(v,w),$

where $B(v,w)$ is the beta function, that is, $B(v,w) = \Gamma(v)\,\Gamma(w) / \Gamma(v+w)$.

The logistic curve has slightly "thicker tails" than the normal distribution to recommend it, it is a symmetric curve, slightly more peaked in the center and thinner in the intermediate regions than the normal. The following comparison of ordinates makes these features clear:

			z score		
Ordinate of	*±4*	*±3*	*±2*	*±1*	*0*
Normal	.0001	.0044	.0540	.2420	.3989
Logistic	.0013	.0078	.0458	.2186	.4535

Although these differences in ordinates appear small, they yield large differences in estimated effects when transformed first to percentiles then to z scores.

The beta distribution is a large family of curves bounded between 0 and 1 for the variate x and encompassing symmetric and asymmetric curves of widely varied shapes. The beta distribution for v = 4 and w = 2 is depicted in Figure 5.6.

By changing v and w, the beta distribution can be given any desired skewness. Thus, it is a useful distribution for describing asymmetric variables. Furthermore, its percentiles have been extensively tabulated (Pearson and Hartley, 1962).

We applied, where appropriate, probit transformations and metric calculation of effect sizes on a body of literature in drug therapy and psychotherapy. The discrepency between the average effect sizes for the two different methods proved to be relatively large, as Table 5.6 reveals. It must be emphasized that the comparison in Table 5.6 is based on two sets of data not necessarily equivalent in all important respects. However, the direction of the difference (favoring the probit transformation by nearly .2 standard deviation unit) is consistent with the expectation that violations

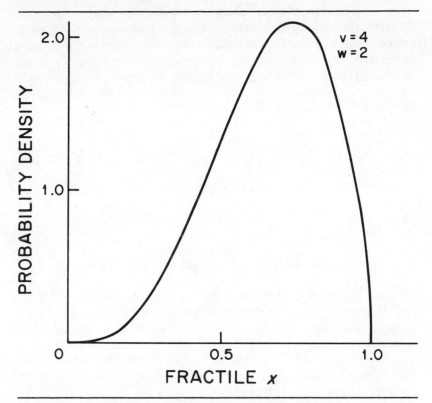

Figure 5.6 Probability density function for the beta variate, B(v,w).

TABLE 5.6 Comparison of Average Effects Calculated by Either
Probit Transformation or Metric Statistics From 112
Experiments on Drug and Psychotherapy

Method	No. of Δ	Average Effect Size, Δ
Probit Transformation	53	.651
Metric Statistics	351	.494

of the normality assumption of the probit method are likely to inflate
effect size estimates, particularly where dichotomies are extreme (.95
versus .05 or worse).

Problem of heterogeneous variances. Suppose that one observes p_e as the proportion of cases exceeding some fixed point, C, on a scale of measurement for which Z_e is normally distributed with mean and standard deviation μ_e and σ_e. The quantity p_c is similarly defined with Z_c having mean and standard deviation μ_c and σ_c. Now if p_e and p_c are transformed into the unit normal deviates, z_e and z_c, that cut off the upper $100p_e\%$ and $100p_c\%$ of the normal curve, then:

$$z_e = (C-\mu_e)/\sigma_e$$

and

$$z_c = (C-\mu_c)/\sigma_c.$$

It is easily shown that:

$$z_c - z_e(\sigma_e/\sigma_c) = \Delta = (\mu_e - \mu_c)/\sigma_c$$

the mean difference standardized against the control group standard deviation. If one knew the value of σ_e/σ_c or had a good hunch about it, then Δ could be easily calculated by weighting z_e by the ratio σ_e/σ_c. But it is more realistic (because σ_e/σ_c will nearly always be unknown) and important to ascertain how Δ is affected if σ_e and σ_c are unknown and heterogeneous. Beginning with $z_c - z_e$ and permitting σ_e and σ_c to differ, one quickly arrives at the expression:

$$z_c - z_e = \frac{C(\sigma_e - \sigma_c)}{\sigma_e \sigma_c} + \frac{\sigma_c \mu_e - \sigma_e \mu_e}{\sigma_c \sigma_e} . \qquad [5.44]$$

It is interesting to note that this expression depends on C, the hypothetical cut-off point used in determining "success" in both the experimental and control groups. The equation has not worked out to any form that is particularly neat or useful. There is probably little point in pursuing it much further. It is sufficient merely to record that heterogeneous variances affect the probit transformation both through their effect on the mean difference and the value of the criterion score. One is advised to be alert to the possibility of unequal variances and to use a transformation such as $z_c - z_e(\sigma_e/\sigma_c)$ when possible.

Probits versus dichotomous variables. It has occurred to some to ask whether the probit transformation of two dichotomies is roughly equivalent to treating the dichotomies as merely a limiting case of an effect size from the manifest variable, for example,

$$\Delta_d = (p_e - p_c) / \sqrt{p_c(1-p_c)}. \qquad [5.45]$$

This expression is simply the mean difference between the two dichotomies standardized by the standard deviation of the control group. The appropriate question to ask is how closely this formulation agrees with the effect size calculated from the probit transformation, namely,

$$\Delta_p = z_c - z_c,$$

where z_e is the unit normal deviate that marks off the upper $(100p_e)\%$ of the area under the normal curve, and z_c is similarly defined. The ratio of Δ_p to Δ_d for various values of p_e and p_c is easily calculated. Values of the ratio for p_e ranging from .1 to .9 in steps of .10 are tabulated below:

Values of the Ratio Δ_p / Δ_d

		p_e, Proportion of Successes in the Experimental Group								
		.1	.2	.3	.4	.5	.6	.7	.8	.9
	.1	–	1.32	1.14	1.04	.96	.92	.90	.91	.96
	.2	1.76	–	1.27	1.20	1.12	1.10	1.09	1.12	1.21
p_c	.3	1.74	1.46	–	1.29	1.20	1.19	1.20	1.25	1.38
proportion	.4	1.70	1.47	1.38	⊤	1.19	1.24	1.25	1.33	1.49
of successes	.5	1.60	1.40	1.31	1.22	–	1.27	1.31	1.40	1.60
in the	.6	1.50	1.34	1.27	1.19	1.24	–	1.33	1.44	1.68
control group	.7	1.38	1.25	1.20	1.17	1.20	1.24	–	1.46	1.74
	.8	1.21	1.12	1.09	1.09	1.12	1.18	1.27	–	1.76
	.9	.96	.91	.90	.92	.96	1.03	1.14	1.32	–

These ratios are disconcertingly large, in most cases. For example, if $p_e = .20$ and $p_c = .10$, the effect size calculated from the probit transformation is nearly one-third larger than the effect calculated from treating the data as a manifest dichotomy. It seems clear that in spite of the problems of nonnormality and heterogeneous variances that may plague the probit transformation, the calculation of effects from dichotomies without consideration of underlying distributions is not an acceptable alternative.

"Crude" measurement (polychotomies). Some ordered trichotomous or even polychotomous measurement is nearly as crude as dichotomous scoring. For example, the results of biofeedback treatment of migraine headache might be judged to be either Worse, No Change, Improved, or Much Improved. The four categories could be scaled 1, 2, 3, and 4 and treated like metric measurement, thus leading to calculation of means and standard deviations for treatment and control groups. But if all patients were either Improved or Much Improved, the collection of 3 and 4 scores is merely a linear transformation of dichotomous scoring and the problems of the previous section arise. It might then be preferable to let the proportion of 4's in both groups serve as the basis of a probit transformation.

The same recommendation might also be well made in the event of polychotomous ordinal measurement that is little different from dichotomous scoring. For example, if the distribution of cases among the four categories Worse, No Change, Improved, and Much Improved is 0%, 4%, 35%, and 61%, respectively, it might make more sense to lump together the first three categories and contrast it with the last, for example, Much Improved = 61%, Less than Much Improved = 39%; then the dichotomy could be transformed as before into a metric effect size via the probit transformation.

Problem of extreme proportions. A vexing problem with probit transformations from dichotomous to metric data arises when n cases reveal either 0 or n "successes." Then the proportion $p = f/n$ equals either 0 or 1, and the corresponding unit normal deviates are infinite $(-\infty$ and $+\infty)$. Consider a typical example. Ten experimental subjects are treated for dyslexia, and at the end of six months each reads sufficiently well to be promoted $(p_e = 10/10 = 1)$. None of the 10 control subjects is promoted $(p_c = 0/10 = 0)$. The corresponding unit normal deviates are $z_e = +\infty$ and $z_c = -\infty$, and $\Delta = \infty - (-\infty) = 2\infty$, which is absurd. Suppose that it was decided arbitrarily to change one case in each sample to avoid this problem. Then p_e would be taken equal to 9/10 and p_c to 1/10. Now the unit normal deviates are 1.282 and −1.282, respectively; and $\Delta = 2.56$. Suppose a compromise between 0 and 1 "success" was struck at .5 so that p_c equaled $.5/10 = .05$ and, similarly, $p_e = .95$. The resulting value of Δ is

1.645−(−1.645) = 3.29. The difference between 3.29 and 2.56 is too large to ignore; and the difference of either from ∞ is too gruesome to contemplate. A method is needed for dealing nonarbitrarily with p's of 1 or 0. One solution is afforded by Bayesian statistics.

We shall assume that p is a sample estimate of π where p = X/n and X is binomially distributed. The Bayesian posterior distribution of π is given by:

$$Pr(\pi|X) = [Pr(\pi) Pr(X|\pi)] / Pr(X),$$

where $Pr(\pi)$ is the prior distribution of π assumed to be uniform on the interval 0 to 1.

Now $Pr(X)$ is given by:

$$Pr(X) = \int_{0}^{1} Pr(\pi) \binom{n}{X} \pi^X (1 - \pi)^{n-x} d\pi \qquad [5.46]$$

Since $Pr(\pi)$ is a constant k, and recognizing that the terms in π integrate to a beta distribution, Equation 5.46 becomes

$$Pr(X) = k \binom{n}{X} B(X + 1, n - X + 1),$$

where $B(u,v) = [\Gamma(u) \Gamma(v)] / \Gamma(u + v)$,

where $\Gamma(u) = (u-1)! = (u-1)(u-2) \ldots 3 \cdot 2 \cdot 1$, when u is an integer. The distribution of X given π is simply the binomial:

$$Pr(X|\pi) = \binom{n}{X} \pi^X (1-\pi)^{n-X}.$$

Thus, the posterior distrubution of π is given by:

$$PR(\pi|X) = \frac{k \binom{n}{X} \pi^X (1 - \pi)^{n-X}}{k \binom{n}{X} B(X + 1, n - X + 1)}.$$

The Bayesian estimate of Π, denoted by $\hat{\Pi}$, is the mean of the posterior distribution:

$$E\,(\pi|X) = \hat{\pi} \;\; = \int_{0}^{1} \frac{\pi\;\pi^X(1-\pi)^{n-X}\;d\hat{\pi}}{B\,(X+1,n-X+1)}$$

$$= \frac{B\,(X+2,n-X+1)}{B\,(X+1,n-X+1)}$$

$$= \frac{\Gamma\,(X+2)\;\Gamma\,(n-X+1)\;\Gamma\,(n+2)}{\Gamma\,(n+3)\;\Gamma\,(X+1)\,\Gamma(n-X+1)} = \frac{X+1}{n+2}\;.$$

This result is the important one: *assuming a uniform prior distribution for π, the Bayesian estimate of π, the binomial parameter, equals $\hat{\pi} = (X+1)/(n+2)$ where n is the sample size and X is the observed number of successes.* (Solutions are also possible for various nonuniform prior distributions of π, especially the beta distribution, for example.)

This result offers a nonarbitrary method of resolving difficulties of probit transformation for the cases of $p=1$ or 0. If $X = 0$ in a binomial sample of n, then whereas $p = 0$, the Bayesian estiamte $\hat{\pi}$ equals $(0 + 1) / (n + 2)$. Likewise, at the other end of the scale, a p of 1 corresponds to a $\hat{\pi}$ of $(n + 1)/(n + 2)$. For example, in the illustration discussed earlier, $p_e = 10/10$ would yield $\hat{\pi}_e = 11/12 = .92$; and $p_c = 0/10$ would give $\hat{\pi}_c = 1/12 = .08$. Hence Δ equals $1.40 - (-1.40) = 2.80$. This solution seems nonarbitrary and reasonable. Having found it, we see no reason why it should not be applied across the board, that is, regardless of the value of $p = X/n$, if a uniform prior distribution of π is reasonable, the $\hat{\pi}$ should be taken to equal $\hat{\pi} = (X + 1)/(n + 2)$.

An interesting problem arises when one's purposes are study integration. Suppose that 10 separate studies of five persons each yielded identical results, one out of five "successes." Each value of p would equal $1/5$, and the average of all the p's or the pooled value across the 10 studies would both equal .20. However, the average of the Bayesian estimates would be $(\hat{\pi}_1 + \ldots + \hat{\pi}_5) / 5 = 5(2/7) / 5 = .29$. The Bayesian correction small samples can be substantial, even though in a pooled sample it would be insignificant, for example, $\hat{\pi}_{pooled} = 11/52 = .21$ versus $10/50 = .20$. Thus the average of many small-sample Bayesian estimates can be quite different from a pooled Bayesian estimate. A pooled estimate would seem preferable, but pooling obviates the examination of study-to-study variation in findings, which is much in the spirit of our approach to integrating research.

OUTCOMES OF CORRELATIONAL STUDIES

In the meta-analysis of correlational studies, one is integrating correlation coefficients descriptive of the relationship between two variables, such as (1) achievement and socioeconomic level or (2) teacher personality and pupil learning. The quantitative description of findings from correlational studies presents fewer complications than do experimental studies.

Illustrations of the integrative analysis of correlational studies will be drawn from a study of the relationship between pupils' socioeconomic status (SES) and their academic achievement. White (1976) collected over 600 correlation coefficients from published and unpublished literature. The coefficients were analyzed to determine how their magnitude was related to varying definitions of SES, different types of achievement, age of the subjects, and so on. White found that the 636 available correlations of SES and achievement averaged .25 with a standard deviation of about .20 and positive skew. SES and achievement correlation was below what was generally believed to be the strength of association of the two variables. The correlation diminished as students got older, r decreasing from about .25 at the primary grades to around .15 late in high school. SES correlated higher with verbal than math achievement (.24 versus .19 for 174 and 128 coefficients, respectively). When White classified the SES and achievement correlations by the type of SES measure employed (see Table 5.7), SES measured as income correlated more highly with achievement than either SES measured by the education of the parents or the occupational level of the head of household. Several reliable trends in the collection of 600 coefficients could help methodologists designing studies and sociologists constructing models of the schooling social system.

It probably matters little whether analysis is carried out in the metric of r_{xy}, r_{xy}^2, or Fisher's Z transformation of r_{xy}. The final results ought to be expressed in terms of the familiar r_{xy} scale, however. There appears to be no good reason to transform r_{xy} to Fisher's Z at the intermediate stages of aggregation and analysis, though this is sometimes recommended. Fisher's transformation was developed to solve an inferential problem, and it would be an unlikely happenstance if it proved to be the method of choice

TABLE 5.7   Average Correlation Between SES and Achievement
             for Different Kinds of SES Measure

SES Measure Consists of Indicators of/	Average r_{xy}*
Parents Income	.315 (19)
Parents Education	.185 (116)
Parents Occupation Level	.201 (65)

* Number of coefficients averaged in parentheses.

for combining correlation measures from several studies. It is frequently recommended that two or more r_{xy}'s be squared, averaged, and the square root taken rather than averaged directly. However, it is fairly easy to show that the choice seldom makes a practical difference. A little algebra applied to the ratio of $(r_1 + r_2)/2$ to $\sqrt{(r_1^2 + r_2^2)/2}$ will show that the discrepancy between the two depends primarily on the size of the difference between r_1 and r_2 and that they must be enormously different for the two averaging methods to differ in any important way. For example, the three coefficients .20, .30, and .40 average .30 directly; and they average .31 if first squared and averaged, and the square root taken. A gap of approximately more than .50 between r_1 and r_2 is needed to separate $(r_1 + r_2)/2$ and $\sqrt{(r_1 + r_2)/2}$ by more than .05. The researcher can safely decide whether the scale of r_{xy} or r_{xy}^2 is more meaningful and work in that metric throughout an integration of correlational studies.

The correlational studies referred to here deal with ordinal, metric variables. Correlational results which involve genuine dichotomies or polychotomies (e.g., sex, ethnic group) should be recast into more informative descriptive measures such as standardized differences among means, and the techniques of "effect size" measurement discussed above may then be applied. Where the two variables correlated are conceived of as having metric properties—even if the technology of measurement at the time fell short of actual metric measurement—then one ought to seek to transform all correlation measures to the scale of Pearson's product-moment correlation coefficient.

When a large field of correlational research is collected, a bewildering variety of statistics is encountered: biserial and point-biserial correlation coefficients, rank-order correlations, phi coefficients, contingency coeffi-

TABLE 5.8 Guidelines for Converting Various Summary Statistics Into Product-Moment Correlations

Reported Statistic	Transformation to r_{xy}	References
a) Point-biserial correlation, r_{pb}	$*r_{xy} = r_{pb} \sqrt{n_1 n_2}/un$ u = ordinate of unit normal distribution n = total sample size	Glass and Stanley (1970, p. 171)
b) $t = \dfrac{\overline{X}_1 - \overline{X}_2}{\sqrt{s^2(\dfrac{1}{n_1} + \dfrac{1}{n_2})}}$	$r_{pb} = \sqrt{\dfrac{t^2}{t^2 + (n_1 + n_2 - 2)}}$ then convert r_{pb} to r_{xy} via a) above	Glass and Stanley (1970, p. 318)
c) t based on extreme	$\rho = \dfrac{t(\sqrt{2/n})}{\sqrt{\dfrac{4z^2}{p^2} + \left[\dfrac{z^2}{p^2} - \dfrac{xz}{p}\right] t^2 \left(\dfrac{2}{n}\right)}}$ n = within cell n. p = proportion cut at each end. z = ordinate on normal curve at the cut. x = standard normal deviate corresponding to p (abscissa value)	Based on Feldt (1961, p. 315)
d) $F = MS_b/MS_w$ for J = 2 groups.	$\sqrt{F} = |t|$ then proceed via b) above.	

149

TABLE 5.8   Guidelines for Converting Various Summary Statistics Into Product-Moment Correlations (continued)

Reported Statistic	Transformation to r_{xy}	References
e) $F = MS_b/MS_w$ for $J > 2$ groups.	1) Collapse J groups to 2 & then proceed via d) above, or 2) $r_{xy} = \eta = \sqrt{SS_b/(SS_b + SS_w)}$	Hays (1973, pp. 683-684)
f) χ^2 only (i.e., no frequencies reported) for a contingency table.	$**r_{xy} \cong P = \left(\dfrac{\chi^2}{\chi^2 + n}\right)^{1/2}$ n = total sample size	Kendall & Stuart (1967, pp. 557 ff)
g) 2×2 contingency table.	Calculate tetrachoric r_{xy} from tables	Glass and Stanley (1970, pp. 165 ff)
h) $R \times C$ contingency table	Collapse to a 2×2 table and proceed via g) above.	
i) Spearman's rank correlation, r_s.	$r_{xy} = r_s$ since the translation of r_s to r_{xy} under bivariate normality is nearly a straight line.	Kruskal (1958)
j) Mann-Whitney U.	Transform U to r-rank-biserial via $r_{rb} = 1 - 2U/(n_1 n_2)$.	Willson (1976)

*$r_{xy} \cong 1.25 r_{pb}$ when $p = n_1/n$ is between .2 and .8 (Magnusson, 1966, p. 205).
**P is Pearson's coefficient of contingency and $p^2 \to \rho^2$ as the number of categories in the table increases. With few categories, the estimate can be unduly low.

cients, contingency tables with chi-square tests, t tests, analyses of variance, and more. In White's analysis of SES and achievement correlational finding was encountered. Of 143 studies, 37 reported t or F statistics, 71 reported Pearson r's, 8 reported chi-square or nonparametric statistics, and 27 presented only graphs or tables of means.

There usually is an algebraic path from the reported statistics to a Pearson correlation coefficient or an approximation to one. Some signposts along the paths are set out in Table 5.8, where it is indicated how one might travel from particular forms of reported data to a product-moment correlation measure.

Another common instance of transforming results involves converting a correlation, r, into a standardized mean difference. For example, Coleman's survey of equality of educational opportunity reported a correlation coefficient between class size, X, and achievement, Y. But most other studies reported the relationship in terms of means and variance of achievement for particular class sizes, leading to the measure Δ_{S-L} described earlier. Knowing only r_{xy} and $\overline{X}$ and s_x, the measure Δ_{S-L} can be calculated assuming a normal distribution of X and a linear relationship of X and Y. Values of S and L must be specified on X; they can be arbitrarily designated as any two convenient percentiles, for example, P and 100-P. Then $S = \overline{X} - zs_x$ and $L = \overline{X} + zs_x$, where z is the unit normal deviate at the percentile 100-P.

From r_{xy}, we can calculate the regression line of Y on X from $b_{yx} = r_{xy}(s_y/s_x)$ and $b_0 = \overline{Y} - b_{yx}\overline{X}$. The mean values of Y corresponding to S and L are calculated by substitution into the regression equation. The within-group variance on Y is simply the variance error of estimate, known to equal $s_y^2(1 - r^2)$. Combining these facts leads to

$$\Delta_{S-L} = 2zr_{xy}(1 - r_{xy}^2)^{-\frac{1}{2}}$$

where z is the unit normal deviate at the Pth percentile of the normal curve (S being at the Pth percentile in the distribution of X and L being at the 100-Pth percentile of X).

The above conversion seems unobjectionable and surely is, provided that X is roughly normally distributed and the regression of Y and X is linear. However, when Y has a curvilinear regression on X, the value of Δ_{S-L} will be somewhat in error.

NOTES

1. The gamma function, $\Gamma(n)$, is defined as $\Gamma(n) = (n-1)!$ where n is a positive integer. If n is even, then $\Gamma(n/2) = (n/2-1)!$ If n is odd, then $\Gamma(n/2) = (n/2-1)$ $(n/2-2) \ldots (1/2)\sqrt{\pi}$.

2. To this point, the dependent or outcome variable has been denoted by X. Now we wish to consider gain scores and covariance analyses where it is conventional to denote the dependent or posttest variable by Y and the pretest or covariate by X.

CHAPTER SIX

TECHNIQUES OF ANALYSIS

The analysis of data in a meta-analysis is properly approached as an instance of multivariate data analysis in which the studies are the units on which measurements are taken and the study characteristics (Chapter 4) and findings (Chapter 5) are the many variables. The point of having come this far in our treatment of meta-analysis is the belief that the import of many studies described in many ways cannot be grasped without the aid of techniques of arranging, ordering, and relating—in short, without the help of statistical methods. Univariate description, frequency tabulations, correlations, linear model estimation, regression analysis, factor analysis, analysis of covariance, discriminant function analysis—any of the methods of statistical analysis that have proved to be useful in extracting meaning from data are potentially useful in meta-analysis. One's attitude toward the data may be exploratory (Tukey, 1977) or confirmatory, descriptive or inferential; it does not matter. We are breaking no new ground here. We are merely illustrating the application of well-known statistical methods in a context in which researchers are prone to forget that they are as useful, indeed necessary, as in more familiar contexts.

In this chapter, we shall first deal briefly with the simple univariate descriptive analysis of study findings. Then we shall describe methods of examining the correlation of study findings and characteristics. Third, the estimation of treatment effects where study findings can be arranged in the manner of factorial experiments will be investigated. Fourth, attention will be given to the special possibilities of integrating study findings where both the independent and dependent variables are measured on quantitative scales. Fifth, problems of statistical inference as they apply in meta-analysis will be discussed.

SIMPLE DESCRIPTION OF STUDY FINDINGS

Once the findings of the studies in a meta-analysis have been measured (whether by means of an effect size, a correlation coefficient, or whatever), all the standard methods of tabulating and describing statistics may be usefully applied: frequency distributions, averages, measures of variability, and the like. In this respect, we much prefer Tukey's (1977) innovative and ingenious methods of exploratory data analysis to the unimaginative lot of techniques presented in most statistical methods textbooks. An illustration might help the reader understand our preference.

El-Nemr (1979) found 59 experimental studies in which were compared traditional teaching of biology and biology taught as a process of inquiry. These studies yielded nearly 250 effect size measures in which inquiry-teaching was compared with traditional teaching of biology. The effect size measures could be classified into seven categories descriptive of type of outcome: science achievement, science process skills, critical thinking skills, laboratory skills, attitudes toward the biology course, interest in science, and "composite" (an average of the preceding outcomes). Plots of the characteristics of the distributions of effect sizes for each outcome category appear as Figure 6.1.

Consider the first category of outcomes in Figure 6.1. The 59 experiments yielded 39 effect sizes based on the measurement of achievement (since achievement was not measured in every experiment). Each effect size compares inquiry (I) and traditional (T) teaching:

$$\Delta_{I-T} = (\bar{Y}_I - \bar{Y}_T) / s_T.$$

The distribution of the 39 achievement effect sizes is described by the lines, letters, and dots above "Achievement" in Figure 6.1. The basic descriptive technique is the "schematic box plot" with auxiliary features. The central box or rectangle marks off the "hinges" (roughly, the first and third quartiles) of the distribution of effect sizes and the median (ordinary definition) lies between the top and the bottom of the box with 25% of those inside the box on either side of it. The hinges for the achievement effect sizes are at .02 and .23, approximately, and the median is at .17. The large black dot inside the box indicates the location of the average of the 39 effect sizes; for achievement, the mean is above the median. The dotted line emanating from both ends of the box measures the distance to the "inner fence," a distance arbitrarily chosen to be one-and-one-half times the length of the box (i.e., 150% of the hinge range). The lowercase letter f marks the inner fence. Data points that lie outside the inner fence are "outliers," and each is denoted by a small dot. At the same distance beyond the inner fence that the inner fence lies beyond the ends of the box, one marks off the "outer fence" with an uppercase F. Data points beyond the outer fence are "far outliers." One casts a suspicious eye at outliers and looks with even greater incredulity on far outliers. They may represent oddities (measurement reporting errors, misprints, miscalculations, and whatever) that ought to be eliminated or given different weight in describing the typical features of the data.

Notice, for example, that among the 39 achievement effect sizes in Figure 6.1, there are 6 outliers and 2 far outliers. If the 2 far outliers are eliminated and the average effect size recalculated, the average drops from .20 to .10. The median drops a little, but less than the 50% drop for the mean. Consider the "Process Skills" outcome category. Here, a substantial discrepancy exists between the median and the mean with the latter one and two-thirds times larger than the former. But the mean is probably distorted greatly by the outlier of 3.0; removing this outlier drops the mean to .41, because of the positive skew in the data for process skills shown by the fact that the median is far closer to the lower hinge than the upper. Generally the means are larger than the medians, except for "Critical Thinking" where the order is reversed. And although the inquiry approach to teaching biology was superior to traditional teaching in most respects, it was no better at stimulating pupils' interest in science.

When descriptive analyses are used, caution must be taken in the interpretation of means (or median) effect sizes in broad categories unless it is clear that those marginal summary statistics are not confounded with other effects because of unbalanced representation of other characteristics of studies. This is a point well-understood in the analysis of subject data in primary research but it has equal force in meta analysis.

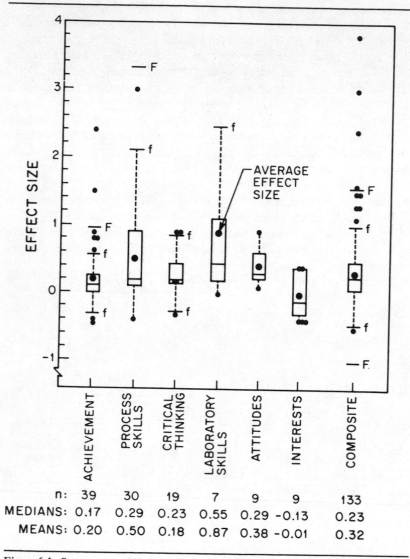

Figure 6.1 Summary statistics for effect sizes in seven classes of outcome from comparisons of inquiry vs. traditional teaching of biology. (After El-Nemr, 1979)

Hartley (1977) integrated the research literature on the effects of individually paced instruction in mathematics. She distinguished four instructional strategies in the literature—computer assisted instruction (CAI), tutoring, individualized learning packets (ILP), and programmed instruction (PI)—which were compared with control. The average effect sizes which she found are reported in Table 6.1. Although these summary statistics suggest, among other things, that CAI was clearly superior to ILP, Hartley also noted that individually paced programs were more effective if they supplemented regular class instruction rather than replaced it. The differences between supplementation and replacement are shown in her summary data reproduced in Table 6.2. From this table it is clear that there was no research on the utility of programmed instruction as a supplement to class instruction. As a replacement program PI was clearly not inferior to CAI. The conclusions invited by a general summary table such as Table 6.1 clearly must be treated cautiously. Hartley's (1977) analysis of the effect sizes observed in studies using varying qualities of research design (from random assignment to no control group) also showed that the different types of research design were differentially represented in the studies of the different instructional techniques. Thus design effects are also confounded in the marginal mean effect sizes for instructional techniques given in Table 6.1.

This confounding in the general conclusions which might be drawn is not unique to meta-analysis. It is simply more readily exposed, and therefore more readily dealt with in meta-analysis than in traditional narrative reviews. One way to remove the confounding is to treat the data

TABLE 6.1   Average Effect Sizes for Individually Paced
Mathematics Instruction

	Technique			
	CAI	Tutoring	ILP	PI
Mean	.409	.597	.158	.110
Standard Deviation	.588	.684	.647	.702
Number of Effect Sizes	89	73	139	89

TABLE 6.2   Average Effect Sizes for Individually Paced
             Mathematics Instruction in Different Types
             of Programs

Programing		*Technique*			
		CAI	Tutoring	ILP	PI
Supplemental Program	Mean	.471	.610		.253
	Standard Deviation	.594	.703		.936
	Number of Effect Sizes	75	68	0	20
Replacement	Mean	.078	.416	.158	.069
	Standard Deviation	.476	.264	.647	.603
	Number of Effect Sizes	14	5	139	69

in a factorial design and to estimate both main and interactive effects. If too many interactions are to be investigated, of course, there will inevitably be many empty cells in the design. Even in the two-way analysis shown in Table 6.2, there was one empty cell. An alternative analytic strategy is to examine the correlations of study characteristics and study findings (effect sizes).

CORRELATING STUDY CHARACTERISTICS AND FINDINGS

The study of the relationship between study characteristics and findings is addressed to such questions as whether the findings are homogeneous for all types of subject (e.g., person) or whether they are positive for some types of subject and negative for others, whether the findings are strong when viewed with certain research methods (e.g., subjective outcome appraisals), whether the short-term findings differ substantially from the long-term results, and so forth. Any one of the many statistical techniques for studying the association or relationship between two variables may find useful application at this stage: contingency table analysis, regression analysis, correlation analysis with its many subspecies (e.g., Pearson's r,

TABLE 6.3   Correlations of Several Descriptive Variables
with Effect Size (n = 833)

Variable	Correlation with effect size
Organization (1 = individual; 2 = group)	−.07
Duration of therapy (in hours)	−.02
Years' experience of therapists	−.01
Diagnosis of clients (1 = psychotic; 2 = neurotic)	.02
IQ of clients (1 = low; 2 = medium; 3 = high)	.15
Age of clients	.02
Similarity of therapists and clients (1 = very similar; . . . ; 4 = very dissimilar)	−.19
Internal validity of study (1 = high; 2 = medium; 3 = low)	−.09
Date of publication	.09
"Reactivity" of outcome measure (1 = low; . . . ; 5 = high)	.30
No. of months posttherapy for follow-up	−.10

point-biserial or biserial correlation, curvilinear correlation). Since study findings will be measured on a metric scale (Δ, r, and so on), metric measures of relationship deriving from Pearson product-moment notions will be the most powerful and useful.

Consider an illustration: In their first meta-analysis of the effects of psychotherapy, Smith and Glass (1977) compiled several hundred effect size measures for nearly 400 controlled-outcome evaluations. Among the characteristics of the studies coded were the 11 for which the linear correlations with effect size are reported in Table 6.3.

The correlations are generally low, although several are reliably non-zero. Some of the more interesting correlations show (1) a positive relationship between an estimate of the intelligence of the group of clients and the effect of therapy and (2) a somewhat larger correlation indicating that therapists who resemble their clients in ethnic group, age, and social level get better results. The effect sizes diminish across time after therapy as shown by the last correlation in Table 6.3, a correlation of −.10 which is closer to −.20 when the curvilinearity of the relationship is taken into account. The largest correlation is with the "reactivity" or subjectivity of the outcome measure. The multiple correlation of the 11 study characteristics with the effect size was equal to about .50; thus, 25% of the variance in study findings can be accounted for by variations in the characteristics of the studies. There is not space here to pause and consider the many implications of the relationships reported in Table 6.3.

A more controversial use of the relationships of study characteristics to findings involves the attempt to equate various classes of studies and then observe comparative results. Imagine a simple hypothetical example. Either medication or hypnotherapy can be prescribed for asthmatic children. A set of 50 controlled experiments on the effects of medication show an average effect size of .75; 60 experiments with hypnotherapy give an average effect size of .40. It is observed, however, that on the average the medication experiments measured effects one month after treatment whereas the hypnotherapy experiments measured outcomes at six months. Furthermore, within each class of experiment, the regression coefficient of Δ onto "follow-up time" is about the same:

(1) Medication: $\hat{\Delta} = .83 - .08$ (No. of months)
(2) Hypnotherapy: $\hat{\Delta} = .65 - .08$ (No. of months)

If the effects of both treatments are estimated for follow-up times of one month, the .35 difference in the uncorrected average comparison (.35 = .75 - .40) shrinks to .75 - .57 = .18 standard deviation unit difference between the means of the treatment and control groups. If the regression of effect size onto follow-up time were heterogeneous in the regression slopes between the two therapies, the estimated order of superiority could change from one follow-up time to another.

In the analysis of psychotherapy effects, the regression of effect size on 10 independent variables was performed separately within three quite different classes of psychotherapy: psychodynamic, systematic desensitization, and behavior modification. The results of the three multiple regression analyses appear in Table 6.4.

Relatively complex forms of the independent variables were used to account for interactions and nonlinear relationships. For example, years experience of the therapist bore a slight curvilinear relationship with outcome, probably because more experienced therapists worked with more seriously ill clients. This situation was accommodated by entering, as an independent variable, "therapist experience" in interaction with "diagnosis of the client." Age of client and follow-up date were slightly curvilinearly related to outcome in ways most directly handled by chang-

TABLE 6.4 Regression Analyses Within Therapies

Independent variables	Unstandardized regression coefficients		
	Psychodynamic (n = 94)	Systematic desentization (n = 212)	Behavior modification (n = 129)
Dianosis (1 = psychotic; 2 = neurotic)	.174	-.193	.041
Intelligence (1 = low; . . . ; 3 = high)	-.114	.201	.201
Transformed age[a]	.002	-.002	.002
Experience of Therapist X Neurotic	-.011	-.034	-.018
Experience of Therapist X Psychotic	-.015	.004	-.033
Clients self-presented	-.111	.287	-.015
Clients solicited	.182	.088	-.163
Organization (1 = individual; 2 = group)	.108	-.086	-.276
Transformed months posttherapy[b]	-.031	-.047	.007
Transformed reactivity of measure[c]	.003	.025	.021
Additive constant	.757	.489	.453
Multiple R	.423	.512	.509
σ_e	.173	.386	.340

[a]Transformed age = (Age - 25) (| Age - 25)$^{1/2}$
[b]Transformed months posttherapy = (No. months)$^{1/2}$
[c]Transformed reactivity of measure = (Reactivity)2·25

ing exponents. These regression equations allow estimation of the effect size a study shows when undertaken with a certain type of client, with a therapist of a certain level of experience, and so on. By setting the independent variables at a particular set of values, one can estimate what a study of that type would reveal under each of the three types of therapy. Thus, a statistically controlled comparison of the effects of psychodynamic, systematic desensitization, and behavior modification therapies can be obtained in this case. The three regression equations are clearly not homogeneous; hence, one therapy might be superior under one set of circumstances and a different therapy superior under others. A full description of the nature of this interaction is elusive, though one can illustrate it at various particularly interesting points.

In Figure 6.2 estimates are made of the effect sizes that would be shown for studies in which simple phobias for persons with high IQ and 20 years of age are treated by a therapist with 2 years' experience and evaluated immediately after therapy with highly subjective outcome measures. This verbal description of circumstances can be translated into quantitative values for the independent variables in Table 6.2 and substituted into each of the three regression equations. In this instance, the two behavioral therapies show effects superior to the psychodynamic therapy.

In Figure 6.3 a second prototypical psychotherapy client and situation are captured in the independent variable values, and the effects of the three types of therapy are estimated. For the typical 30-year-old neurotic of average IQ seen in circumstances like those that prevail in mental health clinics (individual therapy by a therapist with 5 years experience), behavior modification is estimated to be superior to psychodynamic therapy, which is in turn superior to systematic desensitization at the 6-month follow-up point.

Besides illuminating the relationships in the data, the quantitative techniques described here can give direction to future research. By fitting regression equations to the relationship between effect size and the independent variables descriptive of the studies and then by placing confidence regions around these hyperplanes, the regions where the input-output relationships are most poorly determined can be identified. By concentrating new studies in these regions, one can avoid the accummulation of redundant studies of convenience that overelaborate small areas.

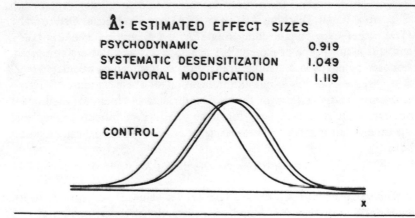

$\hat{\pmb{\Delta}}$: ESTIMATED EFFECT SIZES

PSYCHODYNAMIC	0.919
SYSTEMATIC DESENSITIZATION	1.049
BEHAVIORAL MODIFICATION	1.119

Figure 6.2 Three within-therapy regression estimates of effect for a prototypic therapy client (phobic) and therapy situation.

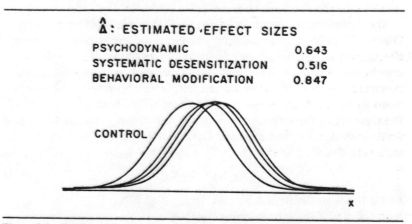

$\hat{\pmb{\Delta}}$: ESTIMATED ·EFFECT SIZES

PSYCHODYNAMIC	0.643
SYSTEMATIC DESENSITIZATION	0.516
BEHAVIORAL MODIFICATION	0.847

Figure 6.3 Three within-therapy regression estimates of effect for a prototypic client (Neurotic) and therapy situation.

LINEAR ANALYSIS OF VARIANCE MODELS FOR ESTIMATION

Collections of experiments often present odd arrays of comparison to one who wishes an integrated summary of effects. For example, an integration of reading instruction research would encounter experiments comparing Initial Teaching Alphabet (ITA) and Traditional Orthography (TO), other experiments comparing ITA and Diacritical Marking (DM), and still a third type of experiment in which TO and DM are compared. For each comparison, a standardized mean contrast can be calculated (e.g., $\Delta = (\overline{X}_{ITA} - \overline{X}_{TO})/s_X$); but the integration of these various Δ's into a estimation of the effects of the three individual instructional methods is not immediately obvious. One fruitful approach is via "effects coding" and the general linear model. For example, the following model can be postulated:

$$\Delta = \beta_{ITA} X_1 + \beta_{TO} X_2 + \beta_{DM} X_3 + e. \qquad [6.1]$$

The variables X_1, X_2 and X_3 take on the values, 1, 0, and -1. If, for example, a particular Δ is based on an experimental comparison of ITA and TO, then $X_1 = 1$, $X_2 = -1$ and $X_3 = 0$. In this way, many Δ's can be regressed onto the X's; and the β's, which are individual effects of the instructional methods, can be estimated.

The technique of "control referencing" that was dealt with briefly in Chapter 5 can be approached more conveniently through use of the linear effects models of this section. Suppose, for example, that there exist n experiments in which treatment A is compared to a control group, n experiments in which B is compared with a control group, and n experiments in which A and B are compared directly without a control group. There are, thus, three types of effect size measure: Δ_A, Δ_B, and Δ_{A-B}. A simple modification of the general linear model like that in Equation 6.1 suffices to describe the effects:

$$\Delta = \beta_A X_1 + \beta_B X_2 + e. \qquad [6.2]$$

$X_1 = 1$ if Δ is of the form A versus Control,
$X_2 = 1$ if Δ is of the form B versus Control,
$X_1 = +1$ and $X_2 = -1$ if Δ is of the form A versus B.
For the equal n's example, the data, the design and the parameter matrices are as follows:

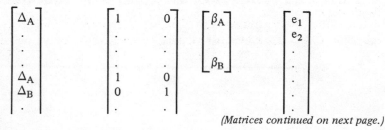

(Matrices continued on next page.)

$$
\begin{bmatrix} \cdot \\ \cdot \\ \Delta_B \\ \Delta_{A-B} \\ \cdot \\ \cdot \\ \cdot \\ \Delta_{A-B} \end{bmatrix}
=
\begin{bmatrix} \cdot & \cdot \\ \cdot & \cdot \\ 0 & 1 \\ 1 & -1 \\ \cdot & \cdot \\ \cdot & \cdot \\ \cdot & \cdot \\ 1 & -1 \end{bmatrix}
+
\begin{bmatrix} \cdot \\ \cdot \\ \cdot \\ \cdot \\ \cdot \\ \cdot \\ \cdot \\ e_{3n} \end{bmatrix}
$$

Denoting the design matrix by X, the least squares estimates of the effect parameters are given by

$$\hat{\beta} = (X^T X)^{-1} X^T \Delta.$$

The form of $(X^T X)^{-1}$ and $X^T \Delta$ are as follows:

$$
(X^T X)^{-1} = 1/n \begin{bmatrix} 2/3 & 1/3 \\ 1/3 & 2/3 \end{bmatrix}, \qquad
X^T \Delta = \begin{bmatrix} \Sigma \Delta_A + \Sigma \Delta_{A-B} \\ \Sigma \Delta_B - \Sigma \Delta_{A-B} \end{bmatrix}.
$$

Therefore, the estimates of the aggregate effect sizes for treatments A and B are given by

$$
(X^T X)^{-1} X^T \Delta = \begin{bmatrix} \hat{\beta}_A \\ \hat{\beta}_B \end{bmatrix} = \begin{bmatrix} 1/3(2\overline{\Delta}_A + \overline{\Delta}_B + \overline{\Delta}_{A-B}) \\ 1/3(2\overline{\Delta}_B + \overline{\Delta}_A - \overline{\Delta}_{A-B}) \end{bmatrix},
$$

where the bar above the delta indicates simple average.

A related, but slightly more complex, problem involves treatment components which can be evaluated separately or in combination in experiments. Consider, for example, the treatment of psychological disorders by either drugs or psychotherapy or both. This experimental literature on drug and psychotherapy addressed the estimation of the separate and interactive effects of drugs and psychotherapy in a variety of ways. The variety was a nuisance. Experiments could be identified which informed one about the drug effect alone, or the drug plus the interaction effect, or the psychotherapy plus the drug plus the interaction effect, and so on in various combinations. An experiment that compares clients' progress under drugs with a group of clients receiving a placebo or nothing estimates the simple drug effect. An experiement that compares two

TABLE 6.5   The Structure of Experiments on the Effects of
             Drug and Psychotherapy

Treatments Compared in the Experiment	Effects Estimated by the Comparison
A. Drug vs. Placebo (or No Treatment)	δ
B. Psychotherapy vs. Placebo	ψ
C. (Drug & Psychotherapy) vs. Placebo	$\delta + \psi + \eta$
D. (Drug & Psychotherapy) vs. Drug	$\psi + \eta$
E. (Drug & Psychotherapy) vs. Psy	$\delta + \eta$
F. Drug vs. Psychotherapy	$\delta - \eta$

groups of clients one of which receives drugs-plus-psychotherapy and the other of which receives only drugs provides an estimate of the psychotherapy plus the interaction effect, since one group has the possible advantage of the separate psychotherapy effect and any benefits that result from combining drugs and psychotherapy. Denote the drug effect in isolation when compared with a placebo or no treatment by δ; denote the separate psychotherapy effect by ψ; and denote the interaction effect of the two by η. Then the comparison of drug therapy and placebo in an experiment estimates δ. The comparison of drug-plus-psychotherapy with psychotherapy estimates $\delta + \eta$ because both sides of the comparison have equal psychotherapy effects. In Table 6.5 appear the possible experimental comparisons of drug and psychotherapy and the effects which these comparisons estimate.

By arranging and averaging the results from experiments of the six different types specified in Table 6.5, the separate and interactive effects of drug and psychotherapy can be estimated. The organization of data and unknown parameters in Table 6.5 can be viewed as a system of six sources of information and three unknown parameters. Least squares estimates of the parameters can be calculated by ordinary methods.

If one wished to maintain a distinction between placebo and no-treatment control groups, there would be 12 lines in Table 6.5 instead of 6 and the structure of effects could change slightly; for example, a Drug versus No-Treatment experiment would estimate the drug plus the placebo effect since the expectancy effect of administering the drug to the experimental group would not be counterbalanced by an expectancy effect for the no-treatment control group.

In a meta-analysis of psychotherapy research, the question was addressed of the main and interactive effects of psychotherapy and drug therapy. A total of 112 studies were collected, each of which addressed the question in part with one or more experimental comparisons. These 112 studies yielded 566 effect size measures (i.e., standardized mean differences). For example, in a study in which drug treatment was compared with combined drug and psychotherapy treatment, a standardized mean difference of the following form would result: $\Delta = (\overline{X}_{D+P} - \overline{X}_D)/s_X$. In Table 6.6 appear the actual average effect sizes calculated from the findings of the 112 experiments.

As an example of how Table 6.6 can be interpreted, consider the first line of entries. A total of 55 comparisons in the 112 studies involved contrasting the scores of persons who received psychotherapy with those who received no treatment or, at most, a placebo. Such comparisons estimate the magnitude of the psychotherapy effect, ψ; the estimate equals .30, that is, the psychotherapy groups averaged .3 standard deviation superior to the control groups on the outcome variables. Consider as a second example the 94 comparisons of drug-plus-psychotherapy with psychotherapy alone. Such comparisons estimate the separate drug effect, δ, and the interactive effect, η, which results when drug and psychotherapy are combined in the same treatment. The psychotherapy effect, ψ, is not reflected in the contrast because it is present on both sides of the comparison. The 94 effect sizes which estimate $\delta + \eta$ have an average of .44. The remainder of the table can be understood in like manner.

From simple inspection, it appears that the drug effect of .51 is more than half again as large as the psychotherapy effect of .30. The interaction effect is slightly more difficult to comprehend from merely inspecting the entries in Table 6.6. That the drug-plus-psychotherapy versus drug comparison, which estimates $\psi + \eta$, is a full .1 standard deviation larger than the .30 estimate of ψ from the first line of the table might lead one to believe that η is positive; but the comparison of the estimates of $\delta + \eta$ and δ (being .44 and .51, respectively) reverses this impression. Inspection is too arbitrary and confusing. Several comparisons in the table contain information about the same parameters; it seems reasonable that every source of information about a parameter should be used in estimating it. A complete and standard method of combining the data in Table 6.6 into estimates of the parameters is needed. Such a method is suggested when one recognizes that the two middle columns of Table 6.6 constitute a system of linear equations, three of them independent and containing three unknowns (ψ, δ, and η). The method of least squares statistical

TABLE 6.6   Average Effect Sizes from Various Experimental Comparisons Made in the Experiments on Drug and Psychotherapy

Comparison	Parameter(s) Estimated	Average Δ	No. of Δ's
Psychotherapy vs. No-Treatment or Placebo	ψ	.30	55
Drug Therapy vs. No-Treatment or Placebo	δ	.51	351
Drug & Psychotherapy vs. Drug	$\psi + \eta$	.41	10
Drug & Psychotherapy vs. Psychotherapy	$\delta + \eta$	.44	94
Drug vs. Psychotherapy	$\delta - \psi$	.10	7
Drug & Psychotherapy vs. No-Treatment or Placebo	$\delta + \psi + \eta$	.65	49

NOTE: ψ denotes the separate or "main" effect of psychotherapy;
δ denotes the separate effect of drug therapy; and
η denotes their interaction.

estimation can be applied to obtain estimates of the separate and interactive effects of drug and psychotherapy.

The data and parameters of Table 6.6 can be written as a set of simultaneous linear equations as follows:

$$
\begin{bmatrix} .30 \\ .51 \\ .41 \\ .44 \\ .10 \\ .65 \end{bmatrix}
=
\begin{bmatrix} 1 & 0 & 0 \\ 0 & 1 & 0 \\ 1 & 0 & 1 \\ 0 & 1 & 1 \\ -1 & 1 & 0 \\ 1 & 1 & 1 \end{bmatrix}
\begin{bmatrix} \psi \\ \delta \\ \eta \end{bmatrix}
$$

Denoting the vector of data by Δ and the design matrix by X, the solution for the parameter estimates is as follows:

$$
(X^T X)^{-1} X^T \Delta =
\begin{bmatrix} \hat{\psi} \\ \hat{\delta} \\ \hat{\eta} \end{bmatrix}
\qquad [6.3]
$$

$$
(X^T X)^{-1} =
\begin{bmatrix} 1/2 & 1/4 & -1/2 \\ 1/4 & 1/2 & -1/2 \\ -1/2 & -1/2 & 1 \end{bmatrix} ,
$$

and

$$
X^T \Delta =
\begin{bmatrix} 1.26 \\ 1.70 \\ 1.50 \end{bmatrix}
$$

Hence, the estimates of the parameters are found from $(X^T X)^{-1} X^T \Delta$ to be

$$
\begin{aligned}
\hat{\psi} &= .31 \\
\hat{\delta} &= .42 \\
\hat{\eta} &= .02.
\end{aligned}
$$

Each effect is expressed on a scale of standard deviation units. Thus, the data of Table 6.6 lead to the conclusion that with the groups of clients studied, psychotherapy produces outcomes that are about one-third standard deviation superior to the outcomes from placebo or untreated control groups. The drug effect is only about a third greater than the psychotherapy effect. An effect of $.31s_x$ will move an average client from the middle of the control group distribution to about the 62nd percentile; an effect of $.42$ would move the average client to only about the 66th percentile. The interactive effect is essentially zero, indicating that when drugs and psychotherapy are employed together, their combined effect will simply be the sum of their separate effects. There is no *special* advantage (η positive) or disadvantage (η negative) of the combination.

Psychometric Scaling of Effects

In Chapter 5, it was seen how reports of studies as crude as whether one group scored higher than another on some measured variable could be translated into a concise statistical representation of study findings. The methods used there were derivative of classic methods of psychometric scaling, as presented by Torgerson (1958), for example. In this section, modern methods of scaling are employed with metric measures of study findings to achieve a more meaningful integration of research studies.

Bassoff (1981) performed a meta-analysis of the relationship between various sex roles and mental health. In the typical study, a group of women would be given a sex-role inventory (e.g., the Bem Sex-Role Inventory) and divided into two groups on the basis of their answers, for example, masculine versus androgynous, feminine versus masculine, high feminine versus low feminine. The two groups thus formed would then be compared on some measure of mental health (e.g., the Minnesota Multiphasic Personality Inventory or the Hopkins Symptom Checklist).

The data in Table 6.7, adapted from Bassoff's Table 2.2 (p. 46), are the standardized mean differences on the mental health measures for women for each pair of sex-role contrasts contained in the literature under review. To depict clearly these relationships between sex roles and psychological health, a system for scaling the sex-role categories along a continuum of psychological adjustment is needed. Shepard's (1962) nonmetric multidimensional scaling procedure, called "analysis of proximities," can be adapted for this purpose. The average Δ (or its inverse) corresponding to a particular comparison is regarded as a measure of the proximity of the two sex roles along the continuum of psychological adjustment. The larger the average Δ, the greater the distance between the two sex roles on the continuum. For example, if Δ is $.60$ for the masculine versus feminine

TABLE 6.7   Standardized Mean Differences Between Various Sex Roles
Averaged Across Several Studies (After Bassoff, 1981)

Sex Roles Compared	Standardized Mean Differences on the Mental Health Measure	No. of Comparisons
Androgynous vs. Masculine	.18	21
Androgynous vs. Feminine	.66	30
Masculine vs. Feminine	.57	20
Masculine vs. Low Masculine	.48	21
Low Feminine vs. Feminine	.05	30
Androgynous vs. Non androgynous	.13	13

distinction, then masculinity (M) and femininity (F) can be regarded as .60 unit apart on the continuum. If the masculine and androgynous (A) distinction has a .10 standardized mean difference on adjustment, and the androgynous and feminine distinction has a .50 Δ on the same criterion, then the three sex roles (M, A, F) can be ordered along a straight line so that the difference between each pair equals the degrees of difference produced when that distinction was measured in standard deviation units on the adjustment scale.

```
F                                              A      M
├─────────────────────────────────────────────┼──────┤
0                                             .50    .60
```

For example, the previous figure perfectly reproduces the findings Δ(M,F) = .60, Δ(M, A) = .10, Δ(A, F) = .50. However, if the data were slightly different, for example, Δ(M, F) = .65, Δ(M, A) = .15, Δ(A, F) = .35, the three sex roles could not be arranged along the continuum in such a way that the difference among pairs of sex roles would exactly reproduce the obtained average Δ. For example, the following scaling

```
F                                              A      M
├─────────────────────────────────────────────┼──────┤
0                                             .40    .65
```

implies that $\hat{\Delta}(M, F) = .65$, $\hat{\Delta}(M, A) = .25$, and $\hat{\Delta}(A, F) = .40$. These $\hat{\Delta}$'s differ from the obtained Δ's by:

$$(|.65 - .65| + |.25 - .15| + |.45 - .35|) / 3 = .25 / 3 = .08$$

on the average. However, by adjusting these three sex roles on the continuum, it is possible to find an arrangement that reproduces $\hat{\Delta}$'s that deviate less from the obtained Δ's. For example, the following arrangement

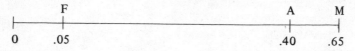

gives $\hat{\Delta}(M, F) = .60$, $\hat{\Delta}(M, A) = .25$, $\hat{\Delta}(A, F) = .35$. The average error for this scaling is:

$$(|.60 - .65| + |.25 - .15| + |.35 - .35|) / 3 = .15/3 = .05.$$

This is a more accurate scaling since the average error in reproducing the observed Δ's has dropped from .08 to .05. Indeed, by trial and error, a better fit—in terms of minimum absolute error $(\Sigma|\Delta - \hat{\Delta}|)$—might yet be found.

Consider, now, the data that Bassoff obtained in her meta-analysis. The following first approximation can be taken as trial #1:

Trial Scaling No. 1

```
0    .05  .09                              .53  .57  .66
├─────┼────┼──────────────────────────────────┼────┼────┤

F    LF   LM                               NA   M    A
```

The starting point is arbitrary and the above scaling of the sex roles along the mental health continuum is taken for convenience because it can be seen to reproduce exactly some of the observed data points. The observed and reproduced Δ's from trial #1 are as follows:

Comparison	Observed	Reproduced from Trial #1
A vs. M	.18	.09
A vs. F	.66	.66
M vs. F	.57	.57
M vs. LM	.48	.48
LF vs. F	.05	.05
A vs. NA	.13	.13

$$\Sigma|\Delta - \hat{\Delta}| = .09$$

The only observed comparison less than perfectly reproduced by the trial #1 scaling is the A versus M comparison which is .09 standard deviation unit off. By moving M further away from A and compensating by lowering LM, an improved scaling might be obtained at trial #2:

Trial No. 2

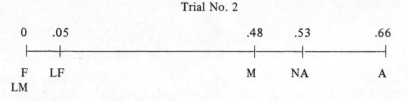

The observed and reproduced Δ's from trial #2 are as follows:

Comparison	Observed	Reproduced from Trial #2
A vs. M	.18	.18
A vs. F	.66	.66
M vs. F	.57	.48
M vs. LM	.48	.48
LF vs. F	.05	.05
A vs. NA	.13	.13

$$\Sigma \mid \Delta - \hat{\Delta} \mid = .09$$

Trial #2 is no more accurate in the aggregate than trial #1 and further iterations will not improve on the net error of .09. Hence, either of the above figures gives a reasonable scaling of the findings. Actually, any adjustment of Masculine down the scale (i.e., to the left) in order to increase the Androgynous-Masculine difference toward the observed .18 while preserving the .48 Masculine-Low Masculine difference will produce a solution with net error of .09. This is true because (1) Low Masculine was not linked empirically with any other sex role (hence, its movement along the scale is immaterial so long as it remains a fixed distance, .48, from Masculine) and (2) the median minimizes the sum of absolute deviations and the median in this case is any position for M between .48 and .57. A sum of squared errors minimization would probably result in a unique positioning of the sex roles on the continuum.

This analysis has been done "by hand" so that the reader might observe more closely the logic; problems of any real size or complexity would be analyzed by the computer methods provided by Shepard and his colleagues. Hearold (1979) also applied nonmetric multidimensional scaling in order to portray statistically a complex set of experimental findings. Her methods and results are too complicated to report here.

INTEGRATING STUDIES THAT HAVE QUANTITATIVE INDEPENDENT VARIABLES

Many bodies of research literature involve the examination of the relationship between dependent and independent variables, both described quantitatively. Where the quantitative character of the independent variable can be preserved, the gain in precision of the integration of findings can be considerable. Examples of problems where this is true include class size and achievement, the duration of effects of any treatment, study time and achievement, and countless laboratory problems in the social sciences. Consider, for example, a research integration problem faced by Underwood (1957) in his work on memory. This example was discussed in a different context in Chapter 2. Over 15 studies were available that addressed the question of the efficacy of recall as a function of the ordinal position of the items to be recalled in a series of lists. Underwood plotted the curve reproduced here as Figure 6.4 and concluded that efficiency of recall was largely a function of interference from items previously memorized. The curve in Figure 6.4 represents a simple problem in research integration; it could be fit adequately with a logarithmic curve or many other alternatives to a straight line. But the problems presented by many other quantitative independent and dependent variables are more complex. Consider the relationship between class size and educational achievement.

A Modification of Multiple Linear Regression

A simple statistic is desired that describes the relationship between class size and achievement as determined by a study. No matter how many class sizes are compared, the data can be reduced to some number of paired comparisons, a smaller class against a larger class. Certain differences in the findings must be attended to if the findings are later to be integrated. The most obvious differences involve the actual sizes of "smaller" and "larger" classes and the scale properties of the achievement measure. The actual class sizes compared must be preserved and become an essential part of the

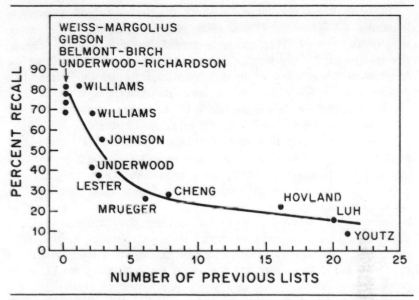

Figure 6.4   Recall as a function of previous lists learned as determined from a number of studies. (After Underwood, 1957)

descriptive measure. The measurement scale properties can be handled by standardizing all mean differences in achievement by dividing by the within-group standard deviation (a method that is complete and discards no information at all under the assumption of normal distributions). The eventual measure of relationship seems straightforward and unobjectionable:

$$\Delta_{S-L} = \frac{\overline{X}_S - \overline{X}_L}{\hat{\sigma}},$$

where:

$\overline{X}_S$ is the estimated mean achievement of the *smaller* class which contains S pupils;

$\overline{X}_L$ is the estimated mean achievement of the *larger* class which contains L pupils; and

$\hat{\sigma}$ is the estimated within-class standard deviation, assumed to be homogeneous across the two classes.

If distributional assumptions about X are needed to add meaning to particular values of Δ_{S-L}, normality will be assumed. For example, suppose $\Delta_{S-L} = +1$. Then assuming normal distributions within classes, the average pupil in the smaller class scores at the 84th percentile of the larger class. These interpretations are occasionally helpful, but seldom critical, and our investment in the normality assumption is not great. It would be no surprise nor any concern if the assumption proved to be more or less wrong, and it is probably not far off in most instances.

There exist several alternative statistical techniques for integrating a large set of Δ_{S-L}'s so as to describe the aggregated findings on the class size and achievement relationship. A large, square matrix could be constructed in which the rows and columns are class sizes and the cell entries are average values of Δ_{S-L}; nearly equal values of average deltas could be connected by lines to form "iso-deltas" in much the manner as economic equilibrium curves are used to depict three-variable relationships. Or a variation of psychometric scaling could be employed: A square matrix of class sizes could be constructed for which each cell entry would be the proportion of times the row class size gave achievement greater than the column class size. This matrix could be scaled by means of Thurstone's Law of Comparative Judgment, which would locate the class sizes along an achievement continuum. (This method was used in Chapter 5 and the results were reasonably satisfactory.) Finally, regression equations could be constructed in which Δ_{S-L} is partitioned into a weighted linear combination of S and L and functions thereof and error. There is much to recommend this latter procedure, and the technique eventually employed is a variation of it. But the regression of Δ_{S-L} onto only S and L requires three dimensions to be depicted. Anything more complex than a simple two-dimensional curve relating achievement to the size of class was considered undesirably complicated and beyond the easy reach of most audiences who hold a stake in the results.

The desire to depict the aggregate relationship as a single-line curve is confounded with the problem of essential inconsistencies in the design and results of the various studies. A single study of class size and achievement may yield several values of Δ_{S-L}. In fact, if k different class sizes are compared on a single achievement test, $k(k-1)/2$ values of Δ_{S-L} will result. This set of Δ's from a single study will form a consistent set of values in that they can be joined to form a single connected graph depicting the curve of achievement as a function of class size. However, various values of Δ_{S-L} arising from different studies can show confusing inconsistencies. For example, suppose that Study #1 gave Δ_{10-15},

Δ_{10-20}, and Δ_{15-20}, and Study #2 gave Δ_{15-30}, Δ_{15-40}, and Δ_{30-40}. A few moments reflection will reveal that there is no obvious or simple way to connect these values into a single connected curve.

The eventual solution to these problems proceeded as follows: Δ_{S-L} was regressed onto a quadratic function of S and L by means of the least squares criterion; then that set of values of $\hat{\Delta}$ that could be expressed as a single, connected curve was found.

The regression model selected accounted for variation in Δ_{S-L} by means of S, S^2 and L. Obviously, something more than a simple linear function of S and L was needed, otherwise a unit increase in class size would have a constant effect regardless of the starting class size S; and the S^2 term seemed as capable of filling the need as any other. The size differential between the larger and smaller class, L-S, was used in place of L for convenience. Thus, the Δ_{S-L} values were used to fit the following model:

$$\Delta_{S-L} = \beta_0 + \beta_1 S + \beta_2 S^2 + \beta_3 (L-S) + \epsilon.$$

Fitting this model by least squares will result in the curved regression surface

$$\hat{\Delta}_{S-L} = \hat{\beta}_0 + \hat{\beta}_1 S + \hat{\beta}_2 S^2 + \hat{\beta}_3 (L-S). \tag{6.4}$$

The problem now is to find the set of $\hat{\Delta}$'s in this surface that can be depicted as a single curved-line relationship in a plane. The property that must hold for a set of $\hat{\Delta}$'s before they can be depicted as a connected graph in a plane is what might be called the *consistency property:*

$$\Delta_{n_1-n_2} + \Delta_{n_2-n_3} = \Delta_{n_1-n_3}$$

for $n_1 < n_2 < n_3$. If this property is not satisfied, then one is in the strange situation of claiming that the differential achievement between class sizes 10 and 20 is not the sum of the differential achievement from 10 to 15 and then from 15 to 20.

When the consistency property is imposed on Equation 6.4, it follows that:

$$\hat{\beta}_0 + \hat{\beta}_1 n_1 + \hat{\beta}_2 n_1^2 + \hat{\beta}_3 (n_2 - n_1) + \hat{\beta}_0 + \hat{\beta}_1 n_2 + \hat{\beta}_2 n_2^2 + \hat{\beta}_3 (n_3 - n_2)$$
$$= \hat{\beta}_0 + \hat{\beta}_1 n_1 + \hat{\beta}_2 n_1^2 + \hat{\beta}_3 (n_3 - n_1). \tag{6.5}$$

Simple algebraic reduction of Equation 6.5 produces the following:

$$\hat{\beta}_o + \hat{\beta}_1 n_2 + \hat{\beta}_2 n_2^2 = 0. \qquad [6.6]$$

A Logarithmic Model

The above modified regression approach for integrating studies with quantitative independent variables is disappointingly complex. Fortunately we have found two simpler alternatives: (1) a logarithmic model and (2) a nonlinear model. The logarithmic model can be illustrated with the class size problem. Assume that the Δ for a comparison of class size 1 and any other class size C has the form

$$\Delta_{1-C} = \beta \log C + e, \text{ where } e \sim (0, \sigma_e^2). \qquad [6.7]$$

Now consider the values of C denoted by S and L which stand in the relationship $S < L$. Then,

$$\Delta_{1-S} = \beta \log S + e,$$

and

$$\Delta_{1-L} = \beta \log L + e.$$

Assuming, quite reasonably that

$$\Delta_{S-L} = \Delta_{1-L} - \Delta_{1-S},$$

one has that

$$\Delta_{S-L} = \beta \log (S/L) + e. \qquad [6.8]$$

Thus, the parameter β can be estimated by simple least squares regression of Δ_{S-L} onto $\log(S/L)$. Then a single curve depicting the relationship of Δ to C can be drawn in a plane defined by the two axes C and Z. We have applied this model in the analysis of class size and achievement with very satisfactory results. It fit the data with lesser mean-square error than did the multiple regression approach described above. Furthermore, this simple logarithmic model presents far more tractable problems of statistical inference than the multiple regression model.

TABLE 6.8   Data on the Relationship of Class-size and Achievement from Studies Using Random Assignment of Pupils.

Study Number	Size of Larger Class L	Size of Smaller Class s	$log_e(L/S)$	Δ_{S-L}	
1.	25.	1.	3.22	.32	$\Delta_{S-L} = \dfrac{\bar{X}_S - \bar{X}_L}{(s_S + s_L)/2}$
2.	3.	1.	1.10	.22	
2.	25.	1.	3.22	1.52	
2.	25.	3.	2.12	1.22	
3.	35.	17.	.72	-.29	
4.	112.	28.	1.39	-.03	
5.	2.	1.	.69	.36	$n = 14$ studies
5.	5.	1.	1.61	.52	$N = 30$ comparisons
5.	23.	1.	3.14	.83	
5.	5.	2.	.92	.22	
5.	23.	2.	2.44	.57	
5.	23.	5.	1.53	.31	
6.	30.	15.	.69	.17	
7.	23.	16.	.36	.05	
7.	30.	16.	.63	.04	
7.	37.	16.	.84	.08	
7.	30.	23.	.27	.04	
7.	37.	23.	.48	.04	
7.	37.	30.	.21	0	
8.	28.	20.	.33	.15	
9.	50.	26.	.65	.29	
10.	32.	1.	3.46	.65	
11.	37.	15.	.90	.40	
11.	60.	15.	1.38	1.25	
11.	60.	37.	.48	.65	
12.	8.	1.	2.08	.30	
13.	45.	15.	1.10	.07	
14.	14.	1.	2.64	.72	
14.	30.	1.	3.40	.78	
14.	30.	14.	.76	.17	
			Average: 1.42	.38	

The Logarithmic Model Illustrated

Consider an illustration from research on class size and achievement. Fourteen experiments were found in which pupils were randomly assigned to classes of different sizes. These 14 studies yielded over 100 separate comparisons of achievement in smaller and larger classes. The multiplicity of findings is due partly to the fact that in one study there may exist several pairs of class sizes and partly to the fact that a single pair of class sizes may have been measured on more than one achievement test. The latter multiplicity was averaged out and the former retained in the summary of 30 data points in Table 6.8.

One might expect class size and achievement to be related in something of an exponential or geometric fashion—reasoning that one pupil with one teacher learns some amount, two pupils learn less, three pupils learn still less, and so on. Furthermore, the drop in learning from one to two pupils could be expected to be larger than the drop from two to three, which in turn is probably larger than the drop from three to four, and so on. A logarithmic curve represents one such relationship:

$$z = \alpha - \beta \log_e C + \epsilon, \qquad\qquad [6.9]$$

where

C   denotes class size,

α is the level of achievement in a "class" of one person (since $\log_e 1 = 0$),

β is the speed of change in achievement as class size increases.

The general relationship represented by Equation 6.9 is depicted in Figure 6.5. Equation 6.9 cannot be fitted to data directly because in a meta-analysis z will not ordinarily be measured on a common scale across studies. This problem can be circumvented, as was illustrated in Chapter 2, by calculating Δ_{S-L} for each observed comparison of a smaller and a larger class within a single study. From Equation 6.9,

$$
\begin{aligned}
\Delta_{S-L} &= (\alpha - \beta \log_e S + \epsilon_1) - (\alpha - \beta \log_e L + \epsilon_2) \qquad [6.10] \\
&= \beta (\log_e L - \log_e S) + (\epsilon_1 - \epsilon_2) \\
&= \beta \log_e (L/S) + e.
\end{aligned}
$$

The model in Equation 6.10 is particularly simple and straightforward. The values of Δ_{S-L} are merely regressed onto the logarithm of the ratio of the larger to the smaller class size, forcing the least squares regression line through the origin.

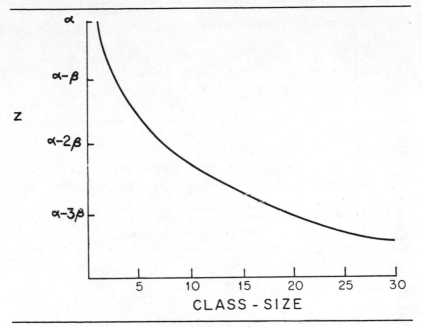

Figure 6.5 Log curve for the model in formula 6.9.

$$\hat{\beta} = \frac{\Sigma \, (\Delta_{S-L}) \, (\log_e \, L/S)}{\Sigma \, (\log_e \, L/S)^2} \, . \qquad\qquad [6.11]$$

A scatter diagram of the data in Table 6.8 appears as Figure 6.6, in which Δ_{S-L} is graphed against $\log_e(L/S)$. The estimate of β for these data equals .26. The value of r is .64, and r^2 = .42. The resulting curve relating class size C to achievement in standard-score units appears as Figure 6.7.

An Alternative Log Model

A model may have advantages if it avoids highly interdependent data sets created (as in the first model) by taking all pairwise differences in a study. Such an alternative model can be developed along the following lines.

Let $\bar{y}_c$ and s_c be the mean and standard deviation of the dependent variable for class size C in one of m studies. For the k class sizes in a particular study, order the groups from $C_1 < C_2 \ldots < C_k$. Arbitrarily set $\delta_k = 0$; then

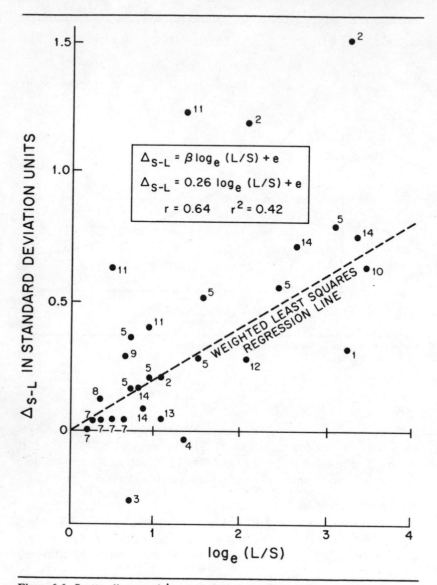

Figure 6.6 Scatter diagram of Δ_{S-L} graphed against Log_e (L/S).

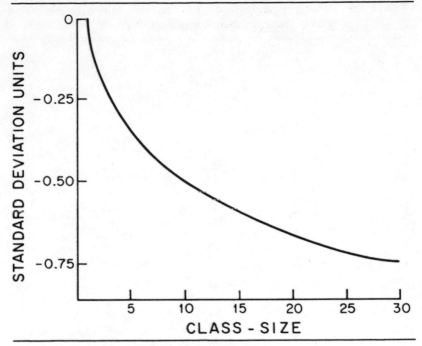

Figure 6.7   Data of Table 6.8 fitted to the Log model.

$$\delta_{k-1} = \frac{\overline{y}_{k-1} - \overline{y}_k}{(s_{k-1} + s_k)/2} \, ,$$

$$\delta_{k-2} = \delta_{k-1} + \frac{\overline{y}_{k-2} - \overline{y}_{k-1}}{(s_{k-2} + s_{k-1})/2} \, ,$$

$$\delta_{k-3} = \delta_{k-2} + \frac{\overline{y}_{k-3} - \overline{y}_{k-2}}{(s_{k-3} + s_{k-2})/2} \text{, and so on.} \qquad [6.12]$$

The data from the 14 class size experiments have been scaled via Equation 6.12 and are recorded in Table 6.9. The following model can be postulated for data of the form in Equation 6.12:

$$\delta = -\beta \log_e C + (\alpha_1 D_1 + \ldots + \alpha_m D_m) + \epsilon, \qquad [6.13]$$

TABLE 6.9   Data on the Relationship of Class-size and Achievement from Studies Using Random Assignment of Pupils.

Study Number	C, Size of Class	δ_c
1.	1.	.32
1.	25.	0
2.	1.	1.44
2.	3.	1.22
2.	25.	0
3.	17.	-.29
3.	35.	0
4.	28.	-.03
4.	112.	0
5.	1.	.89
5.	2.	.53
5.	5.	.31
5.	23.	0
6.	15.	.17
6.	30.	0
7.	16.	.09
7.	23.	.04
7.	30.	0
7.	37.	0
8.	20.	.15
8.	28.	0
9.	26.	.29
9.	50.	0
10.	1.	.65
10.	32.	0
11.	15.	1.05
11.	37.	.65
11.	60.	0
12.	1.	.30
12.	8.	0
13.	15.	.07
13.	45.	0
14.	1.	.95
14.	14.	.17
14.	30.	0

The $\alpha \cdot D$ terms in Equation 6.13 represent dummy variables and arbitrary level parameters for the m separate studies; $D_i = 1$ if a δ in question comes from the ith study, and it equals zero otherwise. The parameters β and $(\alpha_1, \ldots, \alpha_m)$ can be estimated by regressing δ onto $\log_e C$. We have done so for the data in Table 6.9 and obtained a weighted least squares estimate of β equal to .22. The estimates of the α's are unimportant. In this regression, each δ was weighted by k^{-1} so that each of the 14 studies would receive equal weight. The result is virtually identical to that obtained for the model in Equation 6.10.

The model in Equation 6.13 is more general and of more significance than the model in Equation 6.10. Equation 6.13 can be applied in a wide range of circumstances in which studies with quantitative independent variables are integrated. The first log term in Equation 6.13 can be replaced by any mathematical function appropriate to a particular application. The important point about Equation 6.13 is that it simultaneously resolves the problems presented by different scales of measurement of Y and different values of X compared across studies.

Nonparametric Integration When the Independent Variable Is Quantitative

The methods of the previous section assume a model for the relationship between the dependent and a quantitative independent variable. Standardized contrasts of the form $\Delta_{X_1 - X_2}$ are used to estimate the parameters of the model. In many instances, too little will be known about the relationship to hypothesize even an approximate model. Then, perhaps, an approach modeled after Tukey's (1977) methods of exploratory data analysis might be more appropriate. No functional relationship need be hypothesized, and the data themselves will determine the shape of the curve. An example will help clarify the approach, which may differ in details in particular applications.

Andrews et al. (1980) performed a meta-analysis of experimental studies of stuttering therapies. Effect sizes were calculated for 42 studies; all studies were pretest versus posttest designs without control groups. Effects were assessed by comparing the posttest mean against the pretest mean and standardizing by the pretest standard deviation:

$$\Delta_{E-C} = \frac{\overline{Y}_{post} - \overline{Y}_{pre}}{s_{y_{pre}}} . \qquad [6.14]$$

The 42 studies yielded 116 Δ's. These Δ's were categorized by the type of therapy applied, the duration of the therapy, type of outcome measure, and several other features of the therapy and the clients. Differences in average effect were obtained across types of therapy: Prolonged Speech therapy gave a $\bar{\Delta}_{E-C} = 1.65$ for 47 effects; at the other end of the scale, Systematic Desensitization gave a $\bar{\Delta}_{E-C} = .54$ for 5 effects (Andrews et al., 1980).

No correlation was found between the number of months after therapy at which effects were measured and the size of effect. This lack of correlation seemed surprising and prompted the further search for a decay of effect across time that is reported below. The "follow-up time" variable and type of therapy are confounded in the Andrews stuttering data set. For example, Airflow therapy showed an average Δ of .92, but these outcomes were measured at 4.2 months after therapy on the average. On the other hand, Attitude therapy showed a $\bar{\Delta} = .85$ for an average follow-up time of 3.3 months. The only real difference between Attitude and Airflow average effects might be attributable to varying follow-up times for measurement of benefits. Likewise, the effect of different follow-up times may reflect therapy differences. For this reason, the pattern of decay in effects across time should be examined separately within each type of therapy. But another feature of the studies is also confounded with follow-up time and should be likewise controlled. Therapies differed with respect to the attention given to providing for posttherapy maintainence of the gains made during therapy. Andrews and his colleagues classified each study by whether there were *many, some,* or *no* provisions made for maintainence of gains achieved during therapy. Thus, it seemed sensible to cross-classify effects by therapy type and maintainence provisions before examining the data for the decay of treatment phenomenon. Thus, 107 of the 116 effect sizes were cross-classified into the cells of an 8 X 3 (therapy type x maintainence provision) table, and the cell entries were averaged.

The averaging of effects resulted in an 8 X 3 table (see Table 6.10). The typical entry is a triplet of numbers of the form (a, b, c), where a is the follow-up time in months, b is the average $\bar{\Delta}_{o-a}$, and c is the number of values averaged. Within a cell of Table 6.10 the entries were graphed in a connected line. Consider, for example, the cell for Rhythm therapy with many provisions for maintainence. The four data points can be graphed, as shown by the solid line in Figure 6.8. The broken line represents the three data points from Airflow therapy at the second maintainence level. The elevation of either line on the graph is immaterial; only the slope of the

TABLE 6.10   Follow-Up Time, Average Effect Size and Number of Effects Averaged Classified by Type of Therapy and Provisions for Maintenance

Therapy Type	Maintenance Provisions		
	None	Some	Many
Airflow		1, .88, 1 3, .74, 1 16, .86, 1	
Rhythm	0, .66, 1 14, .76, 2		0, 1.26, 7 6, 1.57, 2 9, 1.60, 10 12, .86, 4
Shadow	0, .17, 1 14, .38, 1		
Gentle Onset	0, 1.12, 2 1, 1.38, 1 10, 1.12, 1 25, 1.15, 1		0, 2.37, 2 10, 1.52, 2

TABLE 6.10 Follow-Up Time, Average Effect Size and Number of Effects Averaged Classified by Type of Therapy and Provisions for Maintenance (continued)

Therapy Type	Maintenance Provisions		
	None	Some	Many
Biofeedback			0, .88, 2
			12, 1.03, 2
Attitude	0, .71, 7		
	9, 1.11, 4		
Prolonged Speech	0, 2.02, 6		0, 1.62, 9
	3, 2.42, 2		2, 2.02, 3
	6, 1.27, 2		12, 1.16, 8
	9, 2.17, 3		15, 1.16, 8
	11, 1.77, 1		18, 1.36, 3
Desensitization	0, .69, 1	1, .01, 1	
	1, .89, 1	3, .03, 1	
	20, 1.07, 1		

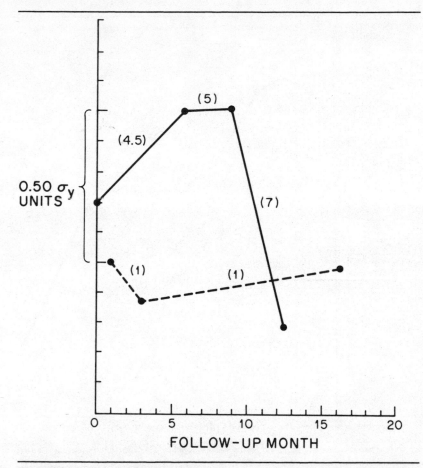

Figure 6.8   Graphs of effects at various follow-up times for two cells of Table 6.10.

line relative to the abscissa is significant. The number in parentheses beside each line is the average of the number of effects, Δ_{o-a}, that exists at each end of the line; for example, the first segment of the solid line is based on 7 Δ's at zero months and 2 Δ's at six months—hence the weight $(7+2)/2 = 4.5$ for the line segment.

One approach to aggregating the data on slopes is to take a weighted average of all the lines above two successive months. For example, the slope of the solid line in Figure 6.8 between months 1 and 2 is +.05 =

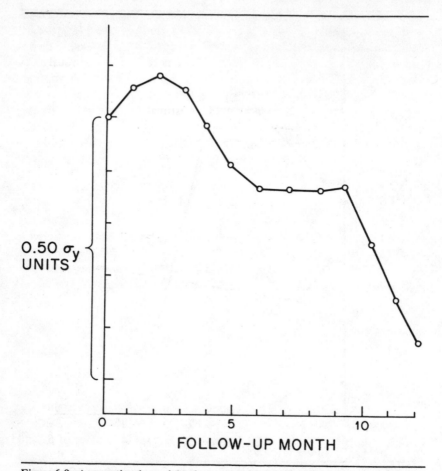

0.50 σ_y UNITS

FOLLOW-UP MONTH

Figure 6.9 Aggregation by weighted averaging of data in Table 6.10 on the decay of stuttering therapy effects.

(1.57 − 1.26)/6 months; the slope of the broken line is − .07. Since the weight for the solid line segment is 4.5 and for the dashed line, 1.0, the weighted average slope between months 1 and 2 is [4.5(.05) + 1.0(−.07)]/(4.5 + 1.0) = + .028.

If the above procedure were repeated for each successive pair of months and for all 12 lines that can be drawn from the data in Table 6.8, a complete aggregate curve is obtained. Such a curve is depicted in Figure

6.9. The curve shows a loss of benefits over the first 12 months after termination of therapy; the average loss is roughly one-half standard deviation. Although the general trend in the curve is unmistakably downward, not every intermediate twist and curve is to be taken seriously as a stable, replicable feature of the true relationship. Even though approximately 20 Δ's are still determining the slope of the aggregate curve in Figure 6.9 at 12 months posttherapy, the estimates of the points on the curve are probably subject to a fairly large sampling error. Inferential techniques, perhaps drawing on Tukey's jackknife procedure (Mosteller and Tukey, 1968), would illuminate the question of the reliability of the determination of the curve.

Aggregating Linear Slopes

An alternative approach was applied to the analysis of deterioration effects. This approach could be characterized as parametric to distinguish it from the nonparametric method illustrated above. Within each cell of Table 6.11 a straight trend line was fit to the (t, $\overline{\Delta}$.) data by means of least squares, that is, the following model was fit by least squares:

$$\overline{\Delta}. = \beta_o + \beta_1 t + \epsilon,$$

where

$\overline{\Delta}$ is the average effect

t is the number of months after treatment that the dependent variable was measured.

These individual cell analyses number 12. In each, estimates of $\hat{\beta}_o$ and $\hat{\beta}_1$ were obtained; in addition, the average number of Δ's for the data points in the cell was obtained. For example, for the cell "Airflow/Some Maintenance Provisions" in Table 6.11, the regression of $\overline{\Delta}$. onto t for the three data points gives $\hat{\beta}_0 = .81025$ and $\hat{\beta}_1 = .00246$. In addition, since each $\overline{\Delta}$. was based on n = 1, the average n is $\overline{n}$ = 1.

In Table 6.11 appear the within-cell regression lines, the follow-up interval spanned and the n weights. The information in Table 6.11 can be integrated into a single curve by taking the $\overline{n}$-weighted average of all slopes, $\hat{\beta}_1$. Only those slopes are averaged at time point t = t_i which were derived on data from a time interval that spans t_i. For example, the aggregate slope at t = 0 is a weighted average of all $\hat{\beta}_1$'s in Table 6.11

TABLE 6.11 Within Cell Regression Lines, Time Interval and $\bar{n}$-weights for the Data in Table 6.10

Therapy/Maintenance Provision Combination	Regression of $\bar{\Delta}$ onto t: $\hat{\beta}_0$	$\hat{\beta}_1$	Time Interval Spanned (in months)	$\bar{n}$-weight
Airflow/Some	.81025	.00246	1, 3, 16	1.00
Rhythm/None	.66000	.00714	0, 14	1.50
Rhythm/Many	1.45685	−.01990	0, 6, 9, 12	5.75
Shadow/None	.17000	.01500	0, 14	1.00
Gentle/None	1.22832	−.00398	0, 1, 10, 25	1.25
Gentle/Many	2.37000	−.08500	0, 10	2.00
Biofeedback/Many	.88000	.01250	0, 12	2.00
Attitude/None	.71000	.04444	0, 9	5.50
Prolonged Speech/None	2.08383	−.02652	0, 3, 6, 9, 11	2.80
Prolonged Speech/Many	1.79433	−.03514	0, 2, 12, 15, 18	6.20
Desensitization/None	.78026	.01472	0, 1, 20	1.00
Desensitization/Some	.00000	.01000	1, 3	1.00

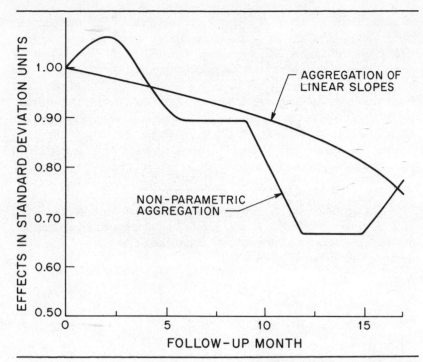

Figure 6.10 Comparison of non-parametric and linear methods of curve aggregation.

except those for "Airflow/Some" and "Desensitization/Some" which were based on intervals that begin at $t = 1$ month posttherapy. Hence, for $t = 0$,

$$\hat{\beta}_1 = [1.50(.00714) + 5.75(-.01990) + \ldots + 1.00(.01472)]$$
$$\div (1.50 + 5.75 + \ldots + 1.00) = -.0094.$$

So the inclination of the curve at $t = 0$ is .0094 unit downward. At $t = 1$, all 12 of the regression slopes in Table 6.9 are averaged because each of the regression lines was determined across a time span that included $t = 1$. The $\bar{n}$-weighted average is

$$\hat{\beta} = [1.00(.00246) + 1.50(.00714) + \ldots + 1.00(.01000)]$$
$$\div (1.00 + 1.50 + \ldots + 1.00) = -.0084.$$

In this manner, the aggregated slope of the curve is determined for each month from $t = 0$ to $t = 17$. The resulting aggregate curve is graphed along with the previously derived nonparametric curve in Figure 6.10.

In Figure 6.10, it is clear that the curve based on the weighted averaging of fitted straight lines is smoother and more regular than the nonparametric curve. This feature seems an advantage since the true curve of effects plotted against follow-up times probably would not follow the jagged, irregular path of the nonparametric curve. But the aggregated curve based on linear slopes appears to have attenuated the size of the effect decay across time. For example, between 2 and 12 months, the nonparametric curves drops about .40 standard deviation unit. Over the same interval, the curve from aggregated linear slopes drops only about .15 standard deviation unit. This difference is so great as to cause one to search for a compromise solution.

Aggregating Quadratic Slopes

Fitting quadratic functions by least squares estimation within each cell of Table 6.10 may produce a more satisfactory aggregate curve. Consider, for example, the cell "Airflow—'Some' Maintenance Provisions." The three pairs of points are as follows:

Follow-up time, t:	1	3	16
Effect size Δ:	.88	.74	.86

These points can be fit to the quadratic equation

$$\overline{\Delta}. = \beta_o + \beta_1 t + \beta_2 t^2 + e.$$

With three points and three parameters in the model, the fit of the equation is perfect:

$$\hat{\overline{\Delta}}. = .9658 - .0911t + .0053\ t^2.$$

For example, at $t = 1$, the predicted effect is .88; at $t = 3$, $\hat{\Delta} = .74$; at $t = 16$, $\hat{\Delta} = .86$.

This single quadratic curve spans the time interval from 1 to 16 months. Its slope at any time t on the interval is given by the value of the derivative of the curve at the point t. In general, the slope of the curve at t, is given by

$$\text{Slope}(t_1) = \hat{\beta}_1 + 2\hat{\beta}_2 t_1.$$

For example, the slope of the quadratic curve for "Airflow–'Some' Maintenance" at 2 months posttreatment is

$$\text{Slope}(t = 2) \quad = \frac{d}{dt}(.9658 - .0911t + .0053t^2)\, ,\bigg|_{t\,=\,2}$$

$$= -.0911 + .0106t \,\big|_{\,t\,=\,2} = -.0699.$$

In words, then, the quadratic curve fit to the data has a slope of .07 standard deviation unit downward at two months posttreatment.

This method of fitting quadratic curves can be applied to each cell of Table 6.10, provided that more than two follow-up times are present in a cell (at least three data points are required to estimate the three parameters of the quadratic curve). Consequently, 6 of the 12 nonempty cells in Table 6.10 must be eliminated. (An alternative approach not explored here would entail fitting straight lines in those cells with only two points and later aggregating their slopes with the slopes from the quadratic curves. This mixing of quadratic and straight-line models is probably preferable to the elimination of two-data-point cells followed here.)

For each cell with sufficient data, a quadratic curve can be fitted via least squares. Then the curve is differentiated to obtain the function describing the slope of the curve at any time t. These slopes can be calculated for each value of t (to the nearest month, for example) across the time interval spanned by the data on which the curve was derived. Finally, for each value of t the slopes of the derived curves can be averaged, or averaged after some appropriate weighting, to form an aggregated curve. For the six quadratic curves fit to the data in Table 6.10, each slope was weighted by the average number of effect sizes in the cell (the same weight function applied in aggregating the data by the nonparametric and linear methods above).

The results of fitting the quadratic curves, the time span over which the curve stretches and the weight (average number of Δ's) for the six cells appear as Table 6.12. Suppose one wished to calculate the aggregate slope of the follow-up curve at t = 16 months posttreatment. From Table 6.12 it is seen that four cells contribute data to determining follow-up effects at 16 months: airflow-some, gentle onset-none, prolonged speech-many, and

TABLE 6.12 Quadratic Curves, Follow-up Time Spans and weights (Average Number of Δ's) for the Data in Table 6.10.

Cell	Time Span (in months)	Weight	$\hat{\beta}_0$	$\hat{\beta}_1$	$\hat{\beta}_2$
Airflow-Some	1 - 16	1.00	.9658	-.0911	.0053
Rhythm-Many	0 - 12	5.75	1.2413	.1741	-.0168
Gentle Onset-None	0 - 25	1.25	1.2471	-.0146	.0004
Prolonged Speech-None	0 - 11	2.80	2.1571	-.0818	.0050
Prolonged Speech-Many	0 - 18	6.20	1.8599	-.0857	.0029
Desensitization-None	0 - 20	1.00	0.6900	.2095	-.0095

desensitization-none. The first derivatives of the quadratic curves for these four cases and the weights associated with each curve are as follows:

	First Derivative	Weight
Airflow-some	$-.0911 + .0106t$	1.00
Gentle-onset-none	$-.0146 + .0008t$	1.25
Prolonged speech-many	$-.0857 + .0058t$	6.20
Desensitization-none	$.2095 - .0190t$	1.00

The aggregate slope at $t = 16$ is found by solving each first derivative at $t = 16$ and then forming the weighted average of the resulting four values:

$$\frac{1.00(.0785) + 1.25(-.0018) + 6.20(.0071) + 1.00(-.0945)}{1.00 + 1.25 + 6.20 + 1.00}$$

$$= \frac{+.0258}{9.45} = +.0027.$$

Thus, the slope of the follow-up curve at 16 months is a rise of .003 of a standard deviation per month—imperceptibly different from a horizontal line. In similar manner, the slopes of the quadratic curves in Table 6.12 were aggregated for each month from 0 to 17 and the composite curve reflecting the proper slope at each month was drawn. This curve, referred to as the "aggregation of quadratic slopes," appears along with the non-parametric aggregated curve in Figure 6.11.

The aggregation of quadratic slopes clearly overcame the manifest shortcoming of the method of aggregating linear slopes, namely, the attenuation of effects. The quadratic curve is much more like the non-parametric curve than was the aggregation of linear slopes.

INFERENTIAL METHODS OF META-ANALYSIS

The role of statistical inference in meta-analyses is somewhat uncertain. Inference at the level of persons within studies (i.e., methods that treat persons as the unit of analysis) seems quite unnecessary; the rejection of hypotheses in such cases is nearly automatic and pro forma since even small integrative analyses encompassing 20 or so studies are likely to involve several hundred persons. The picture changes when one considers "studies" and the variability produced by their characteristics (e.g., loca-

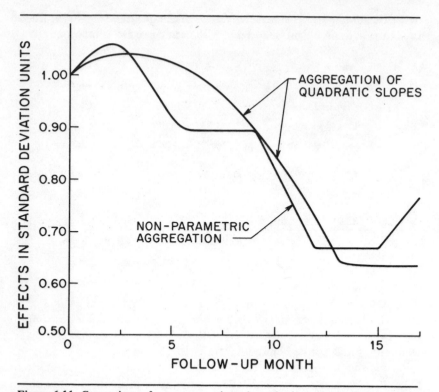

Figure 6.11 Comparison of non-parametric and quadratic methods of curve aggregation.

tion, date, investigator, types of subject, and the like). At this second level, one can readily imagine that even 50 or 100 studies may yield unstable findings, regardless of whether they subsume data from a thousand or many thousand persons. An investigator who subtly communicates his expectations of outcomes to his subjects affects all of them equally, and there is little comfort in there being 100 subjects or 1000. So if any type of statistical inference ought to be undertaken in an integrative analysis, it should be carried out with "study" rather than "person" as the unit of analysis. But the prior question remains: Should meta-analyses use inferential statistics?

The answer is by no means obvious. Inferential statistics seem to work well in two instances: randomized experiments and well-designed surveys with explicit sampling procedures. The classical theory of statistical inference assumes either the definition of a population and rigorous sampling from it or, as Fisher later showed, the randomization of units among conditions of an experiment. There is little doubt in these applications about what is meant when it is asserted that the confidence intervals cover the parameter with 95% probability or that the probability of the hypothesis being rejected incorrectly is 1%.

The typical integrative or meta-analysis seldom meets either condition of valid statistical inference. An attempt is made to locate every study on the topic being examined. Those studies that are located constitute a portion of a population of studies; but one hopes that the proportion is close to 100%, and one is under no illusions about the group of studies in hand being a random or probabilistic sample of the population. Rarely, a meta-analysis will be undertaken on a literature so large that it is impossible to read and analyze it all, even though one can describe, count, and otherwise delineate the population of study. Then one might sensibly draw random (or stratified, cluster, two-stage random) samples of studies and apply classical inferential techniques with a legitimate warrant—as Miller (1977) was forced to do in his meta-analysis of the effects of psychoactive drugs.

The probability conclusions of inferential statistics depend on something like probabilistic sampling, or else they make no sense. There can be no question whether the relationship of a meta-analysis sample of studies to the population is similar to the experimental randomization upon which permutation test theory rests. It is not.

The arguments against inferential techniques in meta-analysis do not satisfy the appetite for some indication of the instability or unreliability of the results. When Smith and Glass (1977) showed their early work on psychotherapy to Tukey, he chided them for not presenting standard errors of the more important averages. Smith and Glass's recitation of the reasons for not broaching the inferential questions left him unconvinced; he felt that regardless of such complications, some rudimentary inferential calculations would be informative and useful. Since then, Smith and Glass have pursued inferential questions at the "study" level and through the application of Tukey and Mosteller's jackknife technique (an all-purpose approach to statistical inference for complex data sets where classical theory is lacking).

Whether the findings from a collection of studies are regarded as a sample from a hypothetical universe of studies, or they are in fact a sample from a well-defined population, problems of statistical inference arise. Significance tests or confidence intervals around estimates of averages or regression planes will indicate where the research literature is conclusive on a question and where the aggregated findings still leave doubts—at least insofar as sampling error is concerned.

The inferential statistical problems of the meta-analysis of research are uniquely complex. The data set to be analyzed will invariably contain complicated patterns of statistical dependence. "Studies" cannot be considered the unit of data analysis without aggregating findings above the levels at which many interesting relationships can be studied. Each study is likely to yield more than one finding. An experiment comparing heterogeneous and homogeneous ability grouping might produce effect-size measures on three types of school achievement at four points in time; thus, 12 of the several hundred effect-size measures in an aggregate data set would have arisen from a single study. There is no simple answer to the question of how many independent units of information exist in the larger data set. One might attempt to impose some type of cluster or multiple-stage sampling framework on the data, but in the end this will probably restrict the movement of an imaginative data analyst. Two resolutions of the problem can be envisioned: one risky, the other complex.

The simple (but risky) solution is to regard each finding as independent of the others. The assumption is untrue, but practical. All inferential calculations could proceed on this independence assumption. The results (standard errors of means, of correlations, and of regression coefficients) could be reported with the qualification that they were calculated under the assumption of independence. This procedure might be useful because the effect of the dependence is almost surely to increase standard errors of estimates above what they would be if the same number of data points were independent. Thus, if 50 effect-size measures from 30 studies yielded an unsatisfactorily large standard error for the mean effect size, then it could be assumed safely that the standard error would be even larger if the complex dependence in the data were accounted for properly.

The matter of statistical efficiency and "lumpy" data can be described more formally by appealing to an analogy with cluster sampling in survey research. Imagine that "studies" are like clusters and effect-size measures (or r's or any other appropriate description of findings) are like observations or cases within clusters. It is well-known from sampling theory (Cochran, 1963) that if m clusters each containing n elements are drawn randomly from a population in which the intracluster correlation of elements is denoted by ρ, then the variance error of the mean of the mn observations is given approximately by:

$$\text{Var}^*(\overline{\Delta}.) \doteq \frac{\sigma_\Delta^2}{mn} [1 + (m-1)\rho], \qquad [6.15]$$

where σ_Δ^2 is the homogeneous within-cluster variance of the observations, and $\text{Var}^*(\overline{\Delta}.)$ is the variance of the mean of nonindependent observations.

The analogy with applications to meta-analysis can be drawn by associating studies with clusters and then ρ becomes the intrastudy correlation of effect sizes, say. It is instructive to notice in the above equation that intracluster (or "intrastudy") correlation changes the variance of the mean, from what would be obtained under independence, by a factor of 1 + $(m-1)\rho$. It is improbable that ρ would ever be negative, hence the conclusion that intrastudy correlation of findings in meta-analyses increases variance errors, thus decreasing the reliability of aggregates from what would be expected under independence.

Fortunately, the results from several extant meta-analyses can be used to investigate what a typical value of ρ might be. Then, the typical inflation of the variance error of the mean can be estimated. In Table 6.13 appear the intrastudy correlation coefficients (of course, these are merely intraclass correlations) calculated from the data of six meta-analyses.

Only one of the six ρ's in Table 6.11 is below .50; they average .63, but they vary greatly about that average. Nonetheless, .60 gives a reasonably typical value of ρ with which to inquire further.

Under the assumption of independence of findings within studies, the variance error of an aggregate average of n findings within each of m studies is given by:

$$\text{Var}(\overline{\Delta}.) = \sigma^2/mn. \qquad [6.16]$$

An intrastudy correlation of findings increases the variance of the mean to:

$$\text{Var}^*(\overline{\Delta}.) = (\sigma^2/mn)[1 + (m-1).6].$$

The ratio of the latter to the former equals:

$$1 + (m-1).6$$

which indicates the inflation of the variance error due to the nonindependence of findings within studies. It is important to note that the inflation factor does not depend on the number of findings, n, within studies, but rather it depends on the number of studies, m.

Another way to view the inflation of the variance error of the mean due to nonindependence is to express the variance of the mean as follows by dropping terms of order $1/m$:

$$\text{Var*}(\overline{\Delta}.) = \sigma^2/mn + (\rho/n)\,\sigma^2 = \sigma^2(1/mn + \rho/n). \qquad [6.17]$$

This formulation shows that, in so far as the simplifying approximations are true, the variance of the mean is increased by $\sigma^2\rho/n$ due to the nonindependence of findings within studies.

The following table illustrates the inflation of $\text{Var*}(\overline{\Delta}.)$ over $\text{Var}(\overline{\Delta}.)$ because of nonindependence. It is based on the typical intrastudy correlation of .60 from Table 6.13 and an assumption of n = 2 findings per study.

No. of Studies	Var(Δ̄.)	Var*(Δ̄.)	Ratio
5	$(\ .10)\sigma^2$	$(\ .34)\sigma^2$	3.4
10	$(\ .05)\sigma^2$	$(\ .32)\sigma^2$	6.4
20	$(\ .025)\sigma^2$	$(\ .31)\sigma^2$	12.4
50	$(\ .01)\sigma^2$	$(\ .304)\sigma^2$	30.4
100	$(\ .005)\sigma^2$	$(\ .302)\sigma^2$	60.4
500	$(\ .001)\sigma^2$	$(\ .3004)\sigma^2$	300.4

The calculations are remarkable. They show, for example, that given an intrastudy correlation of .6 for 50 studies with two findings each, the variance error of the mean of all 100 findings is 30 times larger than the variance error one would suppose to be true assuming independence. Thus, statistical intuitions developed from experience with independent data sets must be held in check when dealing with the kind of nonindependence in data typical of meta-analyses. Furthermore, it is important that statistical techniques applied to meta-analysis take account of the nonindependent structure of the data, either by use of formulas for clustering such as illustrated here or by use of the jackknife technique.

Tukey's Jackknife

An inferential technique which takes account of the interdependencies in a large set of findings in a meta-analysis is Tukey's jackknife method

TABLE 6.13   Intra-Study Correlation Coefficients from Six Meta-Analyses

Investigator(s)	Topic	No. of Studies	No. of Findings Within Studies	ρ
Kavale (1979)	Psycholinguistic training	27	220	.24
Schlesinger, Mumford & Glass (1978)	Treatment of asthma	11	19	.85
Smith (1980c)	Sex-bias in psychotherapy	34	60	.69
Glass et al. (1977)	Teacher indirectness & achievement	19	34	.90
Glass (1977)	Effects of psychotherapy on anxiety	26	39	.51
Smith, Glass & Miller (1980)	Psychotherapy	60	185	.60

(Mosteller and Tukey, 1968). Space does not permit a basic exposition of the jackknife technique. One suggestion and an example must suffice. In calculating the "pseudovalues" in the jackknife method, some portion of the data set is discarded, and the sample estimate of the parameter of interest is calculated. In a meta-analysis, the portion of data eliminated should correspond to all those findings (e.g., effect sizes or correlation coefficients) arising from a particular study. Thus there will be as many pseudovalues as there are studies. The method will be illustrated on a small portion of the data from a meta-analysis of psychotherapy outcome studies.

The data in Table 6.14 represent 39 effect-size measures from 26 experimental studies in which behavioral and nonbehavioral psycho-therapies were compared for their effects on fear and anxiety. The effect-size measure was defined as $\Delta = (\overline{X}_{beh.} - \overline{X}_{nonbeh.})/s_X$. For example, study 1 produced two measures of experimental effect, the first of which shows the nonbehavioral therapy as slightly superior to the behavioral therapy, and the second of which shows the behavioral therapy nearly three-fourths of a standard deviation superior to the nonbehavioral therapy. The first step in establishing a jackknife confidence interval on the mean effect size is to average the 39 effect-size measures to obtain $\overline{X}$. Second, 26 partial means, $\overline{X}_{-i}$, are calculated by eliminating each study in turn; for example, the first partial mean is based on the 37 effect-size measures remaining after the effect sizes from study 1 (-.10, .74) are removed. Third, 26 pseudovalues are calculated as follows: $\hat{\theta}_i = 26\overline{X} - 25\overline{X}_{-i}$. The 26 pseudovalues can safely be regarded as sample of observations of normally distributed independent variables, with expected value approximately equal to the true mean effect size and variance $\sigma_{\hat{\theta}}^2$. Thus, the set of pseudo values, $\hat{\theta}_i$, can be treated as an ordinary sample of data to which t-distribution methods can be applied. The right-hand side of Table 6.14 lists the calculations for the 95% confidence interval on the true effect size; the interval does not quite span zero, indicating a statis-tically reliable superiority of the behavioral therapies. By comparison, a t-method 95% confidence interval on the population mean effect size calculated from the 39 effect-size measures, assuming independent obser-vations, extends from -.10 to +.50.

Statistical inferential methods on the type of data illustrated here could play a role in directing future research. From standard errors of averages and confidence regions around regression planes, one can determine where parameters are sharply estimated by the current body of research studies

TABLE 6.14   Illustration of Application of the Jackknife Technique of Interval Estimation of Mean Effect Size

Study	Effect Size Measures	Pseudo-Values $\hat{\theta}_i = 26\overline{X}. - 25\overline{X}_{-i}$	Calculations
1	-.10		
	.74	.366	N = 39 effect size measures
2	.43		n = 26 studies
	.45	.528	
3	.65	.493	$\overline{X}_{\hat{\theta}}$ = .186
4	.52	.407	
5	.20	.197	$s_{\hat{\theta}}$ = .457
6	-.16	-.040	
7	-.50	-.264	
8	3.35		
	-2.82	.291	95% jackknife confidence
9	.18	.184	interval on μ:
10	.51	.278	
11	-.39	-.191	$_{.975}t_{25}$ = 2.06
12	-.95	-.560	
13	.33	.282	
14	.12	.144	$\overline{X}_{\hat{\theta}} \pm ts_{\hat{\theta}}/\sqrt{n}$ =
15	.08	.118	
16	1.90	1.315	.186 ± (2.06)(.457)/$\sqrt{26}$ =
17	-.44	-.224	
18	- 1.00	-.593	(.002, .371)
19	.06		
	.20		
	.10		
	.00	-.097	
20	.64	.486	
21	.59		
	.96	.980	
22	.05		
	.20	.102	
23	.01	.072	
24	.12		
	.00		
	.14		
	-.28	-.368	
25	-.22	-.079	
26	1.28		
	.24		
	.24	1.016	

and where sample estimates remain poor. The simple cross-tabulation of the characteristics of studies completed is helpful for the same purpose. However, it must be pointed out that the number of studies needed to estimate accurately an aggregate effect size is partly a function of the variance of effect sizes. For example, 5 studies may determine accurately the effect of amphetamines on hyperactive 8-year-olds, whereas 20 studies may be needed to achieve the same accuracy with 12-year-olds if the effects are fundamentally more variable for older children.

The illustration above showed that a confidence interval based on jackknifing on "study" as the unit of analysis was narrower than the confidence interval calculated by traditional methods with individual Δ's as the unit of analysis. This was unexpected and contrary to the illustration to be presented here. It probably is due to the fact that the largest positive and largest negative values of Δ arose from the same study. A recent application of the jackknife to meta-analysis by Haertel et al. (1979) gave results more in accord with expectations. When multiple linear regression weights were jackknifed using "study" as the unit, the t statistics for the significance of the differences of the beta-weights from zero were nearly always smaller for the jackknife estimates than for the conventional estimates (Table 4 of Haertel et al., 1979).

An illustration will indicate the lines along which the jackknife approach to statistical inference in meta-analysis can be applied. The class size and achievement analysis above can serve as the illustration. A total of 108 comparisons of achievement in smaller and larger classes was available to fit the logarithmic curve. These 108 comparisons actually arose from 14 different studies (see Table 6.8). The multiplicity of data arose both from multiple comparisons with a study (a study comparing four class sizes produced six Δ's) and multiple achievement measures for individual comparisons. A traditional inferential analysis that takes no regard of the complex interdependencies of the data set (108 Δ's corresponding to only 30 unique comparisons of class size arising from only 14 studies) would proceed along the following lines. The least squares regression of Δ_{S-L} onto $\log_e(L/S)$ has the solution:

$$\hat{\beta} = \frac{\Sigma \Delta_{S-L}(\log_e L/S)}{\Sigma(\log_e L/S)^2}.$$

For the 108 data points,

$$\hat{\beta} = \frac{108.780}{385.745} = .2820.$$

The estimate of residual variance equals:

$$\hat{\sigma}_e^2 = .1823.$$

From traditional least squares theory, it can be shown that:

$$\sigma_{\hat{\beta}}^2 = \sigma_e^2 \, [\Sigma(\log_e L/S)^2]^{-1}.$$

Thus, in the example,

$$\hat{\sigma}_{\hat{\beta}} = \sqrt{.1823(385.745)^{-1}} = .02174.$$

Assuming normal distributions of estimates of β, the 95% confidence interval on β is given by:

$$\hat{\beta} \pm 1.96 \, \hat{\sigma}_{\hat{\beta}} = .2820 \pm .0430 = (.2390, .3250).$$

The results of the interval estimation prove to be quite different when the jackknife method is used to take account of variation at the study level. The first step in calculating the jackknife interval on β involves the calculation of all 14 pseudovalues, one for each study, by the formula:

$$\hat{\theta}_{-i} = 14\hat{\beta} - 13\hat{\beta}_{-i},$$

where $\hat{\beta}_{-i}$ is the estimate of β calculated by excluding all pairs of Δ_{S-L} and $\log_e L/S$ that arise from the ith study.

Using the earlier calculations on the entire data set, it can be computed that:

$$\hat{\theta}_{-i} = 3.948 - \frac{108.780 - \sum_{1}^{ni} \Delta\log_e(L/S)}{385.745 - \sum_{1}^{ni} (\log_e L/S)^2},$$

where the summation is over all pairs of values of Δ and $\log_e L/S$ that appear in the ith study.

The 14 values of $\hat{\beta}_{-i}$ for the data appear below

Study No.	$\hat{\beta}_{-i}$	$\hat{\theta}_{-i}$
1	.28611	.222057
2	.216408	1.134696
3	.284079	.254973
4	.285092	.241804
5	.283260	.265620
6	.282092	.280810
7	.286599	.222213
8	.281716	.285692
9	.281494	.288578
10	.312188	−.110444
11	.277897	.335339
12	.281980	.282226
13	282685	.273095
14	.293232	.135984

$$\hat{\theta}. = .293760,$$
$$s_{\hat{\theta}} = .265047$$

The 95% confidence interval on β is now calculated by the formula:

$$\hat{\theta}. \pm {}_{.975}t_{df}\hat{\sigma}_{\hat{\theta}} / \sqrt{n},$$

where n is the number of studies and df is $n-1$, in this case, but not generally.

For the data of this illustration, the above formula takes the value:

$$.293760 \pm 2.14 (.265047)/\sqrt{14}$$
$$= .293760 \pm .151590$$
$$= (.1422, .4454).$$

This jackknife interval on β is more than 350% wider than the interval calculated earlier by conventional methods that treated each pair of values Δ and $\log_e L/S$ as an independent data point. The jackknife method appears to be appropriate and equal to the task of handling data sets interlaced with complicated dependencies.

Generalized Least Squares

The methods illustrated on the class size data above are ordinary least squares (OLS) analysis and jackknife (JK) analysis. There exists a third means of analysis that is theoretically more rigorous and may prove superior to the putatively inappropriate OLS and the unknown JK analysis. The third method is the method of generalized least squares (GLS) analysis.

OLS is the traditional method of linear estimation based on a model of independently and normally distributed errors. It is, in fact, a special case of the method of GLS, which permits the errors in the linear model to be correlated. Correlated errors prevail in the type of data that are fitted to the logarithmic model in meta-analyses.

Suppose, to begin with a simple example, that a study of the relationship between class size and achievement is performed where achievement is compared among class sizes of n_1, n_2, and n_3 pupils (assume the n's increase in size from n_1 to n_3). From the logarithmic model,

$$z_{ij} = \beta \log n_j + e_{ij}$$

for the ith pupil in the jth class. It is assumed that e_{ij} are independently and normally distributed with variance σ^2. In order to remove arbitrary scale factors and fit the model, the class means must be paired, differenced and standardized to form delta measures, for example,

$$\Delta_{n_1 - n_2} = \beta \log (n_1/n_2) + (\bar{e}_{\cdot 1} - \bar{e}_{\cdot 2}).$$

Now, the random variable Δ has a normal distribution with mean = $\beta \log(n_1/n_2)$ and variance = $\text{Var}(\bar{e}_{\cdot 1} + \bar{e}_{\cdot 2}) = \sigma^2/n_1 + \sigma^2/n_2$.

There are three possible pairs of the class sizes n_1, n_2, and n_3; thus there are three possible Δ's. However, the deltas are constrained by the restriction that

$$\Delta_{n_1 - n_3} = \Delta_{n_1 - n_2} + \Delta_{n_2 - n_3}.$$

Thus, one of the three adds no information to the remaining two; only two deltas need be considered. (In the more general case of J class sizes, there are $J(J-1)/2$ possible deltas, but only $J-1$ of these are free to vary.) Thus, the available information is completely contained in any nonredundant subset of $J-1$ deltas. It will be convenient to work with only those deltas that are formed by comparing each class size in turn with the smallest class-size, for example,

$$\Delta_{n_1 - n_j}$$

where $n_j > n_1$.

In the three class-size comparison, the deltas will be

$$\Delta_{n_1 - n_2} \text{ and } \Delta_{n_1 - n_3}.$$

We have already seen that $\Delta_{n_1 - n_2}$ has error variance equal to σ^2 $(1/n_1 + 1/n_2)$. Likewise, $\Delta_{n_1 - n_3}$ has error variance equal to σ^2 $(1/n_1 + 1/n_3)$. It remains to determine the covariance of these two deltas:

$$\text{Covar} (\Delta_{n_1 - n_2}, \Delta_{n_1 - n_3}) =$$
$$\text{Covar} (\overline{e}_{.1} - \overline{e}_{.2}, \overline{e}_{.1} - \overline{e}_{.3}) =$$
$$\text{Covar} (\overline{e}_{.1} \overline{e}_{.1}) - 0 - 0 + 0 =$$
$$\text{Var}(\overline{e}_{.1}) = \sigma^2/n_1.$$

It should be clear that in a set of $J-1$ deltas formed by comparing each n_j in turn with n_1, that each delta has variance given by

$$\text{Var}(\Delta_{n_1 - n_j}) = \sigma^2(1/n_1 + 1/n_j),$$

and each pair of deltas has covariance given by

$$\text{Covar}(\Delta_{n_1 - n_j}, \Delta_{n_1 - n_{j*}}) = \sigma^2/n_1.$$

Hence, the set of two deltas in our example has the following variance-covariance matrix of errors:

$$\Sigma_\Delta = \sigma^2 \begin{bmatrix} \dfrac{1}{n_1} + \dfrac{1}{n_2} & \dfrac{1}{n_1} \\[3mm] \dfrac{1}{n_1} & \dfrac{1}{n_1} + \dfrac{1}{n_3} \end{bmatrix} \qquad [6.18]$$

A general linear model could now be stated for the two deltas:

$$\Delta_{n_1 - n_j} = \beta \log(n_1/n_j) + \epsilon$$

where the vector of ϵ's are distributed normally with zero mean vector and variance-covariance matrix in Equation 6.18 above.

Denoting the variance-covariance matrix of errors by Σ_ϵ, then Johnston (1972) shows that the GLS solution for $\hat{\beta}$ is contained in the following quantities:

$$\hat{\beta} = (X^T \Sigma_\epsilon^{-1} X)^{-1} X^T \Sigma_\epsilon^{-1} \Delta, \qquad [6.19]$$

where Δ is the vector of deltas (two, in the example), and X is the matrix of independent variable values—in the example, a 2×1 vector with entries $\log(n_1/n_2)$ and $\log(n_1/n_3)$,

$$\text{Var}(\hat{\beta}) = \sigma_\epsilon^2 (X^T \Sigma_\epsilon^{-1} X)^{-1} \qquad [6.20]$$

and an unbiased estimate of σ^2 is given by

$$\hat{\sigma}_\epsilon^2 = (\Delta - X\hat{\beta})^T \Sigma_\epsilon^{-1} (\Delta - X\hat{\beta})/(N - k), \qquad [6.21]$$

where N is the number of deltas and k is the number of parameters estimated (one, in the example).

In a typical meta-analysis, deltas will arise from more than one study. Thus, there may be two deltas from Study #1 (J=3) and three deltas from Study #2 (J=4). This arrangement of data does not substantially complicate the GLS analysis outlined above. The vector of deltas is now of order 5×1 and the variance-covariance matrix of errors, ϵ, is a block-diagonal matrix of order 5×5:

$$\Sigma_\epsilon = \sigma^2 \begin{bmatrix} \frac{1}{n_1} + \frac{1}{n_2} & \frac{1}{n_1} & 0 & 0 & 0 \\ \frac{1}{n_1} & \frac{1}{n_1} + \frac{1}{n_3} & 0 & 0 & 0 \\ 0 & 0 & \frac{1}{n_1} + \frac{1}{n_2} & \frac{1}{n_1} & \frac{1}{n_1} \\ 0 & 0 & \frac{1}{n_1} & \frac{1}{n_1} + \frac{1}{n_3} & \frac{1}{n_1} \\ 0 & 0 & \frac{1}{n_1} & \frac{1}{n_1} & \frac{1}{n_1} + \frac{1}{n_4} \end{bmatrix}$$

where the n_1 in Study #1 may be different from the n_1 in Study #2 (and likewise for n_2, . . .).

The block diagonal matrix Σ_ϵ in Equations 6.19, 6.20, and 6.21 yields the proper estimate of β, its standard error, and an estimate of error variance. The distribution of $\hat{\beta}$ divided by its estimated standard error is known to be Student's t distribution with degrees of freedom equal to $N-1$, where N is the number of deltas (there being $J-1$ deltas for each study; Johnston, 1972: 210).

The above argument appears to be mathematically complete and appropriate to the inferential problems of fitting and testing the logarithmic model. A Monte Carlo study is not strictly required—failing the discovery of some flaws in the mathematics—but it will be useful to check the validity of the GLS procedure while carrying out a Monte Carlo study to check the usefulness of the OLS and JK solutions. One knows a priori that the OLS and JK confidence intervals do not have complete mathematical justifications; the OLS intervals are likely to be uselessly inexact and, as always, the accuracy of the approximation upon which the JK intervals are based must be checked.

In the following section, the results of a Monte Carlo simulation are presented in which the accuracy of confidence intervals constructed by the GLS, OLS, and JK methods is compared.

Monte Carlo Study

A Monte Carlo study was conducted to check the validity of OLS, GLS, and JK confidence intervals. The structure of the simulation (i.e., number of studies, number of class sizes compared, and the sizes of classes compared) was chosen to duplicate exactly the data set in the meta-analysis of class size and achievement (Glass and Smith, 1979). The data set structure appears in Table 6.15. For example, in Study #1, three class sizes were compared: 1, 3, and 25. This study gives rise to two values of delta: Δ_{1-3} and Δ_{1-25}. In Study #4, two class sizes are compared yielding a single delta: Δ_{28-112}.

Given the above data structure, there are only two parameters of the logarithmic model that need to be specified: the value of β and the error variance σ_e^2 (n.b., this error variance describes error in observations of individuals; it is not the same as the error ϵ). The value of β can be specified without restriction; in the simulations, values of .25, .50, and 1.00 were used. The error variance, σ_e^2, is specified in a roundabout way by

TABLE 6.15 Structure of the Data Set Used in the Monte Carlo Study

Study No.	n_1	n_2	Class Sizes n_3	n_4
1	1	3	25	
2	1	25		
3	17	35		
4	28	112		
5	1	2	5	23
6	15	30		
7	16	23	30	37
8	20	28		
9	26	50		
10	1	32		
11	15	37	60	
12	1	8		
13	15	45		
14	1	14	30	

first specifying a value for the linear correlation between z and $\log(n_1/n_2)$ in the model

$$z = \beta\log(n_1/n_2) + e$$

and then solving for σ_e^2 assuming that z has unit variance. In the simulations reported here, the linear correlation, ρ, between z and $\log(n_1/n_2)$ was taken to be either .65 or .85. Hence, the corresponding error variances equal

$$\sigma_e^2 = \sqrt{1 - .65^2} = .76;$$
$$\sigma_e^2 = \sqrt{1 - .85^2} = .53.$$

The steps in the simulation proceeded as follows:

(1) Having specified values of n_1, n_2, β, and ρ (say, $\beta = .5, \rho = .85$), scores are generated according to the model $z = \beta\log(n_1/n_2) + e$.
(2) Deltas are calculated via $\Delta_{n_1-n_2} = (\bar{z}_1 - \bar{z}_2)/\sigma_z$.
(3) In this way, all the deltas in the 14-study data set specified above are calculated.

(4) The OLS estimate of β is calculated in the usual fashion from the 30 deltas that arise from Table 6.15. The $1 - \alpha$ confidence interval on β is calculated from $\hat{\beta} \pm_{1-\alpha/2} t_{29} \hat{\sigma}_{\hat{\beta}}$.

(5) The JK confidence interval on β is calculated by means of the 14 pseudovalues arising from the data structure in Table 6.13 and then by means of the formula $\bar{\theta}. \pm_{1-\alpha/2} t_{13} \hat{\sigma}_{\hat{\theta}} / \sqrt{14}$.

(6) The GLS confidence interval on β is calculated via $\hat{\beta} \pm_{1-\alpha/2} t_{20} \hat{\sigma}_{\hat{\beta}}$ where the estimates are given in Equations 6.19, 6.20, and 6.21 above.

(7) Each of the three intervals was calculated for each single simulation and it was recorded whether the 90%, 95%, and 99% confidence intervals captured the true value of β. The simulation was repeated 1000 times and the proportions of intervals capturing the parameter were counted.

The results appear in Table 6.16.

The results in Table 6.16 are remarkably similar and the findings are clear. The GLS method is accurate; it yields the confidence coefficient that one expects to have when referencing the $1 - \alpha/2$ percentiles of the proper t distribution. The empirical and theoretical confidence coefficients were never more than .01 unit discrepant—a discrepancy well within the bounds of sampling error for 1000 cases, as it must be since the GLS solution is mathematically correct. By comparison, the OLS confidence intervals were grossly in error. For example with $\beta = 1.0$ and $\rho = .85$, the nominal 90% OLS confidence interval around $\hat{\beta}$ has only .642 probability of capturing the parameter value of 1.0—an error in the expected confidence coefficient of roughly one-third.

The JK confidence coefficients are more accurate than the OLS coefficients but they are probably unacceptably discrepant from theoretical values, in absolute terms, and they are clearly less accurate than the GLS confidence intervals. For example, for $\beta = .50$ and $\rho = .65$, the nominal 90% JK interval has actual confidence coefficient of 84.5%, an error of over 5 percentage points, whereas the GLS interval, as expected, shows an empirical confidence coefficient equal (within sampling error) to the theoretical value.

A Monte Carlo simulation showed the GLS confidence intervals on β of the logarithmic model to be accurate, according to theory. The OLS confidence intervals proved to be grossly inaccurate and unacceptable— victims of the nonindependence of the Δ's from which the logarithmic

TABLE 6.16 Empirical Confidence Coefficients for True α = .10, .05 and .01 for Ordinary Least-squares (OLS), Jackknife (JK) and Generalized Least-squares (GLS) Confidence Intervals

ρ	β	Method of Estimation	Theoretical Confidence Coefficient		
			.90	.95	.99
.65	.25	OLS	.678	.786	.866
		JK	.857	.917	.966
		GLS	.900	.955	.993
	.50	OLS	.646	.740	.871
		JK	.845	.905	.973
		GLS	.909	.949	.987
	1.00	OLS	.641	.744	.876
		JK	.857	.912	.969
		GLS	.910	.956	.988
.85	.25	OLS	.653	.742	.879
		JK	.860	.914	.973
		GLS	.894	.947	.994
	.50	OLS	.647	.771	.876
		JK	.852	.929	.981
		GLS	.906	.947	.991
	1.00	OLS	.642	.734	.869
		JK	.854	.914	.968
		GLS	.897	.943	.983

model is fitted. The JK confidence intervals (although not as inaccurate as the OLS intervals and although possibly capable of being improved by proper normalizing transformations yet to be discovered) were less accurate than the GLS intervals. The method of GLS is an accurate method of interval estimation of β in the logarithmic model which finds frequent application in problems of meta-analysis.

CHAPTER SEVEN

AN EVALUATION OF META-ANALYSIS

The approach to research integration referred to as meta-analysis is nothing more than the attitude of data analysis applied to quantitative summaries of individual studies. By recording the properties of studies and their findings in quantitative terms, the meta-analysis of research invites one who would integrate numerous and diverse 'findings to apply the full power of statistical methods to the task. Thus it is not a technique; rather it is a perspective that uses many techniques of measurement and statistical analysis.

A tenet of evaluation theory is that self-assessment is always more suspect than assessment by a neutral party. There is a tone of false promise in professing to criticize an endeavor in which one has invested heavily. Although we cannot promise to deal with the strengths and weaknesses of the meta-analysis approach with an even hand, we can assure the reader that most of the objections raised against the procedure by critics of earlier applications are recorded and discussed below. Applications of meta-analysis to research in psychotherapy, school class size, special education, and other problems have produced many technical criticisms. Among the persons commenting on meta-analysis are the following: Mansfield and Bussey (1977), Bandura (1978), Eysenck (1978a), Gallo (1978), Jackson (1978), Paul (1978), Presby (1978), Walberg (1978), Rimland (1979), Simpson (1980), Eysenck (1978b), Shapiro (1977), Cook and Leviton (1980), Hunter (1979), and Roid et al. (1979).

The criticisms of meta-analysis can be grouped into four categories.

(1) *The Apples and Oranges Problem.* It is illogical to compare "different" studies, that is, studies done with different measuring techniques, different types of persons, and the like.

(2) *Use of Data From "Poor" Studies.* Meta-analysis advocates low standards of quality for research. It accepts uncritically the findings from studies that are poorly designed or are otherwise of low quality. Aggregated conclusions should only be based on the findings of "good" studies.

(3) *Selection Bias in Reported Research.* Meta-analysis is dependent on the findings that researchers report. Its findings will be biased if, as is surely true, there are systematic differences among the results of research that appear in journals versus books versus theses versus unpublished papers.

(4) *Lumpy (Nonindependent) Data.* Meta-analyses are conducted on large data sets in which multiple results are derived from the same study; this renders the data nonindependent and gives one a mistaken impression of the reliability of the results.

In the remainder of this chapter, these criticisms will be addressed with counterarguments and data accumulated from several extant meta-analyses.

Criticism #1. *The Apples and Oranges Problem. The meta-analysis approach to research integration mixes apples and oranges. It makes no sense to integrate the findings of different studies.*

The worry is often encountered that in combining or integrating studies, one is forcing incommensurable studies together, or trying to make different studies answer the same question, or "mixing apples and oranges." Implicit in this concern is the belief that only studies that are the *same* in certain respects can be aggregated. "A study's dependent variables and those independent variables which are measured must be measured in the same way as, or in a way subject to a conversion into, those employed in the rest of the studies" (Light and Smith, 1971: 449). This thesis should be clarified in at least two ways: "Same" is not defined and the respects in which comparable studies must be the same are unspecified. The claim that only studies which are the same in *all* respects can be compared is self-contradictory; there is no need to compare them since they would obviously have the same findings within statistical error. The only studies which need to be compared or integrated are *different* studies.

Suppose that a researcher wished to integrate existing studies on computer-assisted instruction (CAI) and cross-age tutoring (CAT) to obtain some notion of their relative effectiveness. That studies # 1 and # 2 on CAI used different standardized achievement tests to measure progress in mathematics is a difference that should cause little concern, considering the basic similarity of most standardized achievement tests. He who would object to integrating the findings from these two studies must face a succession of difficult questions which begin with whether he will accept as comparable two studies using *different* forms of the *same* test or whether he will accept as equal two average scores which were achieved by *different* patterns of item responses to the *same* form of the *same* test.

Imagine further that of 100 CAI studies, 75 were in math and 25 in science, whereas of the 100 CAT studies, 25 were in math and 75 were in science. Are the aggregated data on effectiveness from 100 studies each of CAI and CAT meaningfully comparable? It depends entirely on the exact form of the question being addressed. If CAI is naturally much more frequently applied to math instruction than to science (and vice versa for CAT), then the simple aggregation of effectiveness measures may most meaningfully answer the question of what benefits could be expected by a typical school from installing CAI (and using it in the natural manner, which means three times more extensively in math than in science) instead of instigating CAT. If, however, one were more interested in the question of whether CAI was a more effective *medium* than CAT, then such a comparison ought not to be confounded with problems of the difficulties of learning math versus science. In these circumstances, a straightforward aggregation of the findings in each set of 100 studies would not be most meaningful. To compare the media independently of subject taught, one could calculate effectiveness measures separately for math and science within either CAI or CAT. Then total effectiveness measures for CAI and CAT would be constructed by some appropriate method of proportional weighting.

There exists another respect in which critics are inconsistent who criticize meta-analysis as meaningless because it mixes apples and oranges. These same critics, researchers themselves, habitually perform data analyses in their own research in which they lump together (average or otherwise aggregate in analyses of variance, t tests, and whatever) data from different *persons*. These persons are as different and as much like apples and oranges in their way as studies are different from each other. Yet the same critics who object to pooling the findings of studies 1, 2, . . . , 10 see nothing at all objectionable in pooling the results from persons 1, 2, . . . , 100 in their own research. An inconsistency of no small order must be acknowledged at this point, or else the critic of meta-analysis must argue convincingly that the two kinds of aggregating identified are qualitatively different; and he should specify how they are different and why it matters, which will necessarily entail presenting empirical evidence to demonstrate that studies using different populations, measuring instruments, data analyses, and so on are fundamentally incommensurable. (The ironic dilemma posed here is that such an empirical demonstration would be of itself an analysis of exactly the type which we have referred to as a meta-analysis.)

Criticism #2. *Use of Data From "Poor" Studies. The meta-analysis approach "advocates low standards of judgment" of the quality of studies.*

Although Eysenck (1978) saw Smith and Glass (1977) as "advocating" low standards of research quality, other critics have viewed those applying meta-analysis as being incapable of telling the difference between "good" and "bad" studies. Meta-analysis is said to rely on undiscriminating volume of data rather than on quality of design and evidence. In the academic wars waged over the questions of the benefits of psychotherapy, the judgment of "quality of design and evidence" has usually been the ad hoc impeaching on methodological grounds of the studies of one's enemies.

Somewhere in the history of the social sciences, research criticism took an unhealthy turn. It became confused with research design. The critic often reads a published study and second guesses the aspects of measurement and analysis that should have been anticipated by the researcher. If a study "fails" on a sufficient number of these criteria—or if it fails to meet conditions of which the critic is particularly fond—the study is discounted or eliminated completely from consideration. Research design has a logic of its own, but it is not a logic appropriate to research integration. The researcher does not want to perform a study deficient in some aspect of measurement or analysis, but it hardly follows that after a less-than-perfect study has been done, its findings should not be considered. A logic of research integration could lead to a description of design and analysis features and study of their covariance with research findings. If, for example, the covariance is quite small between the size of an experimental effect and whether or not subjects were volunteers, then the force of the criticism that some experiments used volunteers is clearly diminished.

Early work on the effects of psychotherapy (Smith and Glass, 1977) never strayed far from a sensitivity to design and methods in the studies integrated. However, across the field of psychotherapy outcome evaluation, there was basically no correlation between the "quality" of the design and the size of psychotherapy effect (Smith and Glass, 1977: 758, Table 4). Thus any distinctions between "good" and "bad" studies would leave the overall picture unchanged—a fact that should be clear to anyone who understands what the absence of correlation implies. No purpose would have been served by reporting results separately for "good" and "bad" studies since they would have been essentially the same. In a meta-analysis of educational research on the effect of class size on achievement, Glass and Smith (1979) found that quality of research design (essentially the degree of control exercised over the assignment of pupils to classes) was the highest correlate of effects. The sensible course was elected, and results were presented only for the studies in which careful experimental control was exercised.

An early attempt at meta-analysis was characterized somewhat cynically by a critic as follows: "Although no single study was well enough done to prove that psychotherapy is effective, when you put all these bad studies together, they show beyond doubt that therapy works." This skeptical characterization with its paradoxical ring is a central thesis of research integration. In fact, many weak studies can add up to a strong conclusion. Suppose that, in a group of 100 studies, studies 1-10 are weak in representative sampling but strong in other respects; studies 11-20 are weak in measurement but otherwise strong; studies 21-30 are weak in internal validity only; studies 31-40 are weak only in data analysis; and so on. But imagine also that all 100 studies are somewhat similar in that they show a superiority of the experimental over the control group. The critic who maintains that the total collection of studies does not support strongly the the conclusion of treatment efficacy is forced to invoke an explanation of multiple causality (i.e., the observed difference can be caused either by this particular measurement flaw *or* this particular design flaw, *or* this particular analysis flaw, *or* . . .). The number of multiple causes which must be invoked to counter the explanation of treatment efficacy can be embarrassingly large for even a few dozen studies. Indeed, the multiple-defects explanation will soon grow into a conspiracy theory or else collapse under its own weight. Respect for parsimony and good sense demands an acceptance of the notion that imperfect studies can converge on a true conclusion. An important part of every meta-analysis with which we have been associated has been the recording of methodological weaknesses in the original studies and the examination of their covariance of study findings. Thus, the influence of "study quality" on findings has been regarded consistently as an empirical a posteriori question, not an a priori matter of opinion or judgment used in excluding large numbers of studies from consideration. But a critic once asked us, "Why do you study the difference in the findings of 'good' versus 'bad' studies? If you found a difference, wouldn't you reject the 'bad' studies? And if you found no difference, wouldn't the findings of the 'good' studies be the same as those for all studies regardless of quality?" The dilemma was neatly posed, and we hope the answer is comprehensible. Surely, the "good" studies (i.e., those with excellent controls and sophisticated technology) are to be believed if a conflict is observed between findings of good and poor studies (cf. Glass and Smith, 1979). However, if "good" and "poor" studies do not differ greatly in their findings, a large data base (all studies regardless of quality) is much to be preferred over a small data base (only the "good" studies). The larger data base can be more readily subdivided to answer specific subquestions that are inevitably provoked by the answers to the general questions (e.g. "But are behavioral therapies superior to cognitive therapies for children with low I.Q.?"). The smaller data base of "good" studies only is likely to have too few instances to address many subquestions. Moreover, even when the results of "good" and "bad" studies differ, even the bad or not-so-bad studies can be informative; for suppose that 6 studies of quality "10" on a 10-point scale show a correlation of X and Y of .70 on the average, and that 12 studies of quality "9" show an r of .65, studies of quality "8" an r of .60, and so on down to quality "1" an r of .10, say. This pattern is far more informative and lends greater credence to an r of .70 for 6 studies of top quality than would the results of the 6 studies in isolation from all others.

Our experience with meta-analyses of experiments was matched by Yin et al. (1976) in their study of the relationship between case study quality and findings. Yin and his colleagues collected 140 case studies on technological innovations, every study they could find that appeared after

1965. They devised four criteria for judging the quality of the studies: (1) presence of operational measures of innovative device and outcomes, (2) presence of some relevant research design, (3) overall adequacy of evidence in relation to conclusions, and (4) adequacy of evidence in relation to each stated outcome. They correlated research quality, so defined, with study outcomes and concluded:

> To the extent that one objective of our investigation was to examine the widest possible range of reported innovative experiences, there was thus strong reason not to discard the lower quality studies. At the same time, the general lack of relationship between quality and the outcomes of the innovative experience suggested that the inclusion of lower quality studies would not affect the overall conclusions to be drawn from the review [Yin et al., 1976: 153-154].

In an earlier study (Yin and Yates, 1975), the investigators did observe an association between research quality and findings, just as we see a relationship in some literatures and not in others.

Suppose that of 50 experiments on the effects of jogging on life expectancy, 25 are judged to be of poor design and execution, 15 are regarded as moderately well done, and 10 are well-done. Suppose further that the average effect (experimental versus control group difference) is 2.86 years life expectancy favoring the experimental group *in the 10 best designed studies*. Should one base his opinion on the results of these 10 studies and ignore the findings of the other 40? Let us press on and see. Suppose that the effects shown by the 15 moderately well done and 25 poorly done experiments were 2.74 years and 2.60 years, respectively. These findings do, in fact, support the finding of the less numerous well-done studies and make it more credible. Imagine contrariwise that the average effects for the moderately well-done and poorly done experiments were -.47 years and 8.65 years, respectively. Now the finding of the 10 well-done experiments is placed in a context of chaotic error and variability and it is more suspect. People reason and judge with the help of complex patterns and contexts; scholars who are doctrinaire about research quality when they integrate research studies ignore this fact. It is precisely this fact that was ignored in a widely publicized critique of our meta-analysis of the school class size and achievement relationship (Educational Research Service, 1980).

TABLE 7.1   Relationship Between Research Quality (internal Validity)
and Findings in 12 Meta-Analyses of Experimental
Literatures

Investigator (s)	Topic	Relationship Between Internal Validity and Average Experimental Effect Size		
		High	Medium	Low
Hartley (1977)	Computer-based Instruction	n: 11	55	23
		$\overline{\Delta}.$: .311	.389	.503
	Tutoring	n: 52	12	9
		$\overline{\Delta}.$: .584	.306	1.066
Kulik, Kulik & Cohen (1979)	Individual Instruction	n: 22		22
		$\overline{\Delta}.$: .409		.604
Smith (1980c)	Sex bias in psychotherapy	n: 30	26	4
		$\overline{\Delta}.$: −.18	−.01	.77
Smith (1980b)	Effects of aesthetic educ. on basic skills	n: 84	48	117
		$\overline{\Delta}.$: .53	.52	.59
Carlberg (1979)	Spec. ed. room placement vs. reg. room placement	n: 83	187	52
		$\overline{\Delta}.$: −.19	−.11	.02
	Resource room placement vs. reg. room placement	n: 3	31	5
		$\overline{\Delta}.$: 1.13	.12	.56
	Spec. educ. intervention vs. classroom	n: 40	81	35
		$\overline{\Delta}.$: .19	.27	.53
Miller (1977)	Drug therapy for psych. disorders	n: 297	16	37
		$\overline{\Delta}.$: .48	.54	.64

TABLE 7.1 — Relationship Between Research Quality (internal Validity) and Findings in 12 Meta-Analyses of Experimental Literatures (continued)

Investigator (s)	Topic	Relationship Between Internal Validity and Average Experimental Effect Size		
		High	Medium	Low
Hearold (1979)	Effects of TV on anti-social behav.	n: 176	176	176
		$\overline{\Delta}$. : .33	.30	.27
	Effects of TV on "pro-social" behav.	n: 35	35	35
		$\overline{\Delta}$. : .59	.63	.67
		High	Medium	Low
SUBTOTALS		n: 833	667	515
		$\overline{\Delta}$. : .36	.21	.43
Smith, Glass & Miller (1980)	Psychotherapy	n: 1157	378	224
		$\overline{\Delta}$. : .82	.75	.68
TOTALS		n: 1990	1045	739
		$\overline{\Delta}$. : .63	.40	.51

The covariation of research quality with results is, then, an empirical matter of central concern in meta-analysis, as well as being of interest to research methodologists who find meta-analysis too much to swallow. Fortunately, we have several thousand data that can inform us on the general question.

In Table 7.1 appears a summary of the differences in results among studies of varying research quality for 12 different meta-analyses. Each meta-analysis was performed on a literature of comparative experimental findings. The basic unit of measurement for the meta-analysis was the effect size, Δ, and in each instance it was defined so that positive values indicated findings in accord with the favored hypothesis of the field in question (e.g., a positive Δ in Hartley's meta-analysis of computer-assisted math instruction indicated a superiority of CAI over traditional teaching). In each meta-analysis, the rating of High, Medium, or Low research quality was primarily an assessment of internal validity of the experiment.

If Table 7.1 achieves nothing else, it ought to be, at the very least, an effective antidote to rampant a priorism on the matter of which studies should be admitted as evidence in deciding research questions. Some of the meta-analyses in Table 7.1 show a relationship between design quality and findings and others do not. But in those analyses with substantial numbers of cases, the differences in size of average experimental effects between high-validity and low-validity experiments are surprisingly small. The only notable exceptions to this trend in the entire table are Hartley's (1978) tutoring analysis, Smith (1980c) and Carlberg's (1979) resource room analysis; but in each of these instances, as just suggested, the large deviations are probably merely the consequence of small n's in particular categories. As a general rule, there is seldom much more than .1 standard deviation difference between average effects for high-validity and low-validity experiments.

Criticism # 3. *Selection Bias in Reported Research. Meta-analysis is dependent on the findings that researchers report. Its findings will be biased if, as is surely ture, there are systematic differences among the results of research that appear in journals versus books versus theses versus unpublished papers.*

The findings of a dozen meta-analyses can be used to inform us on the severity of one aspect of this criticism. Several investigators working on the integration of experimental literatures compared the effects revealed by experiments depending on whether they were published in journals, books, doctoral or master's theses, or not published at all. The results were tabulated as Table 3.4 in Chapter 3 where these data were used to make a related point.

In every 1 of the 9 instances in which the comparison can be made in Table 3.4, the average experimental effect from studies published in journals is larger than the corresponding effect estimated from dissertations. The bias in the journal literature relative to the dissertation literature is not inconsiderable. As was calculated in Chapter 3, the mean effect size for journals is .64 as compared with .48 for the dissertation literature; hence, the bias is of the order of $[(.64-.48)/.48]\ 100\% = 33\%$. Findings reported in journals are, on the average, one-third standard deviation larger than findings reported in dissertations.

Comparisons of average effect sizes among other sources of publication are less clear, in part perhaps because of the ambiguity in labels such as "unpublished" or "book." In four of six instances, journals gave more favorable results than books. In four of eight instances, the average effect size for journals was larger than for unpublished studies. Unpublished studies seemed to divide along the following lines: (1) one large group of old unpublished studies containing unremarkable results that never caught anyone's attention and (2) a smaller group of new studies circulating through the "invisible college" while waiting to be published.

The compilation of results from various meta-analyses shows that there is substance to the criticism that most disciplines show evidences of a selection bias in what they publish. And the bias may be large in some instances. Smith's (1980c) meta-analysis of sex bias in psychotherapy is particularly relevant, as a final example. The very *direction* of the bias was reversed between the dissertation literature and published journals (from demonstrating a bias in favor of women in the thesis literature to a bias against women in journals); that this reversal was in accord with political ideologies that are presumed to control access to journals makes the case even stronger that disciplines are prone to the temptation to reward findings they approve of by publishing them in more prestigious places.

However, the fact of the existence of selective publication tendencies is not in itself a cogent criticism of meta-analysis, which, after all, is used here to demonstrate the existence and the magnitude of the phenomenon. Indeed, the problem of selective publication cannot be dealt with adequately in integrating a research literature except by meta-analytic means, that is, by collecting *all* of the literature at the outset and analyzing it separately by mode of publication.

There exists another factor with respect to which selection often takes place during research integration, namely, the date on which the studies were published. It is common for reviewers to restrict their attention to a particular span of years and review only studies of that period, for example, "This review will consider all laboratory studies on attention processes published after 1960." The choice of dates is invariably arbitrary and governed by convenience. It behooves us to inquire into the matter of chronological trends in research findings.

TABLE 7.2   Correlation Between Date of Publication and Effect Size
             for Six Meta-Analyses of Experimental Literatures

Investigator(s)	Topic	Correlation Between Date of Publication and Effect Size
Kavale (1979)	Psycholinguistic Training	$r = -.01$ ($n = 25$)
Hall (1978)	Gender effects in non-verbal coding	$r = .28$ ($n = 44$)
Smith (1980	Sex bias in psychotherapy	$r = .29$ ($n = 60$)
Carlberg (1979)	Special education room placement	$r = .02$ ($n = 322$)
	Resource room placement	$r = .32$ ($n = 39$)
	Other special education intervention	$r = .08$ ($n = 156$)
Miller (1978)	Drug treatment of psychological disorders	$r = -.01$ ($n = 358$)
Smith, Glass & Miller (1980)	Psychotherapy	$r = .07$ ($n = 1,764$)

In Table 7.2 appears a compilation of correlations between date of publication and effect size from six meta-analyses of experimental literatures. The average of the eight correlations in Table 7.2 is +.13, indicating that more recently published experiments show a slight tendency toward larger effects than older studies. (The weighted average r, each r weighted by the number of effect sizes in the particular meta-analysis, equals +.07. The unweighted average is probably more sensible because it is not affected by some meta-analyses arbitrarily having more data points.) Assuming a correlation of +.13 between date of publication and effect size and some reasonable parameters for the independent variable (date) and the dependent variable (effect size or Δ), then a linear regression equation can be constructed that relates date of publication to effect size:

$$\hat{\Delta} = .13\ (.67/4)\ \text{date} + .70 - .13\ (.67/4)\ 1970.$$

The above equation contains some assumed values for the means and standard deviations of date and Δ:

Variable	Mean	Standard Deviation
Date	1970	4 years
Δ	.70	.67

Substituting the dates 1965 and 1975, each about one standard deviation away from the mean, into the regression equation gives $\hat{\Delta}$ (1965) = .59 and $\hat{\Delta}$ (1975) = .81.

These calculations indicate that the typical correlation between date of publication and effect size (r - .13) implies that experiments published in 1975 show a .22 average effect size advantage over experiments published in 1965. This difference amounting to [(.81-.59)/.59]100% = 37% is comparable to the difference in average effect size between journals and theses. Thus the concerns about bias that applied in the case of selectivity in publication outlet appear to apply with nearly equal force to the case of selection of studies by date. It would seem ill-advised to begin the integration of an empirical research literature by arbitrarily restricting the studies considered to those published in refereed journals after 1960, for example.

Criticism #4. *Lumpy (nonindependent) Data. Meta-analyses are conducted on large data sets in which multiple results are derived from the same study; this renders the data nonindependent and gives one a mistaken impression of the reliability of the results.*

Of all the technical criticisms of meta-analysis that have been published in the last five years (and most of these criticisms are quite off the mark and shallow), the reminder that meta-analyses are typically carried out on lumpy sets of nonindependent data is quite cogent. The principal implication of this nonindependence is a reduction in the reliability of estimation of averages or of regression equations. For example, if Study #1 gave effects .2, .2, .2, and .2 and Study #2 gave effects .6, .6, and .6, one would have little reason to believe that he had been informed seven times about the aggregate result in question; rather the true "degrees of freedom" would seem to be somewhat closer to 2, the number of studies, than to 7, the number of effects. A facile solution to this problem of nonindependence would be to average all findings within a study up to the level of the study and proceed with a meta-analysis with "studies" as the unit of analysis. No doubt there will be instances in which this resolution of the problem will be satisfactory. But in most instances, it is likely to obscure many important questions that can only be addressed at the "within-study" level of outcome variables, say. The effect on accuracy of estimation of complex interdependencies in a meta-analysis data base was addressed at the end of Chapter 6.

CONCLUSION

Of course, it is unclear what meta-analysis will contribute to the progress of empirical research. One can imagine a future for research in the social and behavioral sciences in which questions are so sharply put and techniques so well-standardized that studies would hardly need to be integrated by merit of their consistent findings. But that future seems unlikely. Research will probably continue to be an unorganized, decentralized, nonstandardized activity pursued simultaneously in dozens of places without thought to how it will all fit together in the end.

What is clear today, that was not so clear to us 10 years ago when we undertook this work, is that the findings of contemporary research fit together poorly. Variance of. study *findings* is only modestly predictable from study characteristics; in nearly all instances, less than 25% of the variance in study results can be accounted for by the best combination of study features. This is *not* like saying that the multiple correlation for predicting college grade-point average is .50—which it is widely known to be. One expects a fairly large residual unpredictability in *individual* human behavior. However, the observations of the dependent variable in a meta-analysis are themselves summary statistics from studies based on hundreds of persons in many instances; hence, the residual unpredictability of study findings is not a simple matter of sampling error or measurement error that reduces the accuracy of predicting someone's grade-point average. Actuaries cannot accurately predict whether Mr. Albert Thanatos will die in the coming year, but they can predict with high accuracy how many persons in a group of 10,000 will die, thus the distinction between accounting for variability in individual versus group phenomena. The condition of most social and behavioral research appears to be that there is little predictability at either the individual or study level.

There are at least two ways to try to understand this state of affairs. First, it may be true that the important conditions that mediate the findings of research studies are simply not reported in written accounts of research. They may be observable in fact, but custom or whatever keeps them from being reported. Thus, the reader of these studies lacks the complete picture, and his judgment of whether the study findings will apply where his interests lie suffers. Second, it is possible that the social and behavioral sciences are at very primitive stages in accounting for their own findings. Perhaps those many things that cause phenomena (statistical correlations, experimental effects) to wax and wane are simply not now understood, recognized, or measured. Of course, they could not, then, be reported in accounts of research. In either case, the reader of the studies is placed in the same position: Findings vary greatly from study to study in ways that cannot be accounted for.

Where does the remedy lie for this affront to scientific aspirations? Better theories? Better measurements? Standardization of research techniques? More complete reports of research studies? Accommodation to an unpredictable world? We have no clear sense of a solution, nor even whether any solution is possible. We only hope that the techniques of research integration that we have devised and illustrated have helped expose the problem rather than created a false sense of a problem. The need for formal techniques of research integration like those presented here will probably grow. Whether future techniques will resemble these is uncertain, but we suspect they will. The approach we call meta-analysis seems to be too plainly reasonable to be false in any simple sense. Whether it will be useful is a different matter.

APPENDIX A

Coding Form Used in the Psychotherapy Meta-analysis

Benefits of psychotherapy

Card one column	Value	Information
1-5	. . . .	Study identification number
6	. . . .	Running comparison number
7-8	. . . .	Running measure number
9	. . . .	Running record number: punch 1 for card 1 Author
10-11	. . . .	Publication date
12	. . . .	Publication form: (1) journal, (2) book, (3) thesis, (4) unpublished
13	. . . .	Training of experimenter: (1) psychology, (2) education, (3) psychiatry, (4) social work, (5) other, (6) unknown
14	. . . .	Blinding: (1) E did therapy, (2) E knew composition of groups but didn't do therapy, (3) single-blind, (4) unknown
15	. . . .	Did E call this an analogue study: (1) yes, (2) no
		Clients
16-17	. . . .	Major diagnosis: (1) neurotic or complex phobic, (2) simple phobic, (3) psychotic, (4) normal, (5) character disorder, (6) delinquent or felon, (7) habituee, (8) mixed, (9) unknown, (10) emotional/somatic complaint, (11) handicapped, (12) depressive label

233

Appendix A (Continued)

Card one Column	Value	Information
18–20	....	List code for label
21	....	Type of phobia: (1) reptile, (2) rodent, (3) insect, (4) speech, (5) tests, (6) other performance, (7) heights, (8) other
22–23	....	Average length of hospitalization in years
24	....	Average intelligence: (1) below average, (2) average, 95–105, (3) above average
25	....	Source of IQ: (1) stated, (2) directly inferred, (3) estimated
26	....	Similarity of client to therapist: (1) very dissimilar, (2) moderately dissimilar, (3) moderately similar, (4) very similar
27–28	....	Mean age to nearest year
29–30	....	Percentage male
31	....	SES: (1) low, (2) middle, (3) high, (blank) unknown
32	....	Solicitation of clients: (1) autonomous presentation, (2) presentation in response to advertisement, (3) solicited by E, (4) committed, (5) referred

Design

33	....	Group assignment of clients: (1) random, (2) matching, (3) pretest equation, (4) convenience sample, (5) other nonrandom
34	....	Group assignment of therapists: (1) random, (2) matching, (3) nonrandom, (4) single therapist, (5) not applicable
35	....	Internal validity: (1) low, (2) medium, (3) high
36	....	Number of threats to internal validity
37–38	....	Percentage mortality from treated groups
39–40	....	Percentage mortality from comparison group
41	....	Is more than one therapy compared simultaneously against control: (1) yes, (2) no
42	....	Number of comparisons in this study
43	....	Number of this comparison
44–45	....	Number of outcome measures within this comparison
46–47	....	Number of this outcome measure (the rest of the record deals with this outcome measure)

Treatment

48–49	....	Type of treatment: (2) placebo, (3) psychodynamic, (4) client-centered, (5) Adlerian, (6) gestalt, (7) systematic desensitization, (8) cognitive/Ellis, (9) cognitive/other, (10) transactional analysis, (11) behavior modification, (12) eclectic/dynamic, (13) eclectic behavioral, (14) reality therapy, (15) vocational/personal development counseling, (16) cognitive behavioral, (18) implosion, (19) hypnotherapy, (20) other

Appendix A (Continued)

Card one column	Value	Information
		Label for therapy type
		Proponent
50–52	....	List code for label
53–55	....	List code for proponent
56	....	Confidence of classification: (1) low . . . (5) high
57	....	Class of therapy
58	....	Superclass of therapy
59	....	Type of comparison: (1) control, (2) placebo, (3) second treatment
60	....	Type of control group: (1) no treatment, (2) waiting list, (3) intact group, (4) hospital maintenance, (5) other, (blank) not control
61–62	....	Type of placebo list code
		Label of placebo type
63–65	....	Second treatment type
66	....	Allegiance of E to therapy compared: (1) yes, (2) no, (3) unknown
67	....	Modality: (1) individual, (2) group, (3) family, (4) mixed, (5) automated, (6) other, (7) unknown
68–69	....	Location of treatment: (1) school, (2) hospital, (3) mental health center, (4) other clinic, (5) other outpatient, (6) private, (7) other, (8) unknown, (9) college mental health facility, (10) prison, (11) residential facility
70–72	....	Duration of therapy in hours
73–75	....	Duration of treatment in weeks
76–77	....	Number of therapists
78–79	....	Experience of therapists in years

Card two column	Value	Information
1–5	....	Study ID
6	....	Running comparison number
7–8	....	Running measure number
9	....	Running record number: punch 2 for card 2
		Effect size
10–12	....	Sample size for treatment group
13–15	....	Sample size for comparison group
16–17	....	Outcome type: (1) fear/anxiety, (2) self-esteem, (3) test measures and ratings of global adjustment, (4) life indicators of adjustment, (5) personality traits, (6) emotional/somatic disorders,

Appendix A (Continued)

Card two column	Value	Information
		(7) addiction, (8) sociopathic behaviors, (9) social behaviors, (10) work-school achievement, (11) vocational/personal development, (12) physiological measures of stress, (13) other
		Label of outcome measure
18-20	....	List code for outcome measure
21-23	....	Number of weeks post-therapy measure was taken
24	....	Reactivity of measure: (1) low . . . (5) high
25-26	....	Calculation of effect size: (1) mean difference over control S.D., (2) MS within, (3) MS total minus treatment, (4) probit, (5) chi square, (6) T table, (7) mean and P, (8) nonparametrics, (9) correlations, (10) raw data, (11) estimates, (12) other
27	....	Source of means: (1) unadjusted post-test, (2) covariance adjusted, (3) residual gains, (4) pre-post differences, (5) other
28	....	Significance of treatment effect: (0) −.001, (1) −.005, (2) −.01, (3) −.05, (4) −.10, (5) .10, (6) .05, (7) .01, (8) .005, (9) .001, (blank) not significant
29-34	....	Treatment group pre-mean
35-40	....	Treatment pre-standard deviation
41-46	....	Treatment post-mean
47-52	....	Treatment post-standard deviation
53-58	....	Comparison group pre-mean
59-64	....	Comparison pre-standard deviation
65-70	....	Comparison post-mean
71-76	....	Comparison post-standard deviation

Card three column	Value	Information
1-5	....	Study ID
6	....	Running comparison number
7-8	....	Running measure number
9	....	Running record number: punch 3 for card 3
10-13	....	T statistic
14-17	....	F statistic
18-22	....	Mean square within, residual, or common
23-24	....	Treatment group percentage improved
25-26	....	Comparison group percentage improved

Appendix A (Continued)

Card three Column	Value	Information
27–30	....	Effect size
31	....	Class of second therapy
32	....	Superclass of second therapy
33	....	Allegiance of E to second therapy
34	....	Modality of second therapy
35	....	Location of second therapy
36–38	....	Duration of second therapy in hours
39–41	....	Duration of second therapy in weeks
42–43	....	Number of therapists in second therapy
44–45	....	Experience of therapists in second therapy
46	....	Other factorial effects tested: (0) none,(1) race, (2) SES, (3)IE, (4) sex, (5) other
47	....	Is this the last effect with this comparison: (1) yes, (2) no
48–51	....	If yes, average effect size within this comparison
52	....	Is this the last effect size in this study: (1) yes, (2) no
53–56	....	If yes, average of all effect sizes in the study

APPENDIX B

STUDY* USED AS CODING EXAMPLE IN CHAPTER FOUR

THE EFFECT OF BEHAVIORAL COUNSELING IN GROUP AND INDIVIDUAL SETTINGS ON INFORMATION-SEEKING BEHAVIOR[1]

John D. Krumboltz
Carl E. Thoresen

192 eleventh-grade pupils were randomly assigned to individual and group counseling settings in which the following four procedures were used by the special counselors: (a) reinforcement of verbal information-seeking behavior, (b) presentation of a tape-recorded model interview followed by reinforcement counseling, (c) presentation of film or filmstrip plus discussion as a control procedure and (d) inactive control. Findings: (a) Model-reinforcement and reinforcement counseling produced more external information-seeking behavior than control procedures. (b) With a male model, model-reinforcement counseling surpassed reinforcement counseling for males but not for females. (c) Group and individual settings were about equally effective on the average but interactions were found with counselor-schools, sex of subjects and treatments.

One interpretation of the counselor's role is that it is his job to help students learn how to make wise decisions (Gelatt, 1962). Students may learn sound decision-making procedures by engaging in these procedures in connection with their own plans.

While it is not possible to specify what the final decision should be for any particular individual, the process in which an individual should engage if he is to maximize the probability of eventually arriving at a wise decision can be specified. Such a process would include considering several alternative courses of action, exploring relevant information about the possible outcomes of each alternative, and weighing the information obtained with more subjective value judgments in an attempt to achieve the outcomes considered most worthwhile.

The present study was designed to investigate ways of increasing the information-seeking behavior of students about their own educational and vocational decisions. The basic problem was to determine which of several behavior change techniques, when applied in either individual or small group settings, would best promote the independent information-seeking behavior of students.

One technique was termed "reinforcement counseling" and has been derived from work in verbal operant learning (Krumboltz, 1963; Schroeder, 1964). Studies in verbal operant learning have clearly demonstrated that the probable frequency of an operant can be increased when it is followed by a positive reinforcer (Greenspoon, 1962; Krasner, 1962). Most of these studies have used a discrete response class, such as personal pronouns or animal responses, with college students in a laboratory setting or with abnormal subjects. Reinforcement effects have usually been assessed immediately without determining whether there is generalization to behavior outside the laboratory. Certain types of verbal and non-verbal stimuli have been identified as positive reinforcers since they increased the frequency of the response class which preceded them.

The second general technique, termed "model-reinforcement counseling," has involved the presentation of a social model who demonstrates the desired behavior. Research evidence has attested to the effectiveness of social models in promoting certain types of learning (Bandura & Walters, 1963). Reinforcement, while not essential to the acquisition of responses, does affect the rate and magnitude of learning from models as well as the subsequent performance of learned responses. Some evidence suggests that more prestigeful and socially powerful models contribute to a greater matching of the models' behavior by observers (Bandura, 1962; Maccoby, 1954; Mussen & Distler, 1959). Studies have indicated that physically present models are not significantly more effective than audio or video presented models (Bandura, Ross, & Ross, 1962; Walters, Llewellyn-

Thomas, & Acker, 1962). Providing a prestigeful social model and positively reinforcing indications of matching responses has been shown to be highly effective in changing the behavior of observers (Krumboltz, 1963; Schroeder, 1964).

The present study, based on prior research in operant learning and social modeling, has certain unique features relevant to counseling:

1. A specific behavioral outcome, information-seeking behavior, was defined in advance, and alternative experimental treatments were designed to promote that particular behavior.
2. The present study was designed to promote a socially meaningful and socially desirable response class rather than a discrete but socially meaningless response class.
3. Treatments were assessed by reports of behavior which occurred outside the counseling interview, not by behavior which occurred during the interview.
4. To promote generalizability of results the experiment was replicated with six different counselors in six different schools.
5. Subjects were normal 11th-grade high school students who had requested special counseling about future plans rather than college students who volunteered for a psychological experiment or abnormal subjects.
6. To control for the "Hawthorne Effect," an additional control group recieved special attention and contact with the counselor but did not recieve the experimental treatments.
7. Each technique was applied in both individual and group counseling sessions to ascertain the effect of the group setting.
8. No attempt was made to disguise the response class that was being reinforced. On the contrary, students were made well aware of the counselor's interest in their vocational and educational explorations.

PROCEDURE

This study was replicated in each of six suburban high schools in the vicinity of Stanford University.[2] All 11th-grade students were asked to indicate if they would be interested in receiving special counseling about their future educational and vocational plans. Between 48 and 63 per cent of the students in each high school volunteered to participate. All students were informed that it might not be possible to provide the special counseling for everyone who requested it. In each high school 20 boys and 20 girls were selected at random from those who volunteered. Two boys and two girls in each high school were assigned at random to each treatment group; four boys and four girls were assigned at random to the inactive control and to the reserve groups. Reserve group subjects were not included in the analysis, so the total N was 192.

Treatments

Subjects were assigned to the two principal treatments, reinforcement counseling and model-reinforcement counseling, applied in both individual and group settings, and to two kinds of control groups plus a group of reserve subjects.

Individual reinforcement counseling. The counselor introduced himself, stressed that the students had volunteered to receive special counseling and said in effect, "The purpose of our getting together is to discuss your ideas about post high school plans. I usually tape record counseling sessions because it helps me remember what was said. If there are no objections, I'll tape record our session. (Pause) A very important part of making future plans is the getting of information—information that is relevant and accurate. Perhaps you have already taken steps to get information about future plans, such as talking to someone who is in the field of work in which you are interested. Well, why don't you tell me about what you have been thinking about in terms of your future plans?"

The counselor carefully listened during the session for any response which he judged to be of an information-seeking type. The counselor reinforced verbally any indication that the subject had sought, was presently seeking or intended to seek information relevant to his own educational or vocational plans. The following are examples of verbal information-seeking responses:

a. "I suppose I ought to find out how much college costs."
b. "Could I talk to an electrician about apprentice training?"

The counselor attempted to reinforce information-seeking responses with some kind of verbal reinforcer. While a stimulus cannot be termed reinforcing until observation establishes that it strengthens the frequency of the preceding operant, it was assumed from past experience that certain counselor responses such as the following were positively reinforcing stimuli:

a. "Yes, that would be a good thing to know."
b. "Excellent idea."
c. "Mm-hmm."

Non-verbal cues such as smiling, forward body posture and head nodding, were also used.

To increase the occurrence of verbal information-seeking responses, the counselors periodically used "cues" (Ryan & Krumboltz, 1964; Rickard, 1961). Such cues were questions designed to increase verbal information-seeking responses. Examples include the following:

a. "How would you handle this question of what college to attend?"
b. "There are several ways of getting information about a particular job. Where would you begin?"

The counselor closed the interview by asking each subject to summarize the specific steps which he might take to seek information about his future plans. The counselor verbally reinforced each summary statement and added any specific steps not mentioned by the subject. The counselor asked subjects if they might begin acting on some of the specific steps before the second interview.

The second counseling interview occurred approximately one week after the first interview. The second session began with the counselor saying in effect, "Hello. I'm happy that we could get together again. At the close of our last interview we mentioned several things which you might do in getting information about your future plans. I'm wondering if you remember what some of these things were? Have you done anything this last week or thought about some ways in which you could get information?" The counselor reinforced any verbal information-seeking behavior on the part of the subject and terminated in a manner similar to that of the first interview.

Group reinforcement counseling. The group reinforcement counseling was virtually identical to the above except that the counselor worked with a group of two boys and two girls. The counselor's introductory remarks included the folloing addition: "I thought that since you all have expressed similar concerns about making future plans and decisions that perhaps together we might be able to help each other. As you all know students often face similar problems and may be able to suggest to one another possible steps in making decisions and choosing alternatives."

The counselor sometimes refrained from interrupting the verbal interaction to reinforce an information-seeking response. Instead the counselor often waited for a pause and then reiterated and reinforced the subject's information-seeking response. The second group counseling session was held one week after the first, and the same reinforcement counseling procedures were utilized.

Individual model-reinforcement counseling. The counselor's introduction to the model-reinforcement counseling was similar to that of the individual reinforcement counseling session with this addition: "But before we start discussing this I thought you might be interested in hearing a tape recording of a boy who faced a problem similar to yours. This student was a very good athlete, active in school clubs and was quite popular. He was concerned about how best to make some decisions about what he was going to do after he graduated from high school. He has been really pleased with his decision and he gave us permission to let other high school students listen to this recorded interview. Let's listen to it. You might have some questions to ask about it when it is over."

A 15-minute edited tape recording of a counseling interview which had been used previously (Krumboltz, 1963; Schroeder, 1964) was then p layed. In this interview the model student verbalized many information-seeking responses, asking questions about possible outcomes and alternatives and suggesting ways in which he might find answers. The model counselor reinforced his question-asking and information-seeking responses and occasionally provided additional suggestions of ways in which he could find the information he sought.

After playing the model tape the counselor said, "Well, why don't you tell me what you've been thinking about in terms of your future plans?" The counseling session continued with the counselor reinforcing any information-seeking response of the subject in the same manner as in the individual reinforcement counseling treatment.

The second counseling session one week later was conducted in the same way as the individual reinforcement counseling second session. No model tape was played in the second session.

Group model-reinforcement counseling. Group model-reinforcement counseling was similar to group reinforcement counseling except that the same model tape recording described above was played during the first session. The counselor then reinforced members of the group for information-seeking responses in the same manner as indicated previously. The second session one week later was the same as described above.

Individual control film discussion. In order to control for the "Hawthorne Effect," an active control group was included in which the counselor provided nonspecific attention to subjects. The counselor acknowledged their request for special counseling and then introduced a film or filmstrip with a comment that viewing and discussing the film might prove helpful. Following the viewing of the film, or filmstrip, the counselor answered any questions. If none were forthcoming, the counselor asked subjects for their reactions to the film or filmstrip. The counselor discussed the general problem of future planning, but no systematic attempt was made to reinforce verbally the subject's information-seeking responses. No second session was held.

Group control film discussion. The group session was similar to the above individual session in procedures. Questions from subjects were referred to other subjects to stimulate a general discussion. Again, no systematic attempt was made to reinforce information-seeking behavior. No second session was held.

Inactive control. Subjects were assigned to the inactive control group from the same pool of volunteers from which the other treatments received subjects. The control group subjects were not contacted by the special counselor in any way. These subjects as well as all others were eligible to participate in their school's regular guidance program.

Reserve pool. In each high school four boys and four girls were assigned to a reserve category in case any member of the other treatment groups was absent or dropped out of school. These subjects were not included in the analysis of the results unless they were drawn to replace some other subject in the experiment.

Training of Special Counselors

The six special counselors were graduate students enrolled in the Counseling Practicum course at Stanford University during the 1962-63 academic year. There were five females and one male. Four were experienced teachers while the other two had had one year of practice teaching experience. One of the six had worked as a parttime secondary counselor for two years.

One counselor was assigned to each high school in October of 1962 on the basis of convenience of location and matching of time schedules. The experiment was conducted in February and March of 1963. For purposes of statistical analysis, these six special counselors and the six participating schools are considered a fixed constant factor and will henceforth be referred to as the counselor-school effect.

The special counselors participated in weekly seminars, read various assignments and spent one-half day per week in their respective schools as part of their training. The rationale of behavioral counseling was discussed and role-playing situations were devised during the weekly seminars. Counselors were provided with interview rating sheets on which to categorize verbal information-seeking responses and other responses during the interviews. Each counselor had practice in exercising the rapid judgment needed in deciding whether or not a given statement was to be classified as an information-seeking response.

Counselors selected subjects from the pool of volunteers in their high school to practice interviewing prior to the beginning of the experiment itself. These practice sessions were tape-recorded and were used for discussion and analysis during the seminar. Regularly scheduled individual interviews were also held between each counselor and one of the instructors.

Criteria

The criterion behavior for this investigation consisted of the frequency and variety of student information-seeking behaviors which occurred outside the counseling interview during a three-week period of time after the first counseling interview. Approximately three weeks after the first counseling interview each of the 192 subjects was interviewed by a member of the evaluation team. These interviewers were not the counselors involved in the study and did not know the type of treatment each subject received. During the interview each subject was asked a series of predetermined questions, some of which were designed to elicit self-reports of information-seeking behavior. Buffer questions were used to disguise the purpose of the interview and to vary the interview format. Each affirmative information-seeking report was followed by other questions to find out precisely how much and what kind of information-seeking behavior was performed by each subject during the specified three-week interval. The following are examples of information-seeking behavior covered by the interview questions:

a. Writing to request a college pamphlet, catalog or an occupational pamphlet.
b. Reading books, magazine articles or other material about occupations or educational institutions.
c. Talking to parents, teachers or other relevant persons who have worked or are working in an occupation or school being considered.
d. Visiting or making definite plans to visit schools or places of employment that are being considered.
e. Seeing the regular high school counselor to gain information relevant to future plans.

While subjects had no known reason to falsify or exaggerate the extent of their recent information-seeking behavior, it was considered essential to verify their self-reports. Previous evidence had demonstrated the validity of self-reports of information-seeking behavior (Krumboltz, 1963; Schroeder, 1964). The names of three subjects from each high school were selected at random for verification. Three names were then assigned to each of six research team members who then conducted follow-up procedures of each subject's self-report. The follow-up procedures included such things as interviewing parents, relatives, teachers, students and employed persons to find out whether the subject had discussed some educational or vocational matter with them, checking with librarians to see whether or not a particular book was checked out during the specified period of time and checking with the regular counselor in the school to see whether appointments had been scheduled by each subject. Of 85 information-seeking behaviors reported by these 18 subjects, 79 were verified and 6 were unconfirmable. None of the reported behaviors was invalidated. Thus, no evidence of falsification of self-reports was obtained, a finding consistent with that of the earlier study.

For each subject two scores were derived from the interview protocol, the *frequency* of information-seeking behavior and the *variety* of information-seeking behavior. The frequency refers to the total number of information-seeking behaviors, e.g., writing to four different colleges for catalogs would give a frequency of four. The variety refers to the number of different *types* of such behaviors, e.g., writing for four different catalogs and talking to three students from Harvard would constitute only two different varieties of information-seeking behavior, though the frequency would be seven.

RESULTS

A 4 X 2 X 6 X 2 analysis of variance was computed using treatments, sex of subjects, counselor-schools and treatment setting as the independent variables. Separate analyses were computed for the frequency and the variety of information-seeking behavior. Both analyses are summarized in Table 1. Three of the four main effects reached at least the .05 level of significance for both criterion variables. The four treatments produced highly significant differences. There were also significant differences between the sexes and among the six counselor-schools. The main effect for treatment setting was not significant for either variable. The interpretation of these main effects is complicated by the presence of several significant interactions. For both variables the interaction between the treatment and sex of subject was significant. In addition, three other interaction effects reached at least the .05 level for the frequency criterion.

The nature of the sex by treatment interaction and the main effects attributable to the four treatments and the two sexes can be seen in Table 2. The original hypotheses in this study stated that the model reinforcement treatment would be more effective than the reinforcement treatment and that the reinforcement treatment in turn would be more effective than the control procedures. No differences were hypothesized between the control film discussion group and the inactive control group. On the average the results were as predicted on both the frequency and the variety variables. The model-reinforcement treatment proved most effective, followed by the reinforcement treatment. The inactive control group was least active. It will also be seen that on the average the females engaged in

TABLE 1   Analyses of Varience of Frequency and Variety of External
Information-Seeking Behavior

Source	df	Frequency MS	F	Variety MS	F
A. Treatment	3	151.48	53.56***	105.52	56.13***
B. Sex and Subject	1	13.55	4.79*	10.55	5.61*
C. Counselor-School	5	15.47	5.47***	5.13	2.72*
D. Setting (Indiv. vs. Group)	1	0.05	0.00	1.88	1.00
AB	3	10.55	3.73*	5.09	2.70*
AC	15	6.21	2.20*	2.99	1.59
AD	3	4.88	1.73	2.14	1.14
BC	5	5.15	1.82	2.00	1.06
BD	1	1.51	.53	2.75	1.47
CD	5	7.47	2.64*	2.01	1.07
ABC	15	3.03	1.07	1.01	0.54
ABD	3	4.23	1.49	1.80	0.96
ACD	15	3.96	1.40	2.07	1.10
BCD	5	8.23	2.91*	3.41	1.81
ABCD	15	3.57	1.26	2.31	1.23
Within Cells	96	2.83		1.88	
Total	191				

*p<.05.
***p<.001.

TABLE 2   Mean Frequency and Variety of External Information-
Seeking Behaviors by Treatment and Sex of Subject

Treatment	Frequency Male	Female	Total	Variety Male	Female	Total
Model-Reinforcement	5.04	5.04	5.04	4.29	4.33	4.31
Reinforcement	3.42	5.33	4.38	3.25	4.66	3.96
Control Film Discussion	2.04	1.96	2.00	1.83	1.87	1.85
Control	1.25	1.54	1.40	1.16	1.54	1.85
Total	2.94	3.47	3.20	2.63	3.10	2.87

both a greater frequency and a greater variety of information-seeking behavior than did the males. The reason for the significant interaction appears to be attributable to the differential effectiveness of the model-reinforcement and the reinforcement treatments for males and females. The hypothesized differences between treatments were tested separately for statistical significance as reported in Table 3. For males the difference between the model-reinforcement and the reinforcement treatments was highly significant with the model-reinforcement treatment proving most effective. For females the differences were slight but in the opposite direction from that predicted. Thus model-reinforcement counseling was more effective than reinforcement counseling for the males but not for the females.

The differences between the reinforcement treatment and the control film discussion group were highly significant for both sexes on both variables in the predicted direction. The control film discussion procedure produced uniformly more information-seeking behavior in all of the groups than did the inactive control procedure, but none of the differences reached the .05 level using a two-tail *t* test.

The nature of the interaction between treatment and counselor-schools can be seen in Table 4. In four of the six schools the direction of the differences was exactly as predicted, but with counselor-schools *E* and *F* the reinforcement treatment produced slightly higher frequencies of information-seeking behavior than did the model-reinforcement treatment. Table 4 also permits inspection of the means associated with each of the six counselor-schools. The differences between these means proved to be significant, as reported in Table 1, but the exact cause for this difference cannot be isolated since subjects were not assigned at random to the six counselor-schools.

The nature of the remaining two significant interaction effects can be seen in Table 5. With four of the six counselor-schools the group setting produced slightly higher mean frequencies than did the individual setting. However, with counselor-schools *E* and *F* the individual setting produced higher frequencies of information-seeking behavior than the group setting. On the average there was no significant difference between individual and group settings, but within certain of the counselor-schools differences between these two settings were large enough to produce the significant interaction effect.

The significant second order interaction involving sex of subject, counselor-school and setting can also be observed in Table 5. The relative effectiveness of group and individual counseling appears to depend not

TABLE 3   t-Values for Hypothesized Differences between Treatments
on Frequency and Variety of External Information-Seeking
Behavior

	Frequency			Variety		
Treatment Comparisons	Males	Females	Total	Males	Females	Total
Model-Reinforcement vs. Reinforcement	3.33***	-0.57	1.94*	2.63**	-0.84	1.25
Reinforcement vs. Control Film Discussion	2.84**	6.94***	6.92***	3.59***	7.06***	7.54***
Control Film Discussion vs. Inactive Control	1.63	0.86	1.74	1.70	0.84	1.79

*p<.05.
**p<.01.
***p<.001.

TABLE 4 Mean Frequency of External Information-Seeking Behavior by Treatment and Counselor-Schools

Counselor-School	Model-Reinforcement	Reinforcement	Control Film	Control	Total
A	5.12	3.12	2.00	0.63	2.72
B	4.38	4.38	3.38	2.00	3.53
C	4.25	3.62	1.50	1.37	2.69
D	7.62	5.12	2.25	2.12	4.28
E	5.50	6.12	1.25	1.25	3.53
F	3.37	3.87	1.62	1.00	2.47
Total	5.04	4.38	2.00	1.40	3.20

TABLE 5 Mean Frequency of External Information-Seeking Behavior by Sex of Subject, Counselor-School and Setting

Counselor-School	Individual Setting			Group Setting		
	Male	Female	Total	Male	Female	Total
A	2.62	2.25	2.44	1.75	4.25	3.00
B	3.75	3.25	3.50	2.63	4.50	3.56
C	2.25	3.12	2.68	2.50	2.88	2.69
D	3.50	3.88	3.69	⁀.75	4.00	4.87
E	3.25	5.50	4.37	2.2⊃	3.12	2.68
F	2.88	2.38	2.63	2.13	2.00	2.06
Total	3.04	3.40	3.22	2.83	3.46	3.14

only on factors associated with the different counselors and schools but also upon the sex of the subjects involved.

The interaction between treatment and setting did not reach conventional levels of significance. However, since the distinction between individual and group settings had most meaning for subjects in the model-reinforcement and reinforcement treatments, a separate breakdown and analysis for these two treatments by setting is summarized in Table 6. The results indicate that for males model-reinforcement counseling was more effective in group settings than it was in individual settings. Reinforcement counseling with males, however, was more effective in an individual setting than it was in a group setting. For females, the settings and treatments produced virtually identical frequncies and varieties of information-seeking behavior. A complete report of all means and standard deviations for all

TABLE 6   Significance of the Differences between Mean Frequencies and Varieties of External Information-Seeking Behavior in Individual and Group Settings

Sex of Subject	Criterion	Treatment	Setting Indiv.	Group	t
M	Freq.	M-R	4.33	5.75	2.07*
M	Freq.	R	4.08	2.75	1.94
M	Var.	M-R	4.08	4.50	.75
M	Var.	R	3.83	2.66	2.09*
F	Freq.	M-R	5.00	5.08	.12
F	Freq.	R	5.33	5.33	.00
F	Var.	M-R	4.41	4.25	.29
F	Var.	R	4.67	4.67	.00

*$p < .05$ (two-tail test).

combinations of independent variables is available elsewhere (Thoresen, 1964).

DISCUSSION

On the basis of these results the following conclusions seem warranted:

1. When model-reinforcement counseling and reinforcement counseling were specifically designed to increase the occupational and educational information-seeking behavior of students, each counseling technique produced more specific information-seeking behavior than that performed by equivalent control groups.
2. The model-reinforcement treatment was more effective for the male students than was reinforcement counseling, but a similar difference for females was not found.
3. Although individual and group counseling settings were equally effective on the average, male subjects receiving model-reinforcement counseling were stimulated more by the group than the individual setting. Reinforcement counseling for males was more effective in the individual than in the group setting.
4. The significant main and interaction effects for counselor-schools indicate that different counselors and/or school settings have differential effects with males and females in group and individual counseling.

One reason why model-reinforcement counseling was more effective for males might be that the model student was a high school male who discussed the field of law, college athletics and ROTC. Such concerns had little direct interest for most females. The model-reinforcement counseling procedure might have been more effective than reinforcement counseling for the females if a female model had been used. A study is currently underway to investigate this possibility. In addition, five of the six counselors were females. The addition of a male model might have lent more authority to the female counselors in the eyes of the male subjects.

In the group settings there were two males and two females. The combination of the tape-recorded male model plus another male counselee might have made the group setting seem particularly relevant to the males. This might explain the superiority of group model reinforcement for males. In the reinforcement counseling treatment, however, most of the males were counseled by a female, a situation which might have been easily tolerable in an individual setting but which might have proved more embarrassing in a group situation with only one other male and two females. Such after-the-fact speculating can only be verified by future experimentation.

The fact that individual and group counseling were not equally effective with each of the counselor-schools cannot be fully explained. It seems quite likely that some of the counselors were more effective in group settings than others, but it could also be that some schools had provided more group work experience for their students than other schools. Most of the special counselors felt more threatened by the group counseling than the individual counseling, and some of them undoubtedly responded to this stress more effectively than others. However, the specific factors which caused group counseling to be more or less effective in some situations than in others need further exploration.

Many questions remain unanswered. What effect would different kinds of models have on the information-seeking behavior of various types of students? Are certain kinds of verbal reinforcers more effective when used by certain counselors than by others? Would a greater or lesser number of counseling interviews have produced greater differences? Would a live model or a model presented by means of both audio and video media have been more or less effective? How does the timing of the counselor's reinforcement affect the amount of information-seeking behavior produced? Would techniques similar to these be equally effective in producing other kinds of behavior change desired by counselees?

This study has demonstrated that counselors can design specific procedures that will result in measurable behavior change on the part of students. In this particular study it was information-seeking behavior that provided the criteria, but counseling itself involves much more than merely promoting information-seeking behavior. In vocational and educational counseling, students need help in formulating reasonable alternatives, discovering the likelihood that they will be successful in each alternative, finding relevant information about where each alternative would lead, considering the relative values associated with each outcome and weighing all these factors carefully in arriving at a tentative decision. Carefully designed procedures for helping students accomplish each of these types of behavior have not yet been devised, but future experimentation may clarify the techniques that will prove most beneficial.

Similarly, a behavioral approach to counseling may prove equally effective with "personal" and "emotional" types of problems. The difficulty for the counselor is one of penetrating the abstract labels which customarily characterize maladaptive behavior to specify the particular change in behavior that the client wishes to make (Krumboltz, 1964). Once the behavior has been defined, a strategy can be developed to increase the likelihood that such a behavior will occur in the future. Work in these directions is just beginning.

Received February 27, 1964.

NOTES

1. This research was supported by a grant to the first author from the Procter and Gamble gift to the Stanford University School of Education and constitutes in part a summary of the Ph.D. dissertation by the second author.
2. The authors are indebted to the counselors, teachers, students and administrators associated with the following high schools: Cubberley, Cupertino, Palo Alto, Ravenswood, San Carlos and Sunnyvale.

REFERENCES

Bandura, A., & Walters, R. H. *Social learning and personality development.* New York: Holt, Rinehart and Winston, 1963.

Bandura, A., & McDonald, F. J. The influence of social reinforcement and the behavior of models in shaping children's moral judgments. *J. abnorm. soc. Psychol.,* 1963, 67, 274-281.

Bandura, A. J., Ross, D., & Ross, S. A. Imitation of film-mediated aggressive models. *J. abnorm. soc. Psychol.,* 1963, 66, 3-11.

Bandura, A. J. Social learning through imitation. In M. R. Jones (Ed.), *Nebraska symposium on motivation.* Lincoln, Neb.: Univer. of Nebraska Press, 1962. Pp. 211-269.

Gelatt, H. B. Decision-making: a conceptual frame of reference for counseling. *J. counsel. Psychol.,* 1962, 9, 240-245.

Greenspoon, J. Verbal conditioning and clinical psychology. In A. J. Bachrach (Ed.), *Experimental foundations of clinical psychology.* New York: Basic Books, 1962. Pp. 510-553.

Krasner, L. The therapist as a social reinforcement machine. In H. H. Strupp & L. Luborsky (Eds.), *Research in psychotherapy,* Vol. II. Washington, D.C.: Amer. Psychol. Assoc., 1962.

Krumboltz, J. D. Counseling for behavior change. Paper presented at the American Personnel and Guidance Association Convention, Boston, Mass., April 1963. (Mimeo.)

Krumboltz, J. D. Parable of the good counselor. *Personnel Guid. J.,* 1964, 43, 118-124.

Maccoby, Eleanor E. Role-taking in childhood and its consequences for social learning. *Child Development,* 1959, 30, 239-252.

Mussen, P. H., & Distler, L. Masculinity, identification, and father-son relationships. *J. abnorm. soc. Psychol.,* 1959, 59, 350-356.

Rickard, H. C. Manipulating verbal behavior in groups: a comparison of three intervention techniques. *Psychol. Rep.,* 1961, 9, 729-736.

Ryan, T. Antoinette, & Krumboltz, J. D. Effect of planned reinforcement counseling on client decision-making behavior. *J. counsel. Psychol.,* 1964, 11, 315-323.

Schroeder, W. W. The effect of reinforcement counseling and model-reinforcement counseling on information-seeking behavior of high school students. Unpublished Ph.D. dissertation, Stanford Univer., 1964.

Thoresen, C. E. An experimental comparison of counseling techniques for producing information-seeking behavior. Unpublished Ph.D. dissertation, Stanford Univer., 1964.

Walters, R. H., Llewellyn-Thomas, E., & Acker, C. W. Enhancement of punitive behavior by audio-visual displays. *Science,* 1962, 136, 872-873.

Classification of a Study by Krumboltz and Thoresen (1964)

Publication date	1964
Publication form	Journal
Training of experimenter	Education (known by institutional affiliation)
Blinding	Experimenter (evaluators) did not do therapy, but did know group composition (no information about blinding of evaluators was given)
Diagnosis	Vocationally undecided (students who asked for counseling about future plans, grouped in "neurotic" diagnostic type)
Hospitalization	None
Intelligence	Average (estimated, in the absence of other information)
Client-therapist similarity	Moderately similar (ages differed, but socioeconomic status of community indicated similarity)

(*continued*)

Appendix B (Continued)

Age	16 (high school juniors)
Percentage male	50% (sample stratified by client sex)
Solicitation of clients	Clients volunteered after being given notice that counseling would be available
Assignment of client	Random (stated)
Assignment of therapist	Random
Experimental mortality	No subjects lost from any group (stated)
Internal validity	High
Simultaneous comparison	Yes (2 treatments groups and placebo group compared against control)
Type of treatment	(1) Model reinforcement—Cognitive behavioral subclass (students were shown tapes of models being reinforced for information-seeking behavior, but students were not reinforced personally)
	(2) Verbal reinforcement—Behavioral subclass (counselors verbally reinforced clients for production of information-seeking statements)
	(3) Film discussion—Placebo (clients saw and discussed a film, to control for nonspecific effects of counselor attention)
Confidence of classification	Rated 5 (highest) (because of thoroughness of description, knowledge of experimenters' theory and previous work)
Allegiance	Equal allegiance paid to each of treatments. No allegiance to placebo condition
Modality	Mixed (students were randomly assigned to individual and group treatments, but modality did not interact with outcome, so the two modes were combined for the meta-analysis)
Location	School (stated)
Duration	2 hours, 2 weeks (2 sessions, time estimated)
Experience of therapists	2 years (estimated by status in counselor-training program plus training for this experiment)
Outcome	Two outcome measures were used: frequency and variety of information-seeking behavior as estimated from responses to structured interview questions. Reactivity was rated "4" for both, because measures were self-report of clients to nonblind evaluators. These were classified as measures of vocational or personal development
Effect size	Statistics reported as treatment means and mean squares from a 4-factor analysis of variance

The effect sizes were as follows:

	Frequency (of information-seeking behavior)	Variety (of information-seeking behavior)
Model reinforcement	1.79	2.01
Verbal reinforcement	1.47	1.77
Placebo	.30	.34

REFERENCES

ABRAMOWITZ, S. I., C. V. ABRAMOWITZ, C. JACKSON, and B. GOMES (1973) "The politics of clinical judgment: What nonliberal examiners infer about women who do not stifle themselves." Journal of Consulting and Clinical Psychology 41: 385-391.

ABRAMOWITZ, S. I., H. B. ROBACK, J. M. SCHWARTZ, A. YASUNA, C. V. ABRAMOWITZ, and B. GOMES (1976) "Sex bias in psychotherapy: A failure to confirm." American Journal of Psychiatry 133: 706-709.

ABRAMOWITZ, S. I., L. J. WEITZ, J. M. SCHWARTZ, S. AMIRA, B. GOMES, and C. V. ABRAMOWITZ (1975) "Comparative counselor inferences toward women with medical school aspirations." Journal of College Student Personnel 16: 128-130.

AGO, Y., Y. IKEMI, M. SUGITA, N. TAKAHASHI, H. TESHIMA, S. NAGATA, and S. INOUYE (1976) "A comparative study on somatic treatment and comprehensive treatment of bronchial asthma." Journal of Asthma Research 14: 37-43.

ALLEN, G. (1970) "The relationship between certain aspects of teachers' verbal behaviour and the number development of their pupils." Presented at the Founding Conference of the Australian Association for Research in Education, Sydney.

ANDREWS, G. (1979) "A meta-analysis of the treatment of stuttering." Presented at the meeting of the American Speech and Hearing Association.

ANDREWS, G., B. GUITAR, and P. HOWIE (1980) "Meta-analysis of the effects of stuttering treatment." Journal of Speech and Hearing Disorders 45: 287-307.

ARNOFF, G. M., S. ARNOFF, and L. PECK (1975) "Hypnotherapy in the treatment of bronchial asthma." Annals of Alergy 34: 356-362.

ASHEM, B. and L. DONNER (1968) "Covert sensitization with alcoholics: A controlled replication." Behavioral Research and Therapy 6: 7-12.

ASHTON, W. D. (1972) The Logit Transformation. London: Charles Griffin.

ASLIN, A. L. (1974) "Feminist and community mental health center psychotherapists' mental health expectations for women." Ph.D. dissertation, University of Maryland.

ATHAPPILLY, K. K. (1980) "A meta analysis of the effects of modern mathematics in comparison with traditional mathematics in the American educational system." Ann Arbor, MI: University Microfilms International.

AZCARATE, C. (1975) "Aggression and minor tranquilizers." Journal of Nervous and Mental Disorders 160: 100-107.

BANDURA, A. (1978) "On paradigms and recycled ideologies." Cognitive Therapy and Research 2: 79-103.

BARENDREGT, J. T. (1957) "A psychological investigation of the effect of group psychotherapy in patients with bronchial asthma." Journal of Psychosomatic Research 2: 115-119.

BARTON, M. A. (1980) "Two new uses of indicator variables in Meta-analysis." Evaluation in Education: An International Review Series 4: 28-30. (Available from Pergamon Press, Maxwell House/Fairview Park; Elmsford, NY 10523.)

BARTON, M. A. and G. V GLASS (1979) "Integrating studies that have quantitative independent variables." Presented at the meeting of the American Educational Research Association, San Francisco, April.

BASSOFF, E. S. (1981) "The relationship between sex-role characteristics and psychological health in new mothers." Ph.D. Dissertation, University of Colorado.

BICKEL, P. J., E. A. HAMMEL, and J. W. O'CONNELL (1975) "Sex bias in graduate admissions: Data from Berkeley." Science 187: 398-404.

BILLINGSLY, D. (1977) "Sex bias in psychotherapy: An examination of the effects of client sex, client pathology, and therapist sex on treatment planning." Journal of Consulting and Clinical Psychology 45: 250-256.

BLANCHARD, E. B., F. ANDRASIK, T. A. AHLES, S. J. TEDERS, and D. O'KEEFE (1980) "Migraine and tension headache: A meta-analytic review." Albany: Headache Project, State University of New York.

BLYTH, C. R. (1972) "On Simpson's paradox and the sure-thing principle." Journal of the American Statistical Association 67: 364-366.

BORGERS, S. B., J. C. HENDRIX, and G. E. PRICE (1977) "Does counselor response to occupational choice indicate sex stereotyping?" Journal of National Association of Women Deans and Counselors 41: 17-20.

BREDDERMAN, T. (1980) "Process curricula in elementary school science." Evaluation in Education: An International Review Series 4: 43-44. (Available from Pergamon Press, Maxwell House/Fairview Park; Elmsford, NY 10523.)

BREDDERMAN, T. (n.d.) "Elementary school process curricula: A meta-analysis." (ERIC Document Reproduction Service No. ED 170 333).

BROVERMAN, I. K., D. M. BROVERMAN, F. E. CLARKSON, P. S. ROSEN-KRANTZ, and S. R. VOGEL (1970) "Sex-role stereotypes and clinical judgments of mental health." Journal of Consulting and Clinical Psychology 34: 1-7.

CADOGAN, D. A. (1973) "Marital group therapy in the treatment of alcoholism." Quarterly Journal of Studies on Alcohol 34: 1187-1194.

CAHEN, L. S. (1980) "Meta-analysis—a technique with promise and problems." Evaluation in Education: An International Review Series 4: 37-39. (Available from Pergamon Press, Maxwell House/Fairview Park; Elmsford, NY 10523.)

CAHEN, L. and N. FILBY (1979) "The class size/achievement issue: New evidence and a research plan." Phi Delta Kappan 60: 492-496.

CARLBERG, C. (1979) "Meta-analysis of special education treatment techniques." Ph.D. dissertation, University of Colorado.

CITRON, K. M., et al. (1968) "Hypnosis for asthma: A controlled trial. Report of the Subcommittee on Hypnotherapy for Asthma." British Medical Journal 71-76.

CLANCY, J., E. VANDERHOFF, and P. CAMPBELL (1967) "Evaluation of an aversive technique as a treatment for alcoholism." Quarterly Journal of Studies on Alcohol 28: 1476-1485.

COCHRAN, W. G. (1963) Sampling Techniques. New York: Wiley.

COEN, K. S. (1974) "Patient sex and clinical evaluation." Ph.D. dissertation, United States International University.

COHEN, P. A. (1980) "A meta-analysis of the relationship between student ratings of instruction and student achievement." Ph.D. dissertation, University of Michigan.

COOK, R. E. (1967) "The effect of teacher methodology upon certain achievements of students in secondary biology." Ph.D. dissertation, University of Iowa.

COOK, T. D. (1974) "The potential and limitations of secondary evaluations," pp. 155-234 in M. W. Apple, et al. (eds.), Educational Evaluation: Analysis and Responsibility. Berkeley, CA: McCutchan.

COOK, T. D. and L. C. LEVITON (forthcoming) "Reviewing the literature: A comparison of traditional methods with meta-analysis." Journal of Personality.

COOPER, H. M. and R. ROSENTHAL (1980a) "Statistical vs. traditional procedures for summarizing research findings." Psychological Bulletin 87: 442-449.

COOPER, H. M. and R. ROSENTHAL (1980b) "A comparison of statistical and traditional procedures for summarizing research." Evaluation in Education: An International Review Series 4: 33-36. (Available from Pergamon Press, Maxwell House/Fairview Park; Elmsford, NY 10523.)

COOPER, H. M., M. BURGER, and T. L. GOOD (1980) "Gender differences in learning control beliefs of young children." Evaluation in Education: An International Review Series 4: 73-75. (Available from Pergamon Press, Maxwell House/ Fairview Park; Elmsford, NY 10523.)

COWDEN, R. C. (1955) "Reserpine alone and as an adjunct to psychotherapy in the treatment of schizophrenia." Archives of Neurological Psychiatry 74: 518-522.

COWDEN, R. C., et al. (1956) "Chlorpromazine alone and as an adjunct to group psychotherapy in the treatment of psychiatric patients." American Journal of Psychiatry 112: 898-902.

CRONBACH, L. J. and L. FURBY (1970) "How should we measure 'change'–or should we?" Psychological Bulletin 74: 68-80.

CRONBACH, L. J., G. C. GLESER, H. NANDA, and N. RAJARATNAM (1971) The Dependability of Behavioral Measurements. New York: Wiley.

DAVIS, J. (1965) "Efficacy of tranquilizing and anti-depressant drugs." Archives of General Psychiatry 13: 552-572.

DAVIS, J., G. KLERMAN, and J. SCHILDKRAFT (1968) "Drugs used in the treatment of depression in D. H. Efron (ed.) Psychopharmacology: A Review of Progress 1957-1967. Public Health Service Publication No. 1836.

DAVIDSON, T. B. (1978) "Meta-analysis of the neuropsychological assessment of children." Ph.D. dissertation, University of Denver.

DONAHUE, T. J. and J. W. COSTAR (1977) "Counselor discrimination against young women in career selection." Journal of Counseling Psychology 24: 481-486.

EDGINGTON, E. S. (1972a) "An additive method for combining probability values from independent experiments." Journal of Psychology 80: 351-363.

EDGINGTON, E. S. (1972b) "A normal curve method for combining probability values from independent experiments." Journal of Psychology 82: 85-89.

Educational Research Service (1980) Class Size Research: A Critique of Recent Meta-Analyses. Arlington, VA: Author.

EL-NEMR, M. A. (1979) "Meta-analysis of the outcomes of teaching biology as inquiry." Ph.D. dissertation, University of Colorado.

EVANGELAKIS, M. G. (1961) "De-Institutionalization of patients (the triad of trifluoperazine group therapy–adjunctive therapy)." Diseases of the Nervous System 22: 26-32.

EYSENCK, H. J. (1978a) "An exercise in mega-silliness." American Psychologist 33: 517.

EYSENCK, H. J. (1978b) "Correspondence." Bulletin of the British Psychological Society 31: 56.

FELDMAN, K. A. (1978) "Using the work of others: Some observations on reviewing, integrating, and consolidating findings," in R. B. Smith et al. (eds.), Handbook of Social Science Research Methods. New York: Irvington.

FELDT, L. S. (1961) "The use of extreme groups to test for the presence of a relationship." Psychometrika 26: 307-316.

FERGUSON, P. C. (1980) "An integrative meta-analysis of psychological studies investigating the treatment outcomes of meditation techniques." Ph.D. dissertation, University of Colorado.

FINNEY, D. J. (1971) Probit Analysis. Cambridge, England: Cambridge University Press.

FLANDERS, N. A. (1970) Analyzing Teacher Behavior. Reading, MA: Addison-Wesley.

FREEDMAN, A. R. (1975) "Age and sex bias in clinical diagnosis." Ph.D. dissertation, Illinois Institute of Technology.

FRIEDERSDORF, N. W. (1969) "A comparative study of counselor attitudes toward the further education plans of high school girls." Ph.D. dissertation, Purdue University.

FURST, N. F. (1967) "The multiple languages of the classroom." Presented at the meeting of the American Educational Research Association, New York.

GAGE, N. L. (1978) The Scientific Basis of the Art of Teaching. New York: Teachers College Press.

GALANTER, R. B. (1977) "To the victim belong the flaws." American Journal of Public Health 67: 1025-1026.

GALLANT, D. M. (1971) "Evaluation of compulsory treatment of the alcoholic municipal court offender," in N. Millie and J. Mendelson (eds.) Recent Advances in Studies of Alcoholism. Washington, DC: Government Printing Office.

GALLANT, D. M., M. FAULKNER, B. STOY, M. P. BISHOP, and D. LANGDON (1968) "Enforced clinic treatment of paroled criminal alcoholics." Quarterly Journal Study of Alcohol 29: 77-83.

GALLO, P. S. (1978) "Meta-analysis–a mixed meta-phor." American Psychologist 33: 515-517.

GILLIAN, J. (1965) "Review of literature," in M. Greenblatt et al. (eds.) Drug and Social Therapy in Chronic Schizophrenia. Springfield, IL: Charles C Thomas.

GLASS, G. V (1978a) "Integrating findings: The meta-analysis of research." Review of Research in Education 5: 351-379.

GLASS, G. V (1978b) "Reply to Mansfield and Bussey." Educational Researcher 7: 3.

GLASS, G. V (1976) "Primary, secondary and meta-analysis of research." Educational Researcher 5: 3-8.

GLASS, G. V, and A. R. HAKSTIAN (1969) "Measures of association in comparative experiments: Their development and interpretation." American Educational Research Journal 6: 403-414.

GLASS, G. V, and M. L. SMITH (1980) "Ask not for whom the bell tolls (a reply to Rimland)." American Psychologist 35: 223.

GLASS, G. V, and M. L. SMITH (1979) "Meta-analysis of research on the relationship of class-size and achievement." Evaluation and Policy Analysis 1: 2-16.

GLASS, G. V, and M. L. SMITH (1978) "Reply to Eysenck." American Psychologist 33: 517-518.

GLASS, G. V, and J. C. STANLEY (1970) Statistical Methods in Education and Psychology. Englewood Cliffs, NJ: Prentice-Hall.

GLASS, G. V, et al. (1977) "Teacher "indirectness" and pupil achievement: An integration of findings." Boulder: University of Colorado, Laboratory of Educational Research.

GOLDBERG, B. J. (1975) "Mental health practice as social control: Practitioners' choices of therapy goals as a function of sex of client, situations, and other practitioners' opinions." Ph.D. dissertation, State University of New York at Stony Brook.

GORHAM, D. R., et al. (1964) "Effects of a phenothiazine and/or group psychotherapy with schizophrenics." Diseases of the Nervous System 25: 77-86.

GROEN, J. J., and H. E. PELSER (1960) "Experiences with and results of group psychotherapy in patients with bronchial asthma." Journal of Psychosomatic Research 4: 191-205.

Group for the Advancement of Psychiatry (1975) Pharmacotherapy and Psychotherapy: Paradoxes, Problems and Progress (Vol. 9). New York: Author.

GULLIKSEN, H. (1956) "A least squares solution for paired comparisons with incomplete data." Psychometrika 21: 125-134.

HAERTEL, G. D., and E. HAERTEL (1980) "Classroom socio-psychological environment." Evaluation in Education: An International Review Series 4: 113-114. (Available from Pergamon Press, Maxwell House/Fairview Park; Elmsford, NY 10523.)

HAERTEL, G. D., H. J. WALBERG, and E. H. HAERTEL (1979) "Social-psychological environments and learning: A quantitative synthesis." Presented at the meeting of the American Educational Research Association, San Francisco.

HALL, J. A. (1978) "Gender effects in decoding nonverbal cues." Psychological Bulletin 85: 845-857.

HARTLEY, S. S. (1980) "Instruction in mathematics." Evaluation in Education: An International Review Series 4: 56-57. (Available from Pergamon Press, Maxwell House/Fairview Park; Elmsford, NY 10523.)

HARTLEY, S. S. (1977) "Meta-analysis of the effects of individually paced instruction in mathematics." Ph.D. dissertation, University of Colorado.

HASTINGS, N.A.J., and J. B. PEACOCK (1974) Statistical Distributions. London: Butterworth.

HAYES, K. E., and P. L. WOLLEAT (1978) "Effects of sex in judgments of a simulated counseling interview." Journal of Counseling Psychology 25: 164-168.

HAYS, W. L. (1973) Statistics for the Social Sciences. New York: Holt, Rinehart & Winston.

HEAROLD, S. (1980) "Television and social behavior." Evaluation in Education: An International Review Series 4: 94-95. (Available from Pergamon Press, Maxwell House/Fairview Park, NY 10523.)

HEAROLD, S. (1979) "Meta-analysis of the effects of television on social behavior." Ph.D. dissertation, University of Colorado.

HEDGES, L. V. (1981) "Distribution theory for Glass's estimator of effect size and related estimators." Journal of Educational Statistics 6.

HEDGES, L. V. (1980) "Combining the results of experiments using different scales of measurement." Ph.D. dissertation, Stanford University.

HEDGES, L. V., and I. Olkin (1980) "Vote-counting methods in research synthesis." Psychological Bulletin 88: 359-369.

HEKMAT, H. (1973) "Systematic versus semantic desensitization and implosive therapy: A comparative study." Journal of Consulting and Clinical Psychology 40: 202-209.

HESS, F. (1979) "Class size revisited: Glass and Smith in perspective." Syracuse, NY: Minoa Central Schools. (ERIC Document Reproduction Service No. ED 168 129.)

HILL, C. E. (1975) "Sex of client and sex and experience level of counselor." Journal of Counseling Psychology 22: 6-11.

HILL, C. E., M. F. TANNEY, M. M. LEONARD, and J. A. REISS (1977) "Counselor reactions to female clients: Type of problem, age of client, and sex of counselor." Journal of Counseling Psychology 24: 60-65.

HOGARTY, G. E., et al. (1974) "Drug and socio therapy in the after care of schizophrenic patients II and III." Archives of General Psychiatry 31: 603-618.

HOLLISTER, L. (1973) Clinical Use of Psychotherapeutic Drugs. Springfield, IL: Charles C Thomas.

HOLLISTER, L. (1969) "Clinical uses of psychotherapeutic drugs: Current status." Clinical Pharmacology and Therapy 10: 170-198.

HONIGFELD, G., et al. (1964) "Behavioral improvement in the older schizophrenic patients: Drug and social therapies." American Geriatrics Society Journal 13: 57-72.

HORAN, P. F., and D. D. LYNN (1980) "Learning hierarchies research." Evaluation in Education: An International Review Series 4: 82-83. (Available from Pergamon Press, Maxwell House/Fairview Park; Elmsford, NY 10523.)

HUNT, G. M., and N. AZRIN (1973) "A community reinforcement approach to alcoholism." Behavior Research and Therapy 11: 91-104.

HUNTER, C. P. (1968) "Classroom climate and pupil characteristics in special classes for the educationally handicapped." Ph.D. dissertation, University of Southern California.

HUNTER, J. E. (1979) "Cumulating results across studies: Correction for sampling error, a proposed moratorium on the significance test, and a critique of current multivariate reporting practice." East Lansing: Michigan State University.

HUNTER, J. E., and F. L. SCHMIDT (1978) "Differential and single group validity of employment tests by race: A critical analysis of three recent studies." Journal of Applied Psychology 63: 1-11.

HUNTER, J. E., F. L. SCHMIDT, and R. HUNTER (1979) "Differential validity of employment tests by race: A comprehensive review and analysis." Psychological Bulletin 86: 721-735.

ITIL, T., and A. WADUD (1975) "Treatment of human aggression with psychotropics." Journal of Nervous and Mental Disorders 160: 83-99.

IVERSON, B. K., and H. J. WALBERG (1980) "Home environment." Evaluation in Education: An International Review Series 4: 107-108. (Available from Pergamon Press, Maxwell House/Fairview Park; Elmsford, NY 10523.)

IVERSON, B. K., and H. J. WALBERG (1979) "Home environment and learning: A quantitative synthesis." Presented at the meeting of the American Educational Research Association, San Francisco.

JACKSON, G. B. (1980) "Methods for integrative reviews." Review of Educational Research 50: 438-460.

JACKSON, G. B. (1978) Methods for reviewing and integrating research in the social sciences. Final Report to the National Science Foundation for Grant No. DIS 76-20309. Washington, DC: Social Research Group, George Washington University, April.

JACOBS, J. A., and J. W. CRITELLI (1980) "Treatment-outcome interactions." Evaluation in Education: An International Review Series 4: 31-32. (Available from Pergamon Press, Maxwell House/Fairview Park; Elmsford, NY 10523.)

JONES, L. V., and D. W. FISKE (1953) "Models for testing the significance of combined results." Psychological Bulletin 50: 375-382.

JOHNSTON, J. (1972) Econometric Methods. New York: McGraw-Hill.

KAHN, A. V. (1977) "Effectiveness of biofeedback and counterconditioning in the treatment of bronchial asthma." Journal of Psychosomatic Research 21: 97-104.

KAHN, A. V., M. STAERK, and B. A. BONK (1973) "Role of counterconditioning in the treatment of asthma." Journal of Asthma Research 11: 57-61.

KAVALE, K. (1980a) "Meta-analysis of experiments on the treatment of hyperactivity in children." Riverside: University of California.

KAVALE, K. (1980b) "Psycholinguistic training." Evaluation in Education: An International Review Series 4: 88-89. (Available from Pergamon Press, Maxwell House/Fairview Park; Elmsford, NY 10523.)

KAVALE, K. (1980c) "The relationship between auditory perceptual skills and reading ability: A meta-analysis." Perceptual and Motor Skills 51: 947-955.

KAVALE, K. (1979) "The effectiveness of psycholinguistic training: A meta-analysis." Riverside: University of California.

KAVALE, K., and C. CARLBERG (1980) "Regular versus special class placement for exceptional children." Evaluation in Education: An International Review Series 4: 91-93. (Available from Pergamon Press, Maxwell House/Fairview Park; Elmsford, NY 10523.)

KAZDIN, A. E., and T. ROGERS (1978) "On paradigms and recycled ideologies: Analogue research revisited." Cognitive Therapy and Research 2: 105-117.

KENDALL, M. G., and A. STUART (1961-1966) The Advanced Theory of Statistics (Volumes 1-3). London: Griffin.

KERLINGER, F. N. (1964) Foundations of Behavioral Research. New York: Holt, Rinehart & Winston.

KING, P. D. (1963) "Controlled study of group psychotherapy in schizophrenics receiving chlorpromazine." Psychiatry Digest (March): 21-26.

KING, P. D. (1958) "Regressive EST, chlorpromazine, and group therapy in treatment of hospitalized chronic schizophrenics." American Journal of Psychiatry 115: 354-351.

KISH, L. (1965) Survey Sampling. New York: Wiley.

KISSIN, B., A. PLATZ, and W. H. SU (1970) "Social and psychological factors in the treatment of chronic alcoholism." Journal of Psychiatric Research 8: 13-27.

KLEIN, D. F., and J. M. DAVIS (1969) Diagnosis and Drug Treatment of Psychiatric Disorders. Baltimore, MD: Williams and Wilkins.

KLERMAN, G. L., and J. COLE (1965) "Clinical pharmacology of imipramine and related anti-depressant compounds." Pharmacology Review 17: 101-141.

KLERMAN, G. L., et al. (1974) "Treatment of depression by drugs and psychotherapy." American Journal of Psychiatry 131: 186-191.

KRAEMER, H. C., and G. ANDREWS "A non-parametric technique for meta-analysis effect size calculation." (unpublished)

KROL, R. A. (1979) "A meta analysis of comparative research on the effects of desegregation on academic achievement." Ann Arbor, MI: University Microfilms International.

KRUMBOLTZ, J. D., and C. E. THORESEN (1964) "The effect of behavioral counseling in group and individual settings on information-seeking behavior." Journal of Counseling Psychology 11: 324-333.

KRUSKAL, W. H. (1958) "Ordinal measures of association." Journal of the American Statistical Association 53: 814-861.

KULIK, J. A., and C. KULIK (1980) "Individualized college teaching." Evaluation in Education: An International Review Series 4: 64-67. (Available from Pergamon Press, Maxwell House/Fairview Park; Elmsford, NY 10523.)

KULIK, J. A., C. C. KULIK, and P. A. COHEN (1980) "Effectiveness of computer-based college teaching: A meta-analysis of findings." Review of Educational Research 50: 525-544.

KULIK, J. A., C. C. KULIK, and P. A. COHEN (1979) "A meta-analysis of outcome studies of Keller's personalized system of instruction." American Psychologist 34: 307-318.

LaSHIER, W. S. (1965) "An analysis of certain aspects of the verbal behavior of student teachers of eighth grade students participating in a BSCS laboratory block." Ph.D. dissertation, University of Texas.

LESSER, E. K. (1974) "Counselor attitudes toward male and female students: A study of "helpers" in conflict. Ph.D. dissertation, University of Rochester.

LEVINSON, T. A., and G. SERENY (1969) "An experimental evaluation of 'insight' therapy for the chronic alcoholic." Canadian Psychiatric Association Journal 14: 143-146.

LEWITTES, D. J., J. A. MOSELLE, and W. L. SIMMONS (1973) "Sex role bias in clinical judgments based on Rorschach interpretations." Proceedings of the 81st Annual Convention, American Psychological Association 495-496.

LIBBEY, M. D. (1975) "Sex-stereotyping in psychotherapist responses in an analogue therapy situation." Ph.D. dissertation, Columbia University.

LIGHT, R. J. (1980) "Synthesis methods: Some judgement calls that must be made." Evaluation in Education: An International Review Series 4: 13-17. (Available from Pergamon Press, Maxwell House/Fairview Park; Elmsford, NY 10523.)

LIGHT, R. J. (1979) "Capitalizing on variation: How conflicting research findings can be helpful for policy." Educational Researcher 8(9).

LIGHT, R. J., and P. V. SMITH (1971) "Accumulating evidence: Procedures for resolving contradictions among different research studies." Harvard Educational Review 41: 429-471.

LORR, M., et al. (1961) "Meprobamate and chlorpromazine in psychotherapy: Some effects on anxiety and hostility of out-patients." Archives of General Psychiatry 4: 381-389.

LUBORSKY, L. (1954) "A note on Eysenck's article 'The effects of psychotherapy: an evaluation.'" British Journal of Psychology 45: 129-131.

LUBORSKY, L., et al. (1975) "Comparative studies of psychotherapies." Archives of General Psychiatry 32: 995-1007.

LUITEN, J. W. (1980) "Advance organizers in learning." Evaluation in Education: An International Review Series 4: 49-50. (Available from Pergamon Press, Maxwell House/Fairview Park; Elmsford, NY 10523.)

LUITEN, J., W. AMES, and G. ACKERSON (1980) "A meta-analysis of the effects of advance organizers on learning and retention." American Educational Research Journal 17: 211-218.

LYNN, D. D., and J. M. DONOVAN (1980) "Medical versus surgical treatment of coronary artery disease." Evaluation in Education: An International Review Series 4: 98-99. (Available from Pergamon Press, Maxwell House/Fairview Park; Elmsford, NY 10523.)

LYSAKOWSKI, R. S., and H. J. WALBERG (1980) "Classroom reinforcement." Evaluation in Education: An International Review Series 4: 115-116. (Available from Pergamon Press, Maxwell House/Fairview Park; Elmsford, NY 10523.)

MACCOBY, E. E., and C. N. JACKLIN (1974) The Psychology of Sex Differences. Stanford, CA: Stanford University Press.

MAGNUSSON, D. (1966) Test Theory. Reading, MA: Addison-Wesley.

MAHER-LOUGHNAN, G. P., N. MACDONALD, A. A. MASON, and L. FRY (1962) "Controlled trial of hypnosis in the symptomatic treatment of asthma." British Medical Journal 5301: 371-376.

MANSFIELD, R. S., and T. V. BUSSEY (1977) "Meta-analysis of research: A rejoinder to Glass." Educational Researcher 6(3).

MASLIN, A., and J. L. DAVIS (1975) "Sex-role stereotyping as a factor in mental health standards among counselors-in-training." Journal of Counseling Psychology 22: 87-91.

MAXFIELD, R. B. (1976) "Sex-role stereotypes of psychotherapists." Ph.D. dissertation, Adelphi University.

MAY, P.R.A. (1971) "Psychotherapy and ataraxic drugs," in A. E. Bergin and S. L. Garfield, (eds.) Handbook of Psychotherapy and Behavior Change. New York: Wiley.

MAY, P.R.A., and H. TUMA (1965) "Treatment of schizophrenia." British Journal of Psychiatry 111: 503-510.

MAY, P.R.A., and H. TUMA (1964) "The effect of psychotherapy and stelazine on length of hospital stay, release rate and supplemental treatment of schizophrenic patients." Journal of Nervous and Mental Disorders 139: 362-369.

McCANCE, C., and P. F. McCANCE (1969) "Alcoholism in north-east Scotland: Its treatment and outcome." British Journal of Psychiatry 115: 189-198.

McGAW, B., and G. V GLASS (1980) "Choice of the metric for effect size in meta-analysis." American Educational Research Journal 17: 325-337.

McLEAN, A. F. (1965) "Hypnosis in 'psychosomatic' illness." British Journal of Medical Psychology 38: 211-230.

MEDLEY, D. M., and H. E. MITZEL (1959) "Some behavioral correlates of teacher effectiveness." Journal of Educational Psychology 50: 239-246.

MILLER, T. I. (1980) "Drug therapy for psychological disorders." Evaluation in Education: An International Review Series 4: 96-97. (Available from Pergamon Press, Maxwell House/Fairview Park; Elmsford, NY 10523.)

MILLER, T. I. (1977) "The effects of drug therapy on psychological disorders." Ph.D. dissertation, University of Colorado.

MOOD, A. M. (1954) "On the asymptotic power efficiency of certain non-parametric two-sample tests." Annals of Mathematical Statistics 25: 514-522.

MOORE, N. (1965) "Behavior therapy in bronchial asthma: A controlled study." Journal of Psychosomatic Research 9: 257-276.

MORRIS, J., and A. BECK (1974) "The efficacy of anti-depressant drugs." Archives of General Psychiatry 30: 667-674.

MOSTELLER, F. M., and R. R. BUSH (1954) "Selected quantitative techniques," in G. Lindzey (ed.) Handbook of Social Psychology: Volume I. Theory and Method. Cambridge, MA: Addison-Wesley.

MOSTELLER, F. M., and J. W. TUKEY (1968) "Data analysis, including statistics," in G. Lindzey and E. Aronson (eds.) Handbook of Social Psychology. Reading, MA: Addison-Wesley, 1968.

NEULINGER, J. (1968) "Perceptions of the optimally integrated person: A redefinition of mental health." Proceedings of the 76th Annual Convention of the American Psychological Association 567-569.

NEWTON, J. R., and L. I. STEIN (ca. 1972) "Implosive therapy." Proceedings of the First Annual Meeting of the National Institute for A.A.A.

PACHT, A. R., R. BENT, T. D. COOK, L. B. KLEBANOFF, D. A. RODGERS, L. SECHREST, H. STRUPP, and M. THEAMAN (forthcoming) "Data-based meta analyses as a tool in literature reviews." Journal of Personality.

PAUL, G. L., and M. H. LICHT (1978) "Resurrection of uniformity assumption myths and the fallacy of statistical absolutes in psychotherapy research." Journal of Consulting and Clinical Psychology 46: 1531-1534.

PEARLMAN, K. (1979) "The validity of tests used to select clerical personnel: A comprehensive summary and evaluation (Technical Study TS-79-1)." Washington, DC: Office of Personnel Management, Personnel Research and Development Center, August. (NTIS No. PB 80-102650).

PEARSON, E. S., and H. O. HARTLEY (1962) Biometrika Tables for Statisticians. Cambridge, England: Cambridge University Press.

PETERSON, P. L. (1980) "Open versus traditional classrooms." Evaluation in Education: An International Review Series 4: 58-60. (Available from Pergamon Press, Maxwell House/Fairview Park; Elmsford, NY 10523.)

PETERSON, P. L. (1978) "Direct and open instructional approaches: Effective for what and for whom?" Working Paper No. 243 of the Wisconsin Research and Development Center for Individualized Schooling, University of Wisconsin, Madison, October.

PETRO, C. S., and J. C. HANSEN (1977) "Counselor sex and empathic judgment." Journal of Counseling Psychology 24: 373-376.

PIETROFESA, J. J., and N. K. SCHLOSSBERG (1973) "Counselor bias and the female occupational role. Detroit, MI: Wayne State University (ERIC #044 749). Reprinted in N. K. Schlossberg and J. J. Pietrofesa, "Perspectives on counseling bias: Implications for counselor education." Counseling Psychologist 4: 44-54.

PINNEY, R. W. (1969) "Presentational behaviors related to success in teaching." Ph.D. dissertation, Stanford University.

POSAVAC, E. J. (1980) "Evaluations of patient education programs: A meta-analysis." Evaluation and the Health Professions 3: 47-62.

POWELL, E. R. (1968) "Teacher behavior and pupil achievement." Presented at the meeting of the American Educational Research Association, Chicago.

PRESBY, S. (1978) "Overly broad categories obscure important differences between therapies." American Psychologist 33: 514-515.

PRICE, G. E., and S. B. BORGERS (1977) "An evaluation of the sex-stereotyping effect as related to counselor perceptions of courses appropriate for high school students." Journal of Counseling Psychology 24: 240-243.

RIMLAND, B. (1979) "Death knell for psychotherapy?" American Psychologist 34: 192.

ROID, G., G. BRODSKY, and D. A. BIGELOW (1979) "Meta-analysis in mental health evaluation research." (unpublished)

ROSENTHAL, R. (1980) "Combining probabilities and the file drawer problem." Evaluation in Education: An International Review Series 4: 18-21. (Available from Pergamon Press, Maxwell House/Fairview Park; Elmsford, NY 10534.)

ROSENTHAL, R. (1979) "The 'file drawer problem' and tolerance for null results." Psychological Bulletin 86: 638-641.

ROSENTHAL, R. (1978) "Combining results of independent studies." Psychological Bulletin 85: 185-193.

ROSENTHAL, R. (1976) Experimenter Effects in Behavioral Research. New York: Irvington.

ROUSSEAU, E. W., and D. L. REDFIELD (1980) "Teacher questioning." Evaluation in Education: An International Review Series 4: 51-52. (Available from Pergamon Press, Maxwell House/Fairview Park; Elmsford, NY 10523.)

SCHLESINGER, H. J., E. MUMFORD, and G. V GLASS (1980) "Effects of psychological intervention on recovery from surgery," pp. 9-18 in F. Guerra and J. A. Aldrete (eds.) Emotional and Psychological Responses to Anesthesia and Surgery. New York: Grune & Stratton.

SCHLESINGER, H. J., E. MUMFORD, and G. V GLASS (1978) "A critical review and indexed bibliography of the literature up to 1978 on the effects of psychotherapy on medical utilization." Denver: Department of Psychiatry, University of Colorado Medical Center.

SCHWAB, D., J. OLIAN-GOTTLIEB, and H. HENEMAN III (1979) "Between-subjects expectancy theory research: A statistical review of studies predicting effort and performance." Psychological Bulletin 86: 139-147.

SCLARE, A., M. B. BALFOUR, and J. A. CROCKET (1957) "Group psychotherapy in bronchial asthma." Psychosomatic Research 2: 157-171.

SHAH, I. (1968) Caravan of Dreams. Baltimore: Penguin.

SHAPIRO, D. A., and D. SHAPIRO (1977) "The 'double standard' in evaluation of psychotherapies." Bulletin of the British Psychological Society 30: 209-210.

SHEARD, M. (1975) "Lithium and aggression." Journal of Nervous and Mental Disorders 160.

SHEPARD, R. N. (1962) "The analysis of proximities: Multidimensional scaling with an unknown distance function. I and II." Psychometrika 27: 125-140; 219-246.

SIMPSON, E. H. (1951) "The interpretation of interaction in contingency tables." Journal of the Royal Statistical Society, Series B. 13: 238-241.

SIMPSON, S. N. (1980) "Comment on 'Meta-analysis of research on class size and achievement.' " Educational Evaluation and Policy Analysis 2: 81-83.

SMITH, M. L. (1980a) "Effects of aesthetics education on basic skills learning." (unpublished)

SMITH, M. L. (1980b) "Publication bias and meta-analysis." Evaluation in Education: An International Review Series 4: 22-24. (Available from Pergamon Press, Maxwell House/Fairview Park; Elmsford, NY 10523.)

SMITH, M. L. (1980c) "Sex bias in counseling and psychotherapy." Psychological Bulletin 87: 392-407.

SMITH, M. L. (1980d) "Teacher expectations." Evaluation in Education: An International Review Series 4: 53-55. (Available from Pergamon Press, Maxwell House/Fairview Park; Elmsford, NY 10523.)

SMITH, M. L. (1974) "Influence of client sex and ethnic group on counselor judgments." Journal of Counseling Psychology 21: 516-521.

SMITH, M. L. (1972) "Responses of counselors to case materials of clients differentiated by gender and ethnic group." Ph.D. dissertation, University of Colorado.

SMITH, M. L., and G. V GLASS (1979) "Class-size and its relationship to attitudes and instruction." Boulder: Laboratory of Educational Research, University of Colorado, July.

SMITH, M. L., and G. V GLASS (1977) "Meta-analysis of psychotherapy outcome studies." American Psychologist 32: 752-760.

SMITH, M. L., G. V GLASS and T. I. MILLER (1980) Benefits of Psychotherapy. Baltimore: Johns Hopkins University Press.

SNEDECOR, G. W., and W. G. COCHRAN (1967) Statistical Methods. Ames: Iowa State University Press.

SNIDER, R. M. (1966) "A project to study the nature of effective physics teaching." Ph.D. dissertation, Cornell University.

SOAR, R. S. (1966) "An integrative approach to classroom learning." Final Report, Public Health Service Grant No. 5-R11-MH 01096 and National Institute of Mental Health Grant No. 7-R11-MH02045.

SOAR, R. S., R. M. SOAR, and M. RAGOSTA (1971) "The validation of an observation system for classroom management." Presented at the meeting of the American Educational Research Association, New York.

SOBELL, M. B., and L. C. SOBELL (1973) "Alcoholics treated by individualized behavior therapy: One year treatment outcomes." Behavior Research and Therapy 11: 599-618.

STORM, T., and R. E. CUTLER (ca. 1970) "Systematic desensitization in the treatment of alcoholics." (unpublished)

SUDMAN, S., and N. M. BRADBURN (1974) Response Effects in Surveys: A Review and Synthesis. Chicago: Aldine.

TAVEGGIA, T. C. (1974) "Resolving research controversy through empirical cumulation: Toward reliable sociological knowledge." Sociological Methods & Research 2: 395-407.

THOMPSON, G. R., and N. C. BOWERS (1968) "Fourth grade achievement as related to creativity, intelligence, and teaching style." Presented at the meeting of the American Educational Research Association, Chicago.

TORGERSON, W. S. (1958) Theory and Methods of Scaling. New York: Wiley.

TORRANCE, E. P., and E. PARENT (1966) "Characteristics of mathematics teachers that affect students' learning." Cooperative Research Project No. 1020, U.S. Office of Education.

TUKEY, J. W. (1977) Exploratory Data Analysis. Reading, MA: Addison-Wesley.

UGUROGLU, M. E., and H. J. WALBERG (1980) "Motivation." Evaluation in Education: An International Review Series 4: 105-106. (Available from Pergamon Press, Maxwell House/Fairview Park; Elmsford, NY 10523.)

UGUROGLU, M. E., and H. J. WALBERG (1978) "Motivation and achievement: A quantitative synthesis." Presented at the meeting of the American Psychological Association, Toronto.

UHLENHUTH, E. H., R. S. LIPMAN, and L. COVI (1969) "Combined pharmacotherapy and psychotherapy." Journal of Nervous and Mental Disorders 148: 52-64.

UNDERWOOD, B. J. "Interference and forgetting." Psychological Review 64: 49-60.

VOGLER, R. E., S. E. LUNDE, and P. L. MARTIN (1971) "Electrical aversion conditioning with chronic alcoholics." Journal of Consulting and Clinical Psychology 36: 450.

WALBERG, H. J. (1978) "Reflections on research synthesis." (unpublished)

WALBERG, H. J., and E. H. HAERTEL (1980) "Research integration: Introduction and overview." Evaluation in Education: An International Review Series 4: 5-10. (Available from Pergamon Press, Maxwell House/Fairview Park; Elmsford, NY 10523.)

WEBER, W. A. (1968) "Relationships between teacher behavior and pupil creativity in the elementary school." Ph.D. dissertation, Temple University.

WHITE, K. (1980) "Socio-economic status and academic achievement." Evaluation in Education: An International Review Series 4: 79-81. (Available from Pergamon Press, Maxwell House/Fairview Park; Elmsford, NY 10523.)

WHITE, K. (1979) "The relationship between socioeconomic status and academic achievement." Presented at the meeting of the American Educational Research Association, San Francisco, April.

WILLSON, V. L. (1980) "A meta-analysis of the relationship between student attitude and achievement in secondary school science." College of Education, Texas A & M University, College Station.

WILLSON, V. L. (1976) "Critical values of the rank-biserial correlation coefficient." Educational and Psychological Measurement 36: 297-300.

WINER, B. J. (1971) Statistical Principles in Experimental Design. New York: McGraw-Hill.

WINNE, P. H. (1979) "Experiments relating teacher's use of higher cognitive questions to student achievement." Review of Educational Research 49: 13-50.

WIRT, M. D. (1975) "Counselor trainee response as a function of client race, attitude, and sex." Ph.D. dissertation, University of Michigan.

WOLINS, L. (1962) "Responsibility for raw data." American Psychologist 17: 657-658.

YEANY, R. H., and P. A. MILLER (1980) "The effects of diagnostic/remedial instruction on science learning: A meta-analysis." Athens: Department of Science Education, University of Georgia.

YIN, R. K., and D. YATES (1975) Street-Level Governments: Assessing Decentralization and Urban Services. Lexington, MA: D. C. Heath.

YIN, R. K., E. BINGHAM, and K. A. HEALD (1976) "The difference that quality makes: The case of literature reviews." Sociological Methods & Research 5: 139-156.

YORKSTON, N. J., R. B. McHUGH, R. BRADY, M. SERBER, and G. S. SERGEANT (1974) "Verbal desensitisation in bronchial asthma." Journal of Psychosomatic Research 18: 371-376.

AUTHOR INDEX

SUBJECT INDEX

ABOUT THE AUTHORS

Gene V Glass is Professor of Education at the University of Colorado—Boulder, where he has been a member of the faculty since 1967. His Ph.D. was earned at the University of Wisconsin in 1965. He is a Fellow of the American Psychological Association; in 1975, he served as President of the American Educational Research Association. Dr. Glass served as Editor of the *Review of Educational Research* (1968-1970), Associate Editor for methodology of *Psychological Bulletin* (1978-1980), and as Editor for Volume 1 of the *Evaluation Studies Review Annual.* He has written widely on statistics, testing, and research methodology. His works include *Basic Statistics for the Behavioral Sciences* (with K. D. Hopkins) and *Design and Analysis of Time-Series Experiments* (with V. L. Willson and J. M. Gottman).

Mary Lee Smith is Assistant Professor at the Laboratory of Educational Research, University of Colorado—Boulder. Before assuming this position in 1979, she acted as an independent researcher, working on such problems as the outcomes of psychotherapy, sex bias in counseling and psychotherapy, the effects of Outward Bound, and the effects of school class size. Dr. Smith has extensive experience developing and applying naturalistic research methods in education. She is the author (with Gene V Glass and Thomas I. Miller) of *Benefits of Psychotherapy* and has published extensively in education and counseling psychology.

Barry McGaw is Professor of Education and Dean of the School of Education at Murdoch University in Perth, Western Australia. He holds B.Sc. and B.Ed. (First Class Hons.) from the University of Queensland and M.Ed., Ph.D. from the University of Illinois. In 1971, while a graduate student at Illinois, he became the first Chairman of the American Educational Research Association Student Representative's Committee and in that capacity participated on the AERA Council. In 1976 he was President of the Australian Asociation for Research in Education.